W9-CMN-840

# FROM  GLADSTONE
# TO LLOYD GEORGE

# FROM GLADSTONE TO LLOYD GEORGE

*Parliament in Peace and War*

BY

ALEXANDER MACKINTOSH

Author of "Joseph Chamberlain: An Honest Biography"

"All I can say is—I saw it."

HODDER AND STOUGHTON
LIMITED          LONDON

To

MY WIFE

# NOTE

In view of recent changes in the composition and character of Parliament, I hope some interest may be taken in the recollections and impressions of a journalist who has for many years observed the House of Commons from the Press Gallery and met its members in the Lobby. I have studied all the statesmen who have played their part in political life since Disraeli fought and lost his last fight with his rival. I have seen the rise of all the living leaders and the fall of more than half-a-dozen Governments.

From the first of Gladstone's speeches which I heard, in 1881, till his last from the Treasury Bench, I was more or less under his oratorical spell. Yet I was fascinated by the career of Mr. Joseph Chamberlain who did so much to frustrate his final ambition; I was thrilled by the boldness and brilliance of Lord Randolph Churchill whose early decline was so lamentable; I admired the dexterity of Mr. Balfour as a leader and found steady satisfaction in the sagacity of Lord Harting-ton, afterwards Duke of Devonshire. "C.B." appealed to me by his courage and pawky humour; I have had abiding respect for Mr. Asquith's talents and qualities; I have followed with palpitating pulse the dazzling life of Mr. Lloyd George. A catholic interest! the reader may say. Yes, but a Cross-Bench temper is perhaps the best for a reviewer of Parliament.

If there is no hero in this volume neither is there a villain. " It is," Carlyle has said, " a much shallower and more ignoble occupation to detect faults than to discover beauties." I have not gone out of my way at any rate to expose faults with more prominence than accuracy demands, although I have not overlooked the wart on the face.

" Examine your words well," wrote George Eliot, " and you will find that even when you have no motive to be false, it is a very hard thing to say the exact truth, even about your own immediate feelings." A Parliamentary chronicler knows how hard it is either to observe truly or to write truly. All I claim is that I have endeavoured to write of what I have seen and heard without unfair partiality and without prejudice.

A. M.

*June,* 1921.

# CONTENTS

## CHAPTER I

## CHAPTER II

## CHAPTER III

## CHAPTER VI

## CHAPTER VII

## CHAPTER XI

## CHAPTER XII

## CHAPTER XIII

# CHAPTER I

## HOW THE WAR FOUND PARLIAMENT

THE first sign on the Parliamentary horizon of the storm which was to shake the world, a little cloud like a man's hand, appeared on the last Monday of July, 1914. Twice or thrice in recent history threatening signals had flashed across the sky, but the alarm had passed without a crash and now people intent on summer pleasures and autumn holidays averted their eyes from the omen in the East. They did not want to know about it; they did not admit it. But to the skilled watcher the cloud gave warning of a terrible possibility. " The moment," said Sir Edward Grey on July 27, " the dispute ceases to be one between Austro-Hungary and Serbia and becomes one in which another great Power is involved, it can but end in the greatest catastrophe that has ever befallen the Continent at one blow." A Navy debate fixed for that Monday in the House of Commons was postponed. At such a moment, declared Mr. Walter Long on behalf of the Opposition, there should be but one voice in the House and the country.

Seldom in our history could the securing of " one voice " have seemed more difficult. Only a week earlier the Sovereign had stated at the conference on the Irish problem that " the cry of civil war is on the lips of the most responsible and sober-minded of my people." Seers gazing into the future of the country had turned with horror, like Allan M'Aulay in *A Legend of Montrose*, from the vision which arose before their eyes.

Partisan contention had been sharp enough in every generation.   Occasionally it had blazed into passion, dividing society and severing friends. The struggle over the first Reform Bill, the quarrel between Peelites and Protectionists, the duels between Disraeli and Gladstone had excited emotions which were sometimes virulent in expression, and the seven years' contest over Gladstone's Irish Home Rule policy had culminated in a physical conflict on the floor of the House of Commons. There were, however, in the national situation in 1914 features more ominous and menacing than any since the cause of the Stuarts was lost.

King George succeeded to the throne at a constitutional crisis, and even in the years of his reign before the Great War it might have been said that uneasy lay the head which wore the crown.   Classes, parties, races, sexes were agitated by alarming antagonisms.   The demands of Labour and women, the controversies which followed the Budget of 1909 and the holding of it up by the House of Lords, the abolition of the veto of that House by an Act carried under the threat of a wholesale creation of peers, the attack on the land system, the forcing forward of measures which were violently opposed, the resistance of Ulster to a Parliament in Dublin : these and other convulsions touched the most sensitive nerves of the State.

There was in the political temper a greater degree of venom even than Burke deplored in his day.   This was displayed in the House of Commons. Intentional disorder prevented the Prime Minister from making a statement in defence of advice he had given to the Sovereign, protracted disturbances were frequent, and after a defeat of the Government Unionists tried to stop the Parliamentary machine with the view to an appeal to the country. Allegations of corruption, rare in modern annals, were brought against ministers. For Mr. Asquith himself a violent fate on a lamp-post was predicted in the event of blood being shed in Ulster.

Towards the precipice of civil war the country plunged rapidly in 1914. Unionists cheered their leader when he declared that if ever any people in the history of the world had a right to resist by force, the men of Ulster in refusing to submit to an Irish Parliament would have that right; Army officers in the Irish Command accepted the option to resign rather than risk the receipt of orders to take part in operations against the northern province; the cry of Parliament and People versus Aristocracy and Army was raised by Radicals and the name of the Sovereign, although Mr. Asquith bore testimony to his constitutional correctness, was dragged into the quarrel. It was in this state of feeling, while Irish Home Rule and Welsh Disestablishment were being carried through their final stages over the head of the peers, that the supreme call came to the country.

On June 28 the Hereditary Archduke of Austria and his wife were murdered at Serajevo. Not suspecting what lay in the lap of that event, the House of Commons, after expressing sympathy with the mourners, proceeded with its acrimonious dissensions. So dangerous were domestic difficulties that on July 10, in debate on the Foreign Office vote, when Radicals impressed upon the Secretary of State the duty of maintaining peace throughout the world, Mr. Bonar Law emphasized rather the obligation on Ministers to keep peace within our own borders. The urgency of this obligation was shown by the steps taken by the Covenanters of Ulster to organize a Provisional Government.

While the Conference of representative men of all parties summoned by the King was engaged at Buckingham Palace on the Ulster question, Austria presented to Serbia the ultimatum which led diplomatists to consider what Russia would do and what would happen if the Tsar stood by the small State in the Balkans which looked to him for protection. On July 24 the Palace Conference broke up " unable to agree." The same day Sir Edward Grey received a copy of the ominous ultimatum and on Sunday the 26th he was informed by our ambassador at Vienna of Austria's diplomatic rupture with Serbia. " War," telegraphed Sir M. de Bunsen, " is thought to be imminent." On that Sunday, as if a malign fate were tying our hands, difficulties at home were aggravated by a collision in Dublin between people and soldiers on the landing of arms by the Irish National Volunteers, who were following the example of the Ulster Covenanters.

In the ever memorable last week of July, the last week of the old world, which opened at Westminster with Sir Edward Grey's warning and the avoidance of naval debate, Parliament watched the cloud in the East with fluctuating hopes and fears. Gradually, although slowly, the consciousness that the attempt to crush Serbia might set all Europe aflame worked itself into minds reluctant to receive it. Yet even during that period there were moments of angry discord in the House of

Commons. On Wednesday, the 29th, the day
after Austria declared war, sharp controversy arose
on the Dublin gun-running incident. In the latter
part of the week domestic differences were driven
out of members' thoughts by the bombardment
of Belgrade, the reports of Russian mobilization
and the suspicions of Germany's secret measures.
Timid people drew their gold from the banks and
those who prided themselves on prudence and may
have recalled the experience of Parisians described
by Mr. Arnold Bennett in *The Old Wives' Tale*,
laid in stocks of food for the few months which
as they supposed a great war might occupy. On
the other hand, a vast number of people left town
for holiday resorts on Saturday, the first of August,
hoping that, after all, the storm might be averted
by Sir Edward Grey's persistent efforts. Events
did not wait on their pleasure.

The storm broke out before Parliament met on
Bank Holiday. Germany had declared war against
Russia on Saturday evening. She had also challenged France to say what her attitude would be
and France had proudly replied she would have
regard to her interests. On Sunday it was known
that German troops had entered the Grand Duchy
of Luxemburg and a demand was made for their
passage through Belgian territory. The world wondered what would be the action of Great Britain.
France turned to us with supreme anxiety. Were
we not under an obligation of honour as her
friend to go to her assistance ?

There were momentous Councils at Downing
Street that holiday week-end and Rumour was busy.
Mr. Asquith and Sir Edward Grey, as was rightly
believed, were for intervention, but financial influences had been brought to bear in favour of

neutrality and several Ministers were hesitating while a few were definitely against war. At last on Sunday, after a Cabinet, the Foreign Secretary gave M. Cambon an assurance that if the German Fleet came into the Channel or through the North Sea to undertake hostile operations against French coasts or shipping, our Fleet would give all the protection in its power. Would we do more ? Would we declare the violation of Belgian territory a *casus belli* ? The Government had to take one of the great decisions of history and sound the House of Commons. That was the position on Monday, the third of August.

Who that was present in the House that day will ever forget the scene and the emotions of the occasion—the crowded Chamber, the eager, excited faces, the grave, calm Foreign Secretary, the world-agitating issue he presented, the high resolve of the representatives of the nation ? So large was the attendance that chairs were brought in and placed between the bar and the table. Three times before I had seen this extra accommodation provided—at the introduction of the Home Rule Bill by its author in 1886, for Mr. Chamberlain's reply to Mr. Asquith's motion of no-confidence in the Conservative Government in 1892, and again in the following year at Mr. Gladstone's submission of his second scheme of Home Rule. Those events, although appealing to the passions of parties, were as stage plays compared with the problem so vital to our destiny submitted on the Bank Holiday afternoon. Every hour was bringing news of events which were dividing Europe into vast, moving armies. Was our own army to enter the field ? Would a war policy be supported by Parliament ? The Russian ambassador, seated in the gallery, his long, fine fingers on the front rail, watched the scene with a searching, nervous glance. " It was not until Grey spoke," the French ambassador told a friend, " that we could breathe."*

The Englishman on whose words the world waited sat still and silent, and aloof from what was occurring around him during the opening proceedings of the House, scanning his notes or with eyes looking far off, absorbed in thought. He had no dramatic pose. Seeing the national duty, he was there to declare it with a full sense of responsibility. No one had more plainly told what was meant by a European war. No one could have more earnestly or sincerely laboured to preserve peace. Yet now he saw that British interests and the obligation of honour in our friendship with France, as well as in our treaty obligations to Belgium, might require us to take up arms. His speech determined the decision of Parliament. The least pretentious, Sir Edward Grey was the most persuasive of speakers. In unadorned, frank words he so framed his indictment that it went home to reason and conscience. The feeling of the House was displayed unmistakably. Cheers, bold and defiant in some quarters and in others austere and solemn, revealed its practical unanimity. And the loudest cheers were for honour.

Party faction suddenly ceased. Political differences were forgotten. Assurance of support to the Government in taking the action for which they were prepared was given by the Unionist leader, and in an oration which excited extraordinary enthusiasm, Mr. John Redmond placed Ireland by the

* *The Times*, December 22, 1920.

side of Great Britain at this hazard of her
career and existence.  So unmistakably was a war
decision approved, except by a minute minority,
that the Government were able in complete reliance
on Parliament to challenge Germany's violation
of the neutrality of Belgium on whose soil her
troops were already marching.  Lord Morley and
Mr. John Burns having retired from the Cabinet,
the Ministers took the appropriate diplomatic
and military steps with a promptitude, precision
and dignified firmness which inspired national
confidence.

Those of us who attended the House of Commons
in those historic days were thrilled by the rapid
succession of dramatic episodes on our entrance
to the quarrel which we were resolved so to bear
that the opposed might beware of us.  I recall Mr.
Asquith's calmly uttered, loudly cheered announcement on August 4 of the ultimatum to Germany,
his laconic intimation on the 5th that " since
eleven o'clock last night a state of war has existed
between Germany and ourselves," his impressive
speech on the 6th in moving the first vote of credit.
No challenge was ever given or accepted by this
country with less bluster.  While we knew that
our quarrel was just, there was in Parliament no
bravado, no bragging, no Jingoism.  If we did not
know how hard was the trial that lay before us we
knew enough to cause anxiety.  We understood
that our strength, material and moral, might be
severely taxed.  Yet no war could have been
engaged in more soberly or with a fuller resolve
to prevail, whatever might be the cost.

For a brief period, on a September afternoon,
the party truce was interrupted at the final stages
of the Irish Home Rule and Welsh Disestablish-

ment bills.  Unionists vehemently urged that these contentious measures should be withheld from the royal assent, but the Government insisted on their being placed at once upon the statute book while making provision to suspend their operation during the war and giving a pledge that before a Parliament was set up in Ireland an amending bill would be introduced for the exclusion of Ulster areas which desired to stay out.  The action of the Ministers was resented by Mr. Bonar Law, who accused them of " taking advantage of our patriotism to betray us," and at the close of his protest the Opposition walked out in a body.  This incident, disagreeable to all parties, being ended, the truce was resumed.

A session remarkable for intensity of interest maintained its dramatic character till the prorogation on September 18.  Usually the Parliamentary year ends in an anti-climax.  On this occasion the curtain fell on a tableau which seemed unreal in the Palace of Westminster.  There were amazing scenes in both Chambers.  In the House of Lords, at the giving of the royal assent to the recently passed statutes, when the Government of Ireland Act was named and the bowing clerk cried *Le Roy le veult*, there burst forth from Irish and Radical members of the other House, in disregard of propriety, a triumphant cheer.  Thus in their enthusiasm, even in the midst of war, they celebrated the placing upon the statute book of a bill which had been carried under the Parliament Act without the assent of the Peers.

Fortunately the echoes of domestic conflict were not heard in the House of Commons.  When members reassembled there after the prorogation ceremony all parties proved their ardent patriotism

by the singing of " God Save the King." The
scene was unconventional, a striking departure
from the formalism of a House so strictly guided
by tradition. Great crises produce great innovations and here indeed was an innovation in Parliamentary practice when strangers and journalists
took part in a demonstration with members. All
stood—occupants of the benches and occupants
of the galleries, the Deputy-Speaker at the table
and the Sergeant-at-Arms at his box, and all
joined gravely with Mr. Will Crooks, who first
raised his voice, in the Anthem which in those most
anxious days had a particularly solemn significance.
Nationalists sang it whole-heartedly now that the
royal assent had been given to Home Rule. Mr.
John Redmond raised his hand at a Hip ! Hip !
Hurrah ! and when a Liberal cried " God save
Ireland," he responded " And God save England
too."

Thus was consummated the national union which
was called for first on July 27, and without which
the Empire could not have been saved in the
storm that had broken out with terrific speed and
fury. As marvellous as *l'union sacrée* of France,
so finely celebrated by Maurice Barrès, was the
union in our own Parliament. The navy debate,
adjourned on Mr. Long's suggestion from the
front Opposition bench, was never held. Nearly
five years passed before Admiralty policy could be
freely discussed without risk to the State, and when
that time came Mr. Long himself was First Lord
under the Prime Ministership of the statesman
whom before the war he distrusted beyond all
others. Burke asked Erskine if in pretending to
call him friend he knew what friendship meant.
With true knowledge of what friendship meant

statesmen in our own day who had been as merciless in party warfare as any politician in any generation learned to call each other friend.

A Government representing only one party proved to be a defective instrument in the carrying on of a great and long war. It was replaced by a Coalition under Mr. Asquith, and this in turn was superseded by a Coalition under Mr. Lloyd George. At each stage there was from one quarter or another much criticism. Nevertheless, so far as the policy of the war was concerned, Parliamentary union lasted till the Armistice. To the supreme issue all other considerations were subordinated. Apart from a very few Socialists and Radicals there was unfaltering unity from that August Bank Holiday which destroyed the dreams of generations. We were compelled to go to war, as was said in the King's speech, for the assertion of Treaty obligations deliberately set at nought and for the protection of the public law of Europe and the vital interests of the Empire, and under each of the three Administrations which ruled between 1914 and 1918, the Parliamentary will remained the same.

To the later chapters of this volume I reserve an account of political developments during the struggle. I proceed now to describe the traditional relationship of party opponents which facilitated their co-operation when the need for it came. Then I shall try to show what manner of men have been, in Burke's words, " the guide-posts and landmarks in the State " since Disraeli's death, and to give some memories of their time. These impressions I record at an epoch of transition when the old order is giving place to a new, and when the pre-war world is already viewed as a far-off, strange, almost incredible state of existence.

# CHAPTER II

A TRUE understanding of the Parliamentary machine cannot be derived solely from what occurs on the floor of the House of Commons. It is necessary to go " behind the Speaker's chair." This phrase has a literal sense and also a wider significance. On the neutral ground behind the chair Whips and others from the front benches occasionally meet to settle the order of business or of debate. Sometimes a great man on the one side beckons to a great man opposite and they go out to arrange a compromise which is afterwards solemnly suggested and adopted across the table. That is the narrow but not unimportant view of what occurs " behind the Speaker's chair." In its wider significance the phrase involves the tradition of our Parliamentary system.

It is only when exceptionally violent that political strife is carried into the social sphere and even then it does not always sever the personal relations of leading opponents. In this respect we claim superior merit. Nowhere else, as we boast in after-dinner speeches, do we find equal tolerance. " We Englishmen are Very Proud of our Constitution, Sir," said Mr. Podsnap to the foreign gentleman. " It Was Bestowed Upon Us By Providence. No Other Country is so Favoured as This Country." Without indulging in Podsnappery, the most candid among us may admit that rarely do we carry our warfare " to the knife and fork." Lord Morley, after a few years' experience, wrote that " the bonhomie of the House of Commons is very superficial," but members, as Mr. Speaker Gully remarked in 1902, know how to distinguish between opinions and men.  " Although," he said, " they might abhor the opinions which they heard, they felt no resentment against the men who held them honestly," and Viscount Bryce, then a leading member of Opposition and as good a party man as ever sat on any bench, testified that great as their differences might be, these did not affect in the least the regard and the respect which they felt for one another.

This traditional temper has been exhibited in an unfavourable light by unsympathetic observers. " What a mockery controversy was in the House ! " wrote Mark Rutherford.  " How often I have seen members, who were furious at one another across the floor, quietly shaking hands outside and inviting one another to dinner ! "  An equally harsh view is presented in *The Party System* by Mr. Hilaire Belloc (for a short time a member) and Mr. Cecil Chesterton.  As a matter of fact, they assert, the Downing Street constitutional conference in 1910, " trumpeted through the Press as if it were a unique event, was only one of the hundred conferences which various members of the two front benches, and especially the two leaders, their secretaries, the two Chief Whips, the confidential hangers-on, and now and then the principal official paymasters habitually hold to settle the affairs of Parliament.  Agreement between the Front Benches is not a rare expedient suited to a special crisis.  It is the normal method

of governing the country." That is a heightened
way of putting the case, but if it be an exaggera-
tion to say that " every move in the silly and
dangerous game is arranged beforehand by the
confederates on the two front benches " there is
ground for the statement that the conference on
the House of Lords was " but a more formal type
of those private conferences between opposing
leaders behind the Speaker's chair and at dinner
parties and social clubs which give "—or at any
rate in the past have given—" their real direction
to the politics and to the destinies of modern
England."

Whatever may happen under new conditions,
hitherto undoubtedly our governing process has
been eased and facilitated by the friendly and
confidential intercourse of opponents. As to the
expediency of this association in private of politicians who differ in public, our statesmen themselves
are not all of one mind. Those of the stricter
school agree with Mark Rutherford that " men
who are totally at variance ought not to be friends,
and if Radical and Tory are not totally, but merely
superficially at variance, so much the worse for
their Radicalism and Toryism." John Bright
maintained that it was difficult to attack in public
a man with whom the orator consorted much in
private. That difficulty, however, has been overcome in many notable instances, and members
of Parliament have prided themselves on the
facility with which they exchange the public for
the private rôle and have, out of hearing of un-
sophisticated constituents, laughed at the Radical
shoemaker who refuses to deal with the Tory
butcher.

Boswell, seeing Dr. Johnson and John Wilkes

literally *tête-à-tête* at Mr. Dilly's, expressed his
rapture. " Such a scene of perfectly easy sociality
between two such opponents in the war of political
controversy would," he wrote, " have been an
excellent subject for a picture. It presented to
my mind the happy days which are foretold in
Scripture, when the lion shall lie down with the
kid." If Wilkes was the kid he had done his best
to propitiate the lion by polite attention. Again,
it is interesting to read in Miss Burney's diary that
Windham loved Dr. Johnson and the latter returned his affection. " Their political principles and
connections were opposite, but Mr. Windham
respected his venerable friend too highly to discuss
any points that could offend him." On such
terms intercourse between opponents is easy enough.
It is not so easy when they meet in controversy
in the House of Commons.

There has been no more painful disagreement
on public affairs than that of Burke and Fox.
When Burke declared his readiness to risk the
desertion of friends for the sake of his views on the
French Revolution, and when Fox called out that
there was no loss of friends, he replied : " Yes, yes,
there is a loss of friends. I know the price of my
conduct. I have done my duty at the price of my
friend. Our friendship is at an end." Thus, as
Lord Morley records, " the once friendly intercourse
between the two heroes was at an end. When they
met in the Managers' box in Westminster Hall on
the business of Hastings's trial, they met with the
formalities of strangers."

Different statesmen, different temperaments !
Walpole, as a biographer points out, stood on easy
terms with men who every day denounced him
as the vilest of wretches. On the other hand, in

the case of Chatham, " disagreement on politics
became a fatal bar to friendly intercourse."
Yet who can say that the one was stauncher
than the other ? Disraeli, who was visited at
Hughenden by Harcourt and Lord Rosebery,
and who occasionally met Dilke and Granville,
and had a liking for Hartington, the Harty-tarty
of his letters, spoke and wrote in his later years
very severely and bitterly of Gladstone, but as
Viscount Bryce says in *Studies in Contemporary
Biography*, he was " not of those who complicate
political opposition with private hatreds. Looking
on politics as a game, he liked, when he took off his
armour, to feel himself on friendly terms with his
antagonists, and often seemed surprised to find
that they remembered as personal affronts the blows
which he had dealt in the tournament." Gladstone
did not look on politics as a game. With him it
was a contest between right and wrong. Always
in earnest, he seemed to regard those who differed
from him as blind to the moral light. The personal
animosity, however, which he felt with regard to
Disraeli, he did not maintain in the case of later
Conservative leaders. For neither the Marquis of
Salisbury nor Mr. Balfour had he unfriendly
feeling.

No statesmen of our time had more vigorous
encounters than those of Mr. Joseph Chamberlain
and Sir William Harcourt, but although their social
intercourse may have been lessened by their
difference on Home Rule, their friendship did not
cease like that of Fox and Burke. Harcourt,
loyal as he was to party, did not by any means in
his friendships keep within party lines. Many,
if not most, of his personal friends were in the camp
of his political opponents. Of Joseph Chamberlain,

the most pugnacious of politicians, it has been said by one who knew him well that he possessed the genius of friendship. " I have never," according to his own confession, " cherished personal animosity to any man, and I have always known how to separate in our political differences the public feeling from the private character." After he had become the ally of the Conservatives and their colleague in Government, he remained on good terms with the ablest of the new Liberals. To this fact witness is borne by the visitors' book at " The Old Cheshire Cheese." In the summer of 1898, when he was Colonial Secretary in Lord Salisbury's Coalition, Mr. Chamberlain and his wife lunched at the tavern in company with Mr. and Mrs. Asquith, Mr. Haldane and Sir Edward Grey.

Asperity is abated by family influences as well as by school memories, business associations, common tastes and recreations. Men of the same kin are not always on the same side. Brothers of Sir William Harcourt and Sir Henry Campbell-Bannerman sat opposite to these statesmen. Mr. Gladstone's eldest brother remained a Tory, the 15th Earl of Derby (son of the Premier), after changing his party connection, served in Mr. Gladstone's second Government, which was stoutly opposed by his brother and successor, Colonel Stanley, and while the Marquis of Lansdowne was leader of the Unionist peers, his brother, Lord Fitzmaurice, was for a time among Liberal Ministers. Marriage sometimes unites the families of prominent opponents, and strong personal friendship throws down the party barrier with a bold disregard of appearances. Mr. Bright might have looked with suspicion at Mr. Churchill and Mr. F. E. Smith (later the Lord Chancellor), when, after pounding one another in debate, they walked from the House arm-in-arm. Neither found it difficult to " attack in public a man with whom the orator consorted much in private."

The amenities of life are easily practised by peers. It is true that debate in the House of Lords is sometimes acrimonious and that members of a Government which touches privilege or land are treated as traitors to their order, but among men belonging to a very select class and moving in a narrow world it is difficult to avoid friendly inter-course. As a rule, too, the peers conduct their controversies with a ceremonious, stately courtesy. Earl Granville, who was Liberal leader in the Upper House during an era of much-hated Gladstonianism, never made an enemy, while he had among political opponents many friends. The Marquis of Salisbury was held in as much personal respect on the one side as on the other, and the same may be said of the Marquis of Lansdowne and the Marquis of Crewe, who led the two parties in hard-fighting days.

Rancour is less common among life-long oppo-nents than among parted colleagues. " Alas ! " cries a stricken heart, " for the loves of statesmen, often ardent and always precarious ! " . " Honeyed words at parting with colleagues," said Sir James Graham on leaving Palmerston's Government in 1855, " are almost always nauseous, generally deceitful, and—like lovers' vows under similar circumstances—unavailing and laughed to scorn." An ex-Premier with painful experience has put the matter in the true light. " Political friend-ships when paths diverge," writes Lord Rosebery, " are more difficult to maintain than men them-selves realize at the moment of separation." This

3

has often proved to be the case. The retiring Minister, although he leaves the Government on public grounds, bears in his sore heart the seed of resentment against colleagues who remain; he takes opportunities—patriotically of course—to show that those who differ from him were wrong, and gradually as he settles in the corner of a back bench and watches old associates in the seats of the mighty, his criticism of their policy become severe and his relations with them strained.

Peel, when he changed his course on the Corn Laws, Mr. Chamberlain, when he left Mr. Gladstone, and Mr. Lloyd George, when he replaced Mr. Asquith, were bitterly attacked by former colleagues. " Love as if you should hereafter hate ; and hate as if you should hereafter love " is an ancient maxim which a cynic might commend to a prudent politician. The second part of it has been observed —not from design, but through temperament— by Mr. Lloyd George. Sharp as his controversies were with Unionists, he was not without friends among them in pre-war times. When he was the incisive critic of their Administration he and Mr. Balfour exchanged some pretty courtesies. At a later period, when Mr. Bonar Law and Mr. Lloyd George were, in the language of the latter, " hammering each other," they were not the enemies that they might have seemed to be. Mr. Bonar Law told Mr. Lloyd George in 1914 that " what he has not realized is that there is some work which gentlemen, whatever their rank in life, will not do," and also said a few weeks before the war that he had used the Exchequer politically to help electioneering. Yet Mr. Lloyd George testified in December, 1918, that during the whole of that period of party strife they were " good and close personal friends."

The rareness of festering wounds in the Parliamentary battle-field is due partly to its rules and conventions. There is an etiquette not only in debate but in the relationship of members, a club-like fellowship, which one generation has handed down to another, and the neglect of which would be resented by any section. The Lobby, the dining-rooms and smoking-rooms and the terrace have their soothing influence. While the old party warfare was at its height one who received and gave the hardest of blows declared that there was no country in the world where such warfare was conducted under stricter and more honourable rules of fair-play and chivalry. The code of conduct has certainly been well fashioned by tradition. And in securing its observance a special duty rests on the Front Benches whose example counts for as much as the authority of the Chair.

In Queen Victoria's reign the leader of " Her Majesty's Opposition " became a clearly defined figure. He acquired a distinct place in the constitutional system as the chief critic of the Government and the responsible mouthpiece and representative of the alternative set of statesmen. The idea that a successful Opposition as such should take the reins was formerly, as Bagehot observes, derided. " Sir," says the sceptic whom he quotes, " I w'd as soon choose for a new coachman the man who shied stones best at my old one." It is not because he shies stones that the new State coachman is chosen ; it is because the country distrusts or is tired of the man on the box and hopes his rival may drive the coach better or safer. To the leader of Opposition official information is sometimes communicated before the House obtains it : he receives a copy of the speech from the throne the night before its delivery; and to a certain degree he shares responsibility for what he does not repudiate. It is his duty to watch the course of affairs, to resist what he considers injurious to the State and to co-operate with the Government on occasions of supreme national emergency.

Consideration for the leader of the Opposition by the leader of the House was familiarly and pleasantly displayed in the time, for instance, of Sir William Harcourt and Mr. Balfour. Harcourt, on one occasion, after announcing the order of business from the Treasury bench, whispered across the table : " Will that suit you, Arthur ? " Similar friendliness was shown by Mr. Balfour when their positions were reversed. In matters which were not vital it was natural for him or any one in his place to consult the convenience of the principal figure with whom he had to cross swords. On Mr. Bonar Law's first appearance in the House as Unionist leader, Mr. Asquith sent a letter to him. Perhaps some day it will be published in the recipient's biography. A letter of courtesy, it was worthy of the chivalry which as a rule characterizes Parliamentary conflict.

" It has long," said Disraeli, in replying to Hartington's first speech as Opposition leader, " been the boast of the House of Commons that even when political passions run high and party warmth becomes somewhat intense, there should exist between those members of both parties who take any considerable share in the conduct of business sentiments of courtesy and, when the public interest requires it, even of confidence, which tend very greatly to facilitate the business of the country to the public advantage." A curious instance of such sentiments and of the friendly

ease of front bench personages engaged in even
deadly public warfare—an instance which might
confirm Mr. Belloc in his view of the party system
—is given by Mrs. Asquith in her *Autobiography*,
where she mentions that on the morning after the
defeat of the Rosebery Government, in which her
husband was Home Secretary, Mr. Brodrick came
to see her. " He was full of excitement and
sympathy, and anxious to know if we minded his
being instrumental in our downfall."

Intimacy of this sort was natural to the limited
range of the society from which, until recently, the
Front Benches were drawn.  From our own level-
ling age we look back with a sense of contrast to
the time when almost all the rulers of the country
belonged to the aristocracy and notably to the
higher landed class.  Burke might aid the Whig
magnates with his genius, but the great Cabinet
offices were for his patrons.  Even as late as Peel's
day it was considered remarkable that a man sprung
from the merchant class should become Prime
Minister.  " Then the world," as we read in *Sybil*,
" was not only made for a few but a very few.  One
could almost tell upon one's fingers the happy
families who could do anything and might have
everything."  Many now living remember the
flutter which was caused when Mr. Broadhurst,
who had worked as a stone-mason, was appointed
an Under-Secretary.  His appointment was considered an act of condescension on Mr. Gladstone's
part.  There was a shaking of privileged heads
even when a Cabinet post was given to Mr. John
Morley, a man of letters, without official training
or powerful family connection.  Understandings
between the Front Benches were, no doubt, comparatively easy when the country was governed

by groups drawn mainly from narrow classes.
Whatever might be the " jealous rivalry of the
oligarchic clans," the patricians, with a common
pride and prejudice, meeting each other in country
houses, could quickly pass the party barrier.

How conditions changed, we all know. The
democratizing of Parliament and Government begun
in the Queen's reign has proceeded steadily.   Front
benches have ceased to be monopolized by men
moving in the same sphere.   Holders of office have
gone home in a crowded tram-car to the suburbs.
But notwithstanding social change, the life of the
House of Commons and the relations of its active
figures have continued in the twentieth century to
be influenced by the traditions of the nineteenth.
There has been the same interdependence of the
front benches.   " Ins " have treated " Outs " as
men who in course of time and political tide might
be called to Downing Street ;  they have recognized
an unwritten obligation to leaders of Opposition.
And the " Outs " in turn, except when carried away
by gusts of passion, have borne in mind the
responsibility which awaited them, and have given
to the Government of the day the support they
themselves hoped in due course to receive.

On the eve of the war a popular sailor, who was
a strong partisan, deplored the friendly association
of Unionists with members of the Government.
Although "not so small-minded " as to say they
should have no private relations with political
foes, Lord Beresford held that there was " no
necessity to take part in recreative sports with
men you call traitors, or to stay with them or dine
with them."   Feeling was at a violent pitch when
advice of this sort could be publicly given.   At the
hour of need, however, even in such conditions of

temper, opponents suspended their quarrels and consulted together in the common cause, subsequently meeting in the same Cabinet and sitting on the same bench with perfect loyalty to each other. Their co-operation in the emergency was rendered easier by, and was in fact a development of, the traditional process which had grown up " behind the Speaker's chair."

# CHAPTER III

## MR. GLADSTONE, LORD SALISBURY, LORD ROSEBERY

WHEN I began to observe the House of Commons (at the opening of the Press Gallery to the Provincial, Scottish and Irish Press in 1881) Mr. Gladstone was Prime Minister for the second time, and with him on the Treasury bench were Mr. John Bright, Lord Hartington, Sir William Harcourt, Mr. Joseph Chamberlain, Sir Charles Dilke, and Mr. Childers. Sir Stafford Northcote, who on Disraeli's elevation to the peerage had succeeded to the leadership of the House, was now leader of the Opposition, with Sir Michael Hicks Beach, Mr. W. H. Smith and Lord John Manners among his colleagues. Lord Randolph Churchill and Mr. Arthur Balfour were below the Opposition gangway, the former bounding into celebrity as founder of the Fourth Party and the latter an uncertain member of it. Mr. Parnell, at the head of a brilliant band of agitators and obstructives, was defying the Government and the House. Of all these men Mr. Balfour alone remains in 1921. Some are almost forgotten.

Vanity of vanities, all is vanity—one is inclined to say—in the political world. Most of its reputations are fleeting. Men who hold high office, who win dazzling victories in debate, who are cheered and courted, hated and envied, fade from fame in a few rapid years. The once familiar names are strange to the new generation. A few, only a few, continue to shine.

Several of the politicians prominent forty years ago hoped, or were expected by friends, to reach the highest position. This or that rising man was selected by observers as a future Prime Minister ; others thought So-and-So more likely. Very few, if any, included Mr. Balfour among those to whom the splendid prize might fall, and Sir Henry Campbell-Bannerman, although on the Treasury bench, had not said or done anything to arouse great expectations. Yet these two alone among the colleagues or critics of Gladstone at that time were destined to win the place to which the ambitious aspired. Mr. Asquith, not then in the House, was little known beyond Oxford and the Courts. Mr. Lloyd George was still in his teens.

## MR. GLADSTONE

Nobody who saw or heard Mr. Gladstone could forget that wonderful face, that wonderful voice. Many of the questions on which he spent his ingenuity and oratory, which excited his audience and on which the future weal or woe of the country appeared to depend, may have disappeared in the mist of memory : the man himself remains conspicuous. What is the impression left on one who watched Mr. Gladstone and heard nearly all his Parliamentary speeches during the last thirteen years of his political activity ? A noble figure, with grave, proud, commanding, awe-inspiring features, attired in an old-fashioned frock-coat, with wide display of shirt front, a broad black tie fastened in a bow and high collar open at the chin ; ever ready in speech, dominating the House of Commons by his personality and genius, vehement in controversy and restless under attack, his great eyes glowing and blazing : a born leader of the multitude, revered by followers, dreaded by opponents, and wherever and whenever he appeared the observed of all observers, arresting attention, arousing tireless curiosity !

Never was the onlooker unoccupied when Gladstone could be seen, never did pen or pencil lack a theme when he could be described. His face, his gestures, his movements, his writing of the letter to the Queen, even his collar as his head sank into it were watched with never lessening interest. After Disraeli left he had no rival in fame ; and whether he sat on the Treasury bench or on the Opposition side of the table he towered above all others.

Which were the greatest of Gladstone's orations in the thirteen years during which I heard him ? Which do I remember most distinctly ? Vivid is my recollection of his speech on the death of Lord Beaconsfield. He was later in arriving than had been expected and the journalists who were for ever assailing him surmised that he was staying away in order to avoid paying a tribute to his dead opponent. At last he entered quickly and as I write I see again the exalted, far-off expression in his eyes, I live again through the deep, solemn thrill of his tones. His eulogy cast a spell on the House. Lord Morley says it cost him " much searching of heart beforehand." Every hearer pronounced it a magnanimous and a generous as well as an eloquent tribute, although on reading it some of the critics could not account for its effect. Gladstone had the power of mesmerizing the House. While listening to his words and watching his face it forgot itself.

" An unparalleled Parliamentary triumph," as the leader of the Fourth Party informed the Marquis of Salisbury, was secured by Gladstone in 1885 on moving a vote of credit for the contingency of war with Russia, when the fear of her advance on India was inflamed by an attack upon the Afghans at Penjdeh. It was an unexpected triumph. Conservatives had planned an assault on Gladstone's " ambiguous " policy, but so mesmeric was his eloquence that, to the dismay of Lord Randolph Churchill, who went away in the middle of his speech to dine, the whole Front Opposition Bench remained " as mute as mummies " and the orator sat down, as Lord Randolph's son records, " while the House was ringing with the united acclamations of Radicals who hated war

and of Tories who hated him." * I have never
seen so complete and conspicuous a collapse of
preparation for an assault. Subsequent events
proved that there was no general confidence in
the policy then laid down, but the vote was passed
without comment.

Varied were the tones, and the scales of rebuke
or remonstrance, in which during the early 'eighties,
when still the revered chief of an undivided Liberal
party, Gladstone dealt with men on the other side.
Sir Stafford Northcote, who had been private
secretary to him at the Board of Trade, he treated
with a courteous condescension ; he was pained
rather than angered when his former *protégé* dared
to challenge him. To Mr. Arthur Balfour as a
young personal friend he referred with amiable
reproach. Randolph Churchill, while appreciating
his greatness, frequently provoked the giant to
wrath and in castigation of that undismayed
assailant he was merciless. Mr. Chaplin, whose
oratorical style was a caricature of his own, drew
his severe and scornful strictures. The Parnellites
caused him deep distress by their obstruction at
Westminster and terrorism in Ireland. Mr. John
Dillon's speeches in particular gave him pain.
One of them he described as heart-breaking.

The long speeches Gladstone delivered in submitting his Home Rule bills were, like his Budget
statements, marvels in exposition. The details
were set off with passages of eloquence, and even
to the details he imparted interest. His rare
power in this respect came partly from the many
lights and hues of his mind and partly from the
magic of his voice. The fact that he himself took

* *Lord Randolph Churchill* ; W. S. Churchill.

delight in details and loved to wander through all
the ramifications of an elaborate subject was a
cause of their attraction to listeners.

Other speeches which he made in the controversy
on these bills, speeches of argument, appeal, denunciation and passion, excited emotions as strong as
he aroused at any period of his career. However
divided were men's opinions on his old-age conversion to Home Rule—whether they thought it
was a mere barter for Parnellite votes or a natural
application of long-held principles to new conditions—all admired the wealth of the resources
which he devoted to the daring and hazardous
adventure. His courage, enthusiasm and faith
kindled hope and zeal in disciples and followers.
At an age when most politicians cast off their
armour and settle into anecdotage or " ermined
insignificance " he fought under the Irish flag
against as powerful opponents as were ever cheered
in Parliament, encountering not only the Conservative leaders, whom he had met in many battles,
but also the Liberal lieutenants who had left him.
Chamberlain, the strongest debater among them all,
was at his best in the closing years of his old
chief's life, but the victory was not always to the
younger man. In the prodigious contests of 1893
the " Grand Old Man " displayed a range of rhetoric
and a readiness of retort which would, even if
limited to a single session, have conferred enduring
fame on any Parliamentarian.

Memories of Gladstone are undimmed although
a quarter of a century with its new figures and
new problems has passed since he went behind the
Speaker's chair for the last time, a beaten man.
I think of him seated on the Treasury bench
listening to debate ; he is attacked, he pauses in

the writing of a letter, gradually he becomes alert, he draws up his shoulders so that his high collar reaches his ears ; he is then " on the pounce," he springs to his feet amid the battle cheers of eager partisans, his eyes blaze, his voice quivers, he bangs the box in front of him, he points the finger of derision, he flings forth his arms and turns with an appeal to members behind him and the House is in a tempest of passion.

The writing of the leader's nightly letter to the Sovereign was a duty on which we saw Gladstone engaged at a late hour. From this duty Disraeli (although he sent many lively communications to the Queen) was excused in his second Prime Ministership and reports of the proceedings of the House were sent, as they have been in recent sessions, by a member of the Government holding a post in the Household. It was an occupation which Gladstone, so long as he performed it, performed with assiduity. He wrote as he sat on the Treasury Bench. He wrote even during stormy scenes when perhaps the fate of his Government was uncertain. Sometimes he would lay down the pad for a moment or hold it in his hand while he rose to correct a critic on a small point, thereby obliging the critic with fresh fuel for controversy.

A mighty man far above his fellows, personal deference was shown to Gladstone by all members, irrespective of party, except the spiteful. Discourtesy to him in extreme old age would have been as strongly resented by Mr. Balfour, the last leader of his opponents, as by any Liberal. He was not so easy of approach as later Prime Ministers in the House of Commons. Few private members ventured to address him. Even many of his official colleagues stood in awe of the great chief.

A word to a follower in the division lobby was a distinction. Yet with all his greatness—or because of his greatness—he was considerate to the humblest. When very old he would move to the end of his bench and place his hand behind his ear to gather the words of an obscure Nationalist below the gangway. "See," said the cynic, "how he fawns upon the Irish." His interest was not assumed and Conservatives as well as friends acknowledged his attention. "I remember," writes Sir Arthur Griffith-Boscawen, "that he sat through my maiden speech, which is more than any of my own leaders did."

A feature of Gladstone's speeches and answers which exposed them to jeers was their verbosity or copiousness (to use a politer word) and ambiguity. It was his habit, as it was the tradition of the older school, to wrap his meaning in phrases and formulas which required a special training for their interpretation. Frequently his statements of policy were so qualified that, in the judgment of the suspicious, it was his purpose to leave a loophole of escape. Colleagues sometimes looked unhappy, as if their pride in him were offended when he laboured to explain away what had been regarded as his declared view. Many of his sentences were extremely long and involved, containing one parenthesis after another. Listeners would wonder how he could bring them to a grammatical end. In this he seldom, perhaps never, failed. They came victoriously out of the tangle. Opponents used to say that Gladstone resorted to intricacies and involutions because he did not know his own mind or did not wish others to know it. Friends, on the other hand, said his qualifications and reservations sprang from fullness and fertility of mind; he could see much more clearly than others, while laying down any proposition, the possible need which might arise for limiting its application.

Conviction, earnestness and the appeal to moral sanction were among the qualities which secured to Gladstone unsurpassed success as a popular orator and leader. " He can persuade himself of almost anything," said a critic who had been a colleague. Therein partly lay the secret of his power. He never spoke from a brief : he spoke as one profoundly convinced. He spoke as one on whose side was righteousness and against whom were the powers of darkness. " Nothing great," wrote Emerson, " was ever achieved without enthusiasm." Gladstone threw heart and soul as well as intellect into whatever he undertook. Although he may thus have exaggerated the issue, he gave to it a loftiness and glamour which stirred generous instincts. Opponents of his policy were enemies of the State if not also enemies of eternal justice ! His appeals to divine guidance were no hypocritical device. If he deceived others he deceived also himself. This power of believing that what he advocated was necessary to the saving of the nation and that what his opponents proposed would be fatal to its highest interests accounted for much of the moral fervour which he aroused. He was as a god to masses of ordinary mortals. Much of the interest of Parliament went out when, baffled in his final endeavour, he resigned the Prime Ministership and left it for ever in March, 1894.

## THE MARQUIS OF SALISBURY

On an August night in 1876 Disraeli " in a long white overcoat and dandified lavender kid gloves, leaning on his secretary's arm," * forsook the scene where he had fought his way over many obstacles to supreme success and where Gladstone, then resting from leadership, remained for eighteen years longer. The zenith of his career he spent in the calm atmosphere of what Victorian writers called the Guilded Chamber and here he had his final experience in the valley of Opposition. From the front crimson bench on the left of the throne he looked across the table at the colleagues of the great antagonist who had driven him from power. His last polemical speech in the House of Lords, on the withdrawal from Candahar, was the only speech from that strange man of genius I ever heard. He impressed me by the sombreness of his tone. A fortnight later he spoke in support of the vote of condolence on the murder of the Emperor Alexander of Russia and in a few weeks his place was empty.

It would have been difficult then to choose a successor to the commandership-in-chief of the Conservatives whom Disraeli had led in wonderful ways. That was a choice which would ultimately depend on the Queen's selection for the Prime Ministership when they returned to office. All that had immediately to be done, the party being in Opposition, was for its members in the House of Lords to appoint their own leader, who would act with Sir Stafford Northcote. Even for this post opinion did not point at first in one direction.

* *The Life of Sir Charles W. Dilke :* Gwynn and Tuckwell.

There was discussion, at any rate in the Press, before the decision was taken. An impassioned denunciation by Lord Cairns of the Transvaal policy of the Government drew attention to the combative qualities of the ex-Lord Chancellor, although he had found in 1869 his semi-judicial position inconsistent with party leadership; Lord Cranbrook, who as Gathorne Hardy defeated Gladstone at Oxford, possessed qualification as a vigorous debater and a favourite of the country party; and there was some talk of the Duke of Richmond as a safe man who had experience of the leadership.

Cautious Conservatives were doubtful of the discretion of the Marquis of Salisbury. His capacity had been proved, and he had won a European reputation as Foreign Secretary, but everybody remembered Disraeli's saying that he was " not a man who measures his phrases " and that he was " a great master of gibes and flouts and jeers." Everybody recalled that when the paper duty was being discussed he ridiculed the idea of a person of any education learning anything from a penny paper. Everybody recalled how, after he had said that certain devices were more worthy of an attorney than a statesman, he made an apology —to the attorneys. Although applauded in the heat of debate, his gibes left in prudent politicians a feeling of distrust. They were afraid that he would be reckless not only in phrase but in action. The Marquis's claim, however, could not long be resisted. His intellectual distinction, his knowledge, his fitness to cope with the statecraft of Gladstone, as well as his high character, were thoroughly recognized. Moreover, it turned out on inquiry, as Mr. Traill has recorded in his biography, that the misgivings which his name

and personality inspired in anxious minds were not
shared by those who knew him best.  It is probable
that some of the peers who acquiesced in his election
as leader, an election which was unanimous, calculated that his rashness would be held in check by
his very circumspect colleague in the other House
with whom he was to share the control of the party.

The dual control, with uncertainty as to the
choice of the Sovereign for the Prime Ministership,
lasted till 1885 when, on the fall of the Liberal
Government, Queen Victoria sent for the Marquis.
From that date he exercised complete authority
in the Conservative domain.  His authority was
challenged by Lord Randolph Churchill, but the
challenge proved fatal to Lord Randolph.  Not
only was the Marquis's supremacy in his own party
maintained and strengthened, but he was undis-
puted chief of the Coalition of Conservatives and
Liberal Unionists.  He was fortunate in having
as his principal ally in the Coalition so disinterested
a statesman as the Duke of Devonshire and in
having as the party leader in the House of Commons,
after Lord Randolph Churchill, first the faithful Mr.
Smith and then his own nephew, Mr. Balfour.  Mr.
Joseph Chamberlain, who at an earlier period had
exchanged sharp words with " my lord Salisbury,"
may not always have been a comfortable colleague,
but, so far as the world saw, the Marquis was not
greatly disturbed by the adventures of his former
arch-critic.

" He is rough of tongue in public debate," wrote
Gladstone of Lord Salisbury in 1876, " but a great
gentleman in private society."  Rough of tongue
he remained.  Often as a party leader, when watchful
pens pounced on his words, he indulged in quips
and sallies which startled nervous friends and

were quoted against him by critics. " A salis-bury " became the synonym for a blazing indis-cretion. His comparison of intractable Irish to races like the Hottentots who were incapable of self-government provided Liberals with a Press and platform weapon of which they made plentiful use, and his allusion to an Indian candidate for Parliament as " a black man " enabled leader-writers to argue anew that he was " not a man who measures his phrases." As a rule, however, he dealt with high subjects in a high manner and in some of his caustic sayings the opponents of his domestic policy found good sense, as when he advised people afraid of Russia's advance to study large maps and when he suggested that in our Near East policy as between Turkey and Russia we had backed the wrong horse. In course of time he was universally respected as one of the steadying forces of Europe and his foreign policy gradually secured the confidence even of those who had previously imagined him to be a danger to the State.

Although during the last nine years of Glad-stone's public life Lord Salisbury, after his first appointment as Prime Minister, was the supreme chief of the Conservative party, he was not the Liberal leader's most familiar antagonist. It was by colleagues and friends in the House of Commons that the incessant and sometimes bitter fray was carried on. Lord Salisbury flouted Gladstone's policy and Gladstone solemnly reproached Lord Salisbury, but the struggle between them was devoid of personal bitterness. Each respected the character of the other and they had a link in their devotion to the Church of England. A few weeks before his death, while waiting for the summons which was not of this world, Gladstone wrote a letter to Lady Salisbury on her husband's narrow escape in a carriage accident. At a time of international dangers and anxieties he saw that the Marquis's life was precious to England. And no finer tribute was paid to Gladstone himself when the final summons came than that of the Conservative Prime Minister who described him as " a great Christian statesman " and acted as a pall-bearer at his funeral.

All who appreciated political knowledge and dialectical skill enjoyed the duels of Lord Salisbury and the statesman who throughout a period of thirty-six years (except when Earl Russell was Prime Minister) led the Liberal peers. Earl Granville, one of the last of the aristocratic Whigs who ruled through the great families and the country houses, was an important figure in Queen Victoria's reign. Liberals honoured him for the patience and pluck with which he kept their flag flying in a field where the forces against him steadily grew, and the House of Lords as a whole honoured him because, as an opponent testified, " no political leader ever lived who was more closely and entirely identified with the assembly in which he sat." His duels with the Marquis were not unequal. With manner bland and soft enough to earn for him the title of " pussy Granville " he got in many a neat blow.

When I think of the Marquis I recall a man big in frame, with coat hanging clumsily from his bent shoulders and hat deep on his great head ; he strides heavily to his place in the House of Lords, thrusts his hat beneath the bench regardless of its fate ; he listens and meditates, by and by his knees bob up and down, then we know his mind is busy on a speech ; he rises, fills a glass of water and drinks, and placidly proceeds to pour forth his thoughts with face turned towards the reporters' gallery. He does not indulge in any gestures. He has no notes. Only when about to give a quotation he draws a slip from his pocket. The literary grace of his speeches is pleasing to the fastidious listener. Every sentence is as perfect as if he had written it carefully. He does not soar to eloquence, but he is luminous, piquant and incisive and he seasons his argument with irony, occasionally uttering a gibe which causes a gentle flutter and which runs through the corridors to the country.

I never saw the Marquis in the peers' gallery of the House of Commons. While that Chamber has held its spell over many who have gone from it to the other place, Lord Salisbury showed no desire to look down on the arena in which he laid the foundation of his fame. When the business of the peers was finished he passed out at once through the central hall where strangers stared at the well-known, heavy figure ; he never crossed to the Commons. It was easy to believe that he did not recognize all his colleagues. A Prime Minister who sits in the House of Lords has few opportunities of becoming familiar with a subordinate member of his Government in the other House, unless they meet in society or the clubs. Lord Salisbury was not a club-man and preferred Hatfield to the West End of London.

For over twenty years he ruled the House of Lords. Once or twice, when he made concessions to his Radical ally, a group of Tory peers revolted, but the revolt proved futile. Few statesmen have possessed so much power as he exercised from the time of his first Ministry in 1885 till he laid down his official burden in 1902. During that period, with the exception of six months in 1886 and 1892–1895, he was at the head of affairs, and when in Opposition the readiness of the House of Lords to do his will enabled him to control and check Liberal legislation. Protests were made against the action of the peers under his leadership, but at a later time, when they had other guides, it was remembered that he had never challenged the clearly established opinion of the country.

## THE EARL OF ROSEBERY

Once a peer, always a peer ! That has been the misfortune of the Earl of Rosebery. Contact with the rough and ready world of the House of Commons would have called forth his popular qualities and they would have been developed by its discipline, but he succeeded his grandfather in the year of his majority, and as he once pathetically said, the doors of the House of Lords open only inwards. There were times probably when his thoughts turned wistfully to the popular Chamber with its quick and animated life and decisive functions. His footsteps often led to its gallery. With its environment he might have been a happy leader.

" An orator, a courtier, a wit and a man of letters "—Macaulay's description of Lord Chesterfield : is it not also a partial description of Lord Rosebery ? He was all these characters and more. Richly endowed by nature and favoured by fortune his capacity to charm was not equalled by any man of our time.

> " What'er he did, was done with so much ease,
> In him alone 'twas natural to please."

But did he turn the talents with which he was entrusted to full account ? He won all that the world has to offer in position and fame, and yet his career disappointed those who in his early and middle age were dazzled by his brightness. After a brief political leadership he retired to his splendid tent ; looking out from it he saw that his reappearance was eagerly hoped for and awaited ; he made an occasional sally and then secluded himself again, leaving no inspiring impulse behind ; his followers gradually fell away and turned to another standard.

A plainer, homelier, more steadfast Scot succeeded where the gifted Earl failed.

Over forty years have passed since the most brilliant young man in Great Britain, who at the age of twenty-seven had presided at the Social Science Congress and who was married to a Rothschild, captured the affection of the Liberal party by his devotion in the Midlothian campaign to the hero whom it carried back to power. On the formation of the Government in 1880 he declined the Under-Secretaryship for India. He wrote to Lord Hartington, who would have been his chief, that he did not wish at that time to begin an official career, and according to Lord Fitzmaurice's *Life of Lord Granville*, he feared that public opinion would see in the post an equivalent for the electoral support he had given to Gladstone. He went to the Home Office as Under Secretary in 1881, with an eye specially on the affairs of Scotland, which had not then a separate Department, but he could not get on with his chief, Sir William Harcourt, and he resigned in 1883. His prestige and popularity soon brought the offer of a higher place. It was only, however, in February, 1885, on the fall of Khartoum, when his first thought was how to help the Ministers, that he entered the Cabinet. His action was thought to be disinterested and chivalrous, for the Government was doomed; and it fell on the following June.

Although he began in subordinate offices, Lord Rosebery had no reason to complain of his progress. Instead of the experienced Granville, he was appointed Foreign Secretary in the Gladstone Government of 1886. To have reached that high and distinguished position at the age of thirty-eight was an achievement worthy of his abilities and reputation. And when Joseph Chamberlain was dissociated from the official Liberal party the Earl's prospects looked more glittering than ever. He was now regarded in many quarters as the natural heir to the Gladstonian mantle and while the party was in opposition the heir grew in favour. A House of Lords which threw cold water on his zeal for its reform provided no adequate sphere for his political activities out of office, but as the first Chairman of the London County Council "John Burns's pal" and "the coronetted Social- ist" dived deep into Radical hearts. Once more Foreign Secretary in 1892, he was by the choice of the Queen, and with the approval of nearly all his Cabinet colleagues, called in 1894 to succeed Gladstone as head of the Government.

From this period, when he won the Derby and the Prime Ministership and his name was on every tongue, the dissensions which eventually closed his career began to be openly and recklessly displayed. Although London Radical newspapers had recom- mended him for the place vacated by the chief whom he held in honour and affection, a section of Liberal members who would have preferred Har- court vehemently objected to its being held by a peer. Distrust of his leadership extended to others when in his first speech as Prime Minister in the House of Lords he accepted the doctrine that before Home Rule could be adopted England as the predominant partner must be convinced of its justice. Gladstone's bill had been carried by a majority of the elected representatives of the United Kingdom and the requirement of a purely English majority was resented by the Irish Nation- alists and by their zealous Liberal allies.

Personal as well as political differences sapped

Lord Rosebery's new position. In his book on Pitt, published in 1891, he wrote : " It would be too much to maintain that all the members of a Cabinet should feel an implicit confidence in each other ; humanity—least of all political humanity— could not stand so severe a test. But between a Prime Minister in the House of Lords and the leader of the House of Commons such a confidence is indispensable ! Responsibility rests so largely with the one, and articulation so greatly with the other, that unity of sentiment is the one necessary link that makes a relation, in any case difficult, in any way possible." There was not between Lord Rosebery and Harcourt, the leader of the House of Commons, that necessary confidence or unity of sentiment. Both were relieved when the Government fell in the snap division on cordite.

Misfortune usually draws a party together, but disagreement among Liberals did not lessen or abate in rancour during the early years of their wandering in the wilderness. Besides a suspicion of Lord Rosebery's attitude towards Home Rule there were wider grounds of difference. His Imperialism was disliked by those who feared the enlargement of our responsibilities ; he had been, unlike many Radicals, opposed to the evacuation of Egypt long before events put that step out of the question, and he insisted upon our retention of Uganda when a powerful section denounced it. Another cause of dissension was his desire to mend and strengthen rather than end or fetter the House of Lords. Personal rivalries, if not intrigues, accentuated the difficulties and so deep were the discords that he threw up the leadership in 1896 and severed his responsible connection with the party that he adorned.

For nearly ten years he was " a dark horse in a loose box." Nobody knew what he might do. When it was asserted that he had left the Liberal party he retorted that the fact would be more correctly stated if it were alleged that the party had left him. The party might have returned to him if he had cared to lead it where it desired to go, but he was not prepared to say with the leader of the Jacobin mob : " *Je suis leur chef, il faut que je les suive.*" A considerable number of Liberals, including several ex-members of Government, continued to look to him for guidance, and when Harcourt, in turn, threw up the leadership of the Opposition in the House of Commons and was succeeded by Campbell-Bannerman, there appeared a prospect of reconciliation.

The prospect varied frequently, brightening for a time and then passing into obscurity. In 1901, when the rank and file of the party which he had left or which had left him was drawing together, Lord Rosebery protested that he would never voluntarily return to the arena of politics. " I must," as he told the City Liberal Club, " plough the furrow alone." At the end of the year it seemed that he might abandon that lonely life. Lively and flattering interest was aroused by his appearance on the political platform at Chesterfield. The country read into his speech a desire for Liberal re-union. It was mistaken. As Campbell-Bannerman informed Sir Henry Fowler,* Lord Rosebery still " declined to come into consultation " with the leaders of the Opposition. Early in 1902 he revived the distrust of Liberals by telling them " you have to clean your slate." To a clean slate the men who were content to repeat the lessons

* *The Life of Lord Wolverhampton.*

taught by Gladstone were resolutely opposed. They refused to rub out what had been written. " C.B." was now so firm in the leadership that he felt in a position to ask the ex-Prime Minister whether he " speaks to us from the interior of our political tabernacle or from some vantage ground outside." Lord Rosebery promptly replied that he remained outside Sir Henry's tabernacle " but not, I think, in solitude."

A new tabernacle was set up in the form of the Liberal League, with Lord Rosebery as President and Mr. Asquith and Sir Edward Grey among the Vice-Presidents. Several young men who were making their mark in debate joined the League, which was intended to maintain a prudent Imperialism as part of the Liberal faith. Both sections of the party, however, found increasing opportunities of acting in concert and hope of the re-union of leaders was once more revived. At Leicester, in November, 1903, Lord Rosebery agreed to " let bygones be bygones," and Campbell-Bannerman hailed with cordial satisfaction the discovery that he was " ready to share the labour and responsibility of public life in active co-operation with a united Liberal party." Alas ! the vision faded again. When the Unionist Administration was at the point of death and an appeal to the country was imminent, Lord Rosebery, observing that " C.B." had hoisted the flag of Home Rule, declared that he could not serve under that banner.

This was the end. It was for the staunch and steady leader of Opposition in the House of Commons and not for the ex-Prime Minister that King Edward sent when Mr. Balfour resigned and in his Government Lord Rosebery's friends accepted office. There remained for Lord Rosebery one more renunciation—the renunciation of attendance in the assembly of which he was the finest ornament. From the time that his friends took service under " C.B." he ploughed his lonely furrow—an attractive, yet pathetic figure.

Lord Rosebery's speeches were good to read; they were still better to hear. A musical voice, rich in tone, gave additional charm to the words, and the listener had the pleasure of watching the distinguished face with the grave, beautiful eyes. There was always something fresh and suggestive in his addresses whatever the subject might be. In literary flavour they excelled; wit sparkled in them and on questions of the day light was flashed by phrases as piquant as Mrs. Mountstuart Jenkinson's. Nothing in Parliamentary debate was more delightful than Lord Rosebery's raillery of the haughty, learned and eloquent Duke of Argyll, the great Whig who left Gladstone soon after the new Scottish star rose in the firmament. With banter and irony for a generation he set the country laughing at dull, pompous men. To see and hear Lord Rosebery was the desire of many a visitor to Westminster from our own country and America. He had always a good audience and a good Press for his speeches, but Peers disliked the vehemence which in his later years he displayed. He banged the box on the table and occasionally he raised his voice to a higher pitch than they considered genteel and then lowered it to a dramatic whisper. Such a display of feeling was more appropriate to a vulgar House than to the sedate and solemn Chamber. The icy tones of the Marquis of Lansdowne were more congenial to the ears of the patricians.

From a cross bench in the final stage of his political life Lord Rosebery watched the two violently conflicting sides. With hands clasped behind head he listened and meditated. He rarely conversed with any one. Perhaps nobody shared his confidence. Each time he moved to the table to speak there was a flutter among the peers and the sketch-writers were pleased at the prospect of " copy." Occasionally, when he had been expected to take part in debate, he left the House during its progress. Men said he liked to do what was unexpected and not to do what was expected. For a considerable period the " orator of the Empire " was heard much more frequently elsewhere than in the House of Lords. His speeches in that capacity gave admirable expression to national sentiment. Viscount Morley has mentioned his " excellent short books." His " Appreciations and Addresses " display the variety of literary and historical interests in which he found solace ; they display his culture, his lore, his fancy, the ripeness and richness of his mind. He has, what Henry James found in Hawthorne, a natural sense of language—a " turn for saying things lightly and yet touchingly, picturesquely yet simply, and for infusing a gently colloquial tone into matter of the most unfamiliar import." This is true of his speeches, as of his books.

At last the gifted peer who had piqued so much curiosity and won so much admiration, but had so few opportunities in his brief official career of directly influencing the policy of the country, left the House of Lords just as he had left the Liberal party, dissatisfied with its position and seeing for himself in it no useful function. In May, 1911, on the second reading of the Parliament Bill, he struck a farewell note. "We who are speaking here to-night," he said, "feel that we are speaking for the last time in this House as we have known it, and perhaps for the last time in these walls at all." His voice was heard a few months later on a most critical occasion. He hated the Parliament Bill, but when it came to be a question of the peers dying in the last ditch in resistance to the limitation of their powers, he declared on August 10, in "perhaps the most painful speech" of his life, that he could not risk the danger to which they were liable to be exposed by insisting upon their own proposals. So he voted that the House "do not insist" and disappeared from an assembly whose veto was clipped by his old Liberal friends. The War came and leaders of all parties were called to Downing Street, but Lord Rosebery did not return there and his name was rarely mentioned.

A shining and a splendid life he has had, but not the life hoped for by those partisans who honoured him and who would have loved him if he had cared for their love. To quote again his book on Pitt : "Time and circumstance and opportunity paint with heedless hands and garish colours on the canvas of a man's life ; so that the result is less frequently a finished picture than a palette of squeezed tints." Perhaps in his own case the unfinish of the picture was due partly to " time and circumstance " and partly to his temperament— his fastidiousness, his proud sensitiveness, his impatience with dull men, his lack of that discipline or pliability of mind which is so necessary to a political leader.

# CHAPTER IV

### THREE DRAMATIC FIGURES

As I look far back over the period covered by these notes my memory is haunted by the figures of three men who produced a sense of drama in the arena of Parliament—the figures of Lord Randolph Churchill, Mr. Parnell and Mr. Joseph Chamberlain. Seldom have three such men acted together on the same stage. In their time they were, apart from Gladstone, the most arresting, challenging, forceful personalities. Endowed with political genius and animated by great political aims and ambitions, they played exciting parts during an era in which the emotions of Parliament were unusually keen and its proceedings unusually interesting.

What tricks Fortune plays us ! How little can we read the future ! Who in the early 'eighties foresaw the fate of these three men—Joseph Chamberlain, the hope of the Radicals and their nominee for the succession to the Liberal leadership; Randolph Churchill, the most popular man in the Conservative party in the country and its most brilliant champion in the House of Commons; Parnell, the " uncrowned king of Ireland," the autocrat of the Home Rule members.¦ A few years passed and what then ? A miscalculated resignation and Churchill fell from power to political isolation. Parnell, famed for self-control, risked his career for a woman and a divorce case cost him his throne. Chamberlain, the Radical hero, became the ally of the Tories and instead of succeeding Gladstone served as the colleague of Lord Salisbury.

## LORD RANDOLPH CHURCHILL

Only one other man in the last forty years has by aggressive speech and tactics in Parliament attained such notoriety and success as Lord Randolph Churchill enjoyed in the stirring years 1880–1885 when with Sir Henry Drummond Wolff, Mr. Gorst and to some extent Mr. Arthur Balfour as colleagues he fought Gladstone, the giant, wrestled with the fighter from Birmingham, promoted Tory democracy and prodded the Conservative " old gang." " There are two great parties in the State," casually remarked a member in the good old-fashioned way. " Three ! " exclaimed Parnell. " Four ! " cried Churchill. Merrily laughed the House at his claim, but the Fourth Party which sprang into life in the Bradlaugh controversy flourished on its audacity, made an indelible mark on Parliamentary annals and left a fame which still endures.

I recall Lord Randolph standing at the corner of the front bench below the Opposition gangway, very smartly attired, twirling his heavy moustache, his hands at his waist, one foot thrust forward on the heel, his handkerchief obtruding from outer breast-pocket as he assailed the Liberal Ministers or turned with a jeer or rebuke on the leaders at his right hand. For these Conservative seniors —" the blameless and respectable gentlemen on the front Opposition bench "—he had no reverence or deference. Two of them he disdainfully likened to a drapery firm ; one he taunted with a " double-barrelled name, so often associated with mediocrity," He flouted " bourgeois placemen," he mocked the " old men who croon over the fires at the Carlton." Their methods were too cautious and conventional for him.   With his own small guerilla group he was always dashing into battle against " the Moloch of Midlothian."

With the diligence which is necessary to Parliamentary success Lord Randolph spent a great deal of time at the House of Commons, he and his friends kept a suspicious eye on all the proceedings of the Government, he acted thoroughly on the principle that it was the duty of an Opposition to oppose. His speeches were well-informed, incisive and vigorous.   He was a master of invective.   Grave argument he relieved by raillery, vivid personal touches and picturesque phrases which appealed to the public.   Outraged Liberals sneered at " the mischievous son of a duke," " the cheeky boy," the " randy," the " dandy " ; they shouted with glee when the representative of Woodstock was referred to by Mr. Jacob Bright as the member for Woodcock ; Gladstone, in irritation, likened him to an insect.   Conservatives of the old school at the same time shook their grave heads in displeasure at his forwardness, and grand-motherly newspapers solemnly rebuked him when he could not be ignored. But he had the instinct for the Parliamentary opportunity.   He struck at the right moment and struck hard ; he caught the imagination of the public and snubs and scoldings only increased his notoriety.   In a few years the Fourth Party achieved its leader's aim.   His spirit gradually spread through the Conservative ranks.   They followed the fighter.

In June, 1885, on the defeat of the Government whose prestige he had done more than any other opponent to destroy, Lord Randolph was master of the situation.   He had brought up to date Disraeli's education of the Tory party.   A " Conservative working man " had been the butt of the Liberal scoffer, but Lord Randolph, the aristocrat, made Tory democracy a real force. His influence was then greater than that of any of the elder Conservative statesmen who had frowned at him. In the formation of Lord Salisbury's first Government his voice was potent. It was on his insistent demand that Sir Michael Hicks Beach, instead of Sir Stafford Northcote, who was banished to the other place, was appointed leader of the House of Commons. In policy he exercised a startling influence. It was largely on account of his attitude and the co-operation with him of the Parnellites that the Conservative Government which came into existence with their support allowed the Irish Crimes Act to expire.

For himself the political king-maker accepted the post of Secretary of State for India. Staid persons who had thought him too rash and flighty for high office shuddered at the appointment. They did not know their man. He showed a true sense of responsibility and a dignity gratifying to his friends.

> " Consideration like an angel came
> And whipp'd the offending Adam out of him."

His tenure of the Indian Secretaryship, although brief, gave confidence in his capacity and conduct as a Minister and opened the way for him to a still higher place. On Gladstone's return (after the General Election) to office early in 1886 with an Irish Home Rule policy which secured the Nationalist vote, Lord Randolph took an active part in the promotion of a Conservative alliance with the Liberal Unionists. He joined with them in spirited attacks on the proposals of " an old man in a

hurry " ; he declared that " Ulster will fight and
Ulster will be right." Few members were surprised
when on the victory of the Unionists at the polls
in the summer of 1886 and the formation of
Lord Salisbury's second Government he received
the place which corresponded with his authority,
becoming Chancellor of the Exchequer and leader
of the House of Commons. He was then only
thirty-seven.

In his leadership, short as was its span, Lord
Randolph raised expectation high by dexterity,
tact and courtesy. The House admired, wondered
at and liked him. He seemed certain, indeed, to
become one of the most brilliant leaders it had ever
had. While his new manner was dignified, conciliatory and persuasive, he continued to proclaim
a democratic policy in striking phrases. I remember
the sensation he excited and the speculation which
followed when he came in during a debate and
declared that the great sign-posts of policy in the
development of a genuinely popular system of
government in all the countries of the United
Kingdom were " equality, similarity and simultaneity." For simultaneity in the treatment of
Ireland and England the older Tories were not
prepared, but Lord Randolph's words had received
the approval of his principal colleagues and they
undoubtedly expressed his own firm intention. His
far-reaching Dartford programme in October—a
programme which provoked the jealousy of Radicals
and reminded a critic of the palmy days of Gladstone
—manifested his bold, resourceful statesmanship.

If ambition or self-confidence led him astray and
if, like smaller men, he forgot that nobody in this
world is indispensable, it was in a great cause—
the cause of economy—that he took in December,

1886, the fatal step of resignation, which he announced to the Prime Minister on the note-paper of Windsor Castle, where he was a guest, and which, to the Queen's indignation, he disclosed to *The Times* before it was communicated to Her Majesty. The two terms of office of this remarkable man with political powers of a high order counted together only a single year.

A note of pathos runs through the remainder of Lord Randolph's career. Seated behind the Government which he had left he found himself politically isolated. Worse than that of " an old man in a hurry " became the plight of a young man in a hurry whose plans had been foiled. It was his doom for several years on a back bench to listen to the homilies of Mr. W. H. Smith, his successor in the leadership of the House, and to the Budget statements of Mr. Goschen, the new Chancellor of the Exchequer, whom he had forgotten in his outlook and whose acceptance of office in the Conservative Government had greatly assisted Lord Salisbury. Sometimes Lord Randolph disagreed with the Ministers, sometimes he quarrelled with their zealous friend, Mr. Chamberlain. He offended the Liberal Unionists by sneering at them as a useful kind of crutch and Mr. Chamberlain in turn ridiculed an independent programme which he submitted as a " crazy quilt." The breach between the ex-leader and former colleagues was widened by his censures of the Government in respect of the Commission they set up to inquire into " Parnellism and Crime." His denunciation of their extra-constitutional methods caused bitter resentment.

While attacking the Government on this subject in 1890 he paused to whisper a request for a glass of water. None of those near him moved to show the courtesy which as a rule is so readily offered. The request being repeated, a young member below the Ministerial gangway who heard it hurried out. When he returned and handed the glass which he had brought to the former hero of his party, Lord Randolph said in an aside : " I hope this will not compromise you." Such was the strain in the relations of parted colleagues ! It is easy to keep on good terms with an opponent ; to forgive a friend is an exercise of virtue rare in a politician.

As Lord Randolph watched the rise of his Fourth Party comrade, Mr. Balfour, and noted his growing favour with the Conservative ranks he may have realized that the chance of his own return to leadership was gone. There was never, in fact, any movement to recall him. On Mr. Smith's death in 1891 Mr. Balfour was, with the enthusiastic assent of the party, appointed to the vacant place, and in due course the leadership of the House led to the Prime Ministership. Long ere that happened Lord Randolph had passed from politics.

Before he went from the scene he acted again with his friends when they were out of office. In 1893, on Mr. Balfour's invitation, he took a place beside them on the front Opposition bench and those who remembered his early achievements hoped that with his genius for Parliamentary attack he might again play an effective rôle. Alas ! his speech on the introduction of the second Home Rule Bill dispelled that hope. The Prince of Wales (afterwards King Edward) came to hear Lord Randolph, the House was crowded, reconciled friends warmly cheered. A few passages of vigorous invective, a few trenchant phrases occurred in his speech, but instead of the audacious, confident, inspiring leader there was a man with broken voice and trembling hands. He was more like his old self at the close of debate on the Welsh Church Suspensory Bill, delivering an attack on Gladstone which irritated the veteran and aroused the enthusiasm of Unionists. This proved only a flicker. Disease had fastened upon Lord Randolph and at the age of forty-five his fiery spirit was extinguished in January, 1895.

There have been few politicians whose death has caused so much sorrow. Till he passed away many men did not know how they had loved " Randy." All mourned the early end of one who for a short space occupied a great position and whose latter years were years of disappointment. " But what has been has been, and I have had my hour," wrote Dryden, in lines copied out by Lord Randolph (as his son tells us) about 1891. Lord Randolph had had his hour. It was an hour of glorious life. Placemen recall his career to point a placeman's moral. But men indifferent to place may think of his resignation not as a warning to ambitious climbers, but as the event in his public life which was most to his honour.

## MR. PARNELL

When I think of Mr. Parnell I think chiefly of his power of inspiring dread in the House of Commons. He was a strange, perplexing, baffling man. Till we knew of the events of the secret life which brought him to the divorce court we might have described him " self-school'd, self-scann'd, self-honour'd, self-secure." His self - repression in public, his chilly aloofness, his apparent absorption in one definite aim, his haughty disregard of English opinion was amazing. In the most violent debates, seated among excited, shouting colleagues, he looked as calm as if he were unconcerned. But " fire that's closest kept burns most of all." I have never heard so passionate an utterance as that of Parnell when he gave expression to his political and national hate. Picking his phrases slowly and using scarcely any gestures he attacked " Buckshot Forster " or Earl Spencer and challenged the authority of Parliament with a ferocity of feeling which made the flesh creep.

Strong speeches and stormy scenes are frequent enough. The effect of Parnell's defiances of British rule and Parliamentary tradition was unique. It may be hard now in restless, revolutionary times to realize the shivering horror which he caused. We were then less accustomed to the challenge of settled ways. Everything was supposed to be for the best or nearly the best in the best of all countries under the best of all constitutions. We lived by precedent. And here came a leader who " held up " the House of Commons. His National League and Land League in Ireland with their boycotting and tyranny and his ruthless obstruction at Westminster invested him with a dæmonic character which terrified conventional Liberals and Conservatives trained in the strict school of Victoria.

The absoluteness of his authority over his followers exceeded that of any British leader. They were not meek, feeble or stupid men. Among them were able writers, barristers, orators, debaters who were astute politicians and masters of every move in the Parliamentary game. Their history after Parnell's fall revealed their difficult, fractious character. From him in the fulness of his power they bore despotism. He held aloof from nearly all of them in private and rarely conferred with any in the House. His reserved manners were uncongenial to warm Irishmen ; they were annoyed by his mysterious disappearances and by his absence at critical times, and some of them disagreed at certain points with his policy. But he took usually his own course. His colleagues might mutter when he was away, but when he re-appeared they were submissive. The storm rose or fell according to his will. They obstructed in obedience to his call ; at a sign from him their fire was instantly quenched.

Although Parnell lacked not only the eloquence but the fluency of many of the Irishmen he could make his meaning mercilessly clear. " We must show those gentlemen," he said of British members, " that if they don't do what we want they shall do nothing else." This was the doctrine of obstruction which in practice brought the Parliamentary machine nearly to a stand-still and delayed legislation and embarrassed the Government while the machine was being readjusted. What again could be more effective in its callousness than the famous passage in which Parnell advocated what became known as boycotting ? "When a man," he said at Ennis, "takes a farm from which another has been evicted, you must show him on the roadside when you meet him, in the streets of the town, at the shop counter, in the fair, in the market place, and even in the house of worship, by leaving him severely alone, by putting him into a moral coventry, by isolating him from his kind as if he were a leper of old—you must show him your detestation of the crime he has committed." How well Irishmen understood this language was quickly proved in the treatment of Captain Boycott, a landlord's agent, who served ejectment notices upon a number of tenants.

During the period between Gladstone's adoption of Home Rule and the O'Shea divorce Parnell maintained in his relations with the Liberals the attitude of a reconciled, forgiving enemy. He left more effusive persons to gush over "the union of hearts." Although friendly enough to his new allies, he was rather frigid. The advances came from the Liberals, the men whom he had denounced and obstructed and opposed, but who now—in some cases heartily and in other cases reluctantly—admitted the justice of his demand. On various occasions he manifested indifference to their good opinion. He distressed British allies by his cool treatment of *The Times* articles on Parnellism and Crime. There were, on the other hand, no bounds to *their* delight at the exposure of the forgery of the letter attributed to him, condoning the Phœnix Park murders.

His popularity reached its height in Liberal circles after that dramatic episode in 1889. "Because," said Lord Salisbury, "a Nationalist journalist has forged the signature of the Nationalist leader, that is no proof that the latter possesses every statesmanlike quality and virtue." Sentiment, however, was powerful. Parnell was regarded politically as an injured innocent and the cause of which he was the advocate benefited by the sympathy which Pigott's forgery aroused on his behalf.

When the prospects of Home Rule thus glowed brightly they were suddenly overcast by a cloud of the darkest hue. Never were politicians more painfully embarrassed than the Liberals were in November, 1890, when Captain O'Shea obtained divorce from his wife on the ground of her adultery with his friend, Parnell, and the details of the intrigue became known. In his struggle to retain his leadership after Gladstone's refusal further to co-operate with him had led to his deposition by a majority of his party, Parnell not only displayed harsh contempt for the colleagues who had thrown him over, but revealed in the most truculent manner his genuine indifference to Liberal opinion. Trying to turn the immediate issue from a personal and moral question to a question of policy, he appealed to Irishmen to save him from " the English wolves now howling for my destruction." Dilating on the inadequacy of Home Rule proposals which he had hitherto supported and thereby giving plausibility to the Unionist contention that the Irish had concealed their real designs, he waged war at the head of a small band of faithful adherents against all parties in Parliament.

A politically hunted man, defiant, dangerous and haggard, he presented a painful contrast to the Parnell at whose voice Parliament had trembled. How the struggle might have ended if he had lived much longer no person could say. There were many observers who believed that amid the factions of Ireland he would ultimately by his fame and genius recover his leadership. Death ended his struggle in October, 1891. The temple which he had raised with masterly hand he pulled down in his fall. The divorce in which he figured and his repudiation of the Gladstonian scheme diverted sympathy from and excited fresh distrust of the Home Rule movement. What connection there is between personal morality and public policy the cynic and the philosopher may ask, but just as Parnellism gained from the exposure of a forgery so it suffered for many years from its founder's relations with another man's wife.

## MR. JOSEPH CHAMBERLAIN

Before the Great War the political drama staged at St. Stephen's had an interest and occasionally a thrill which a Parliament with an all-powerful Coalition majority does not produce. It appealed not only to the serious-minded, but to the seeker after excitement. The fate of classes, the fate of the Kingdom, appeared to depend on the play of parties, on the clash of combatants on the Parliamentary stage, their accusations and retorts, their debates and divisions. In that drama for thirty years Joseph Chamberlain was conspicuous, performing with zest and arresting attention in each rôle he undertook. " With a masculine understanding and a stout and resolute heart," Burke said of Grenville, and it may be said of Chamberlain, " he had an application undissipated and unwearied. He took public business not as a duty which he was to fulfil, but as a pleasure he was to enjoy ; and he seemed to have no delight out of this House except in such things as some way related to the business that was to be done within it."

When first I saw the man who was so greatly to influence the course of politics he was on the Treasury bench beside Sir Charles Dilke. On that bench, in 1881, John Bright often sat at Gladstone's elbow, but he did not associate much with the restless Birmingham colleague who belonged to the newer school of Liberalism. The Marquis of Hartington lounged there, respected by supporters of the Government for his party loyalty and by all men for his honest patriotism, and frequently in the Whig leader's company was Sir William Harcourt, sharing his antipathy to the Parnellites, who regarded Chamberlain as the best friend of

Ireland in the Cabinet. With Chamberlain and Dilke seemed to lie the future of Liberalism. Enemies of the former—and they were numerous —used to say that Dilke supplied him with his information and Jesse Collings or Schnadhorst, the party organizer, with his ideas. Never, as events proved, were sneers more stupid.

There was something unmistakably aggressive in that keen and eager face which I watched from the first with lively curiosity. Chamberlain's career in and out of the House had already made him notorious. Whether people spoke of " Joey " with love or disdain they knew he was no more lightly to be meddled with than the Scottish thistle. No one provoked him with impunity. While he was President of the Board of Trade I saw him receiving deputations and was amused by the manner in which he looked at his visitors through his intimidating eye-glass. Instead of listening blandly to long speeches and replying with elaborate evasiveness, he would quickly by questions probe to the root of the matter. And the part the monocle played was by no means unimportant.

In his years of office as a Liberal Minister, 1880–1885, Chamberlain advanced by steady, sure strides in reputation and power. By his influence over the Caucus which had been organized throughout the country on the Birmingham model, by his initiative in policy, by his pungent oratory and by his strength of character, this man of the middle class, the product of Nonconformity, of trade and of municipal training, became one of the chief personages of the State and one of the accepted champions of the common people. As an administrator he was energetic and efficient. As a legislator he might have been more successful if he had been less provocative. He piloted several useful measures, but the interested opposition to his principal project, the Merchant Shipping Bill, was too strong for him. Never was he a mere placeman or head of a Department. With a clear, confident ambition, a firm will and a zeal for reform, unchastened by fear of change, he claimed and established for himself a position as leader of the Radicals and as their representative in the Cabinet.

The " daring duckling " of the Liberal brood, while the Whigs shivered on the edge of the pond on which he ventured so boldly he was gazed at with alarm and hatred by the Conservatives. His policy—to pass from metaphor—was presented from the platform in speeches which have never been surpassed in all the elements of popular appeal and aroused the enthusiasm of the classes who hoped for a new earth. They were delighted by his pugnacity, by his sallies against Peers and Privilege. The more that he grew in favour with the populace the more he was attacked by the classes who would rather have the conditions that existed than fly to others that they knew not of. To all attacks Chamberlain replied with a gay audacity. Instead of being subdued he waxed bolder and bolder. When set free from official restraint by the defeat of the Government in 1885 he stumped the country with a programme unauthorized by his party leader or colleagues. Now the hope of the poor, the landless and the discontented, he was scolded by the Whigs and denounced by Conservatives as a sort of Jack Cade.

A rapid and painful reaction in Liberal feeling with regard to Chamberlain occurred when he left

Gladstone on his chief's adoption of Home Rule. It was tenser than the Conservative reaction against Churchill on his resignation. It extended to a larger section of the party than recoiled from Mr. Lloyd George at Mr. Asquith's overthrow. The Radicals, as a rule, who had hoped most from Chamberlain, turned into his most bitter assailants. They lamented " the lost leader " ; they imputed to him motives of personal chagrin. They thought that he was annoyed because his own programme was not adopted and that he hoped immediately to be leader himself. They were amazed and exasperated by his co-operation with his former opponents.

There is a tendency among people who knew and admired him only in the latter part of his career to assume that his Radical stage was merely a stage of political immaturity and that he left it when he reached years of wisdom. They forget he was fifty when he broke from the official Liberal party and nearly sixty when he became a Unionist Minister. Between these events, sitting as a Liberal among Liberals and changing with them from side to side of the House, he employed his art and craft to frustrate and discredit those who supported Home Rule. From its defeat in 1886 till 1892 he sat on the front Opposition bench beside Gladstone and his lieutenants, hotly attacking them, defending the Conservative Government and exchanging recriminations with the Irish who called him " Judas," and in the three following years, while the Liberals were in office, he was their most persistent and damaging enemy.

However men differed with regard to his conduct there was no question as to his pre-eminence as a debater. With an agreeable, well-toned voice and a full store of good English and apt, homely illustration at the command of a quick and subtle brain, with a power of invective traced by an eminent critic, Sir W. Robertson Nicoll, to the *Letters of Junius*, and with an instinct for political warfare and a merciless determination to overcome his enemy, Chamberlain's contributions to debate were always vivid, piquant and animated. No speaker was more lucid. He discarded the circumlocutory style and introduced a method which was direct, simple and unmistakable. I have never known a member who could more certainly hold the attention and interest of the House. During the speeches of almost every other man in my time figures have here and there flitted out. Rarely did Chamberlain lose his grip.

The debates of 1893 on the second Home Rule Bill were the finest I ever heard and Chamberlain's attacks had a more sustained pungency than any others within my ken. His duels with Gladstone, his raids upon the Nationalists, his spirited incitements maintained the vigour and passion of the protracted struggle. I recall the crowded Chamber, the " Grand Old Man," with Morley, Harcourt and Asquith on the Treasury bench ; Balfour, Goschen and Hicks Beach on the other side of the table. Chamberlain, orchid in coat, monocle in position, rises from the corner of the third bench below the Ministerial gangway. Members behind the Government glare at him ; Nationalists jeer. His voice vibrates with derision and invective as he pounces on an exposed argument or turns upon a rash interrupter with unerring swoop. How the Gladstonians cheer their own glorious leader when with imperious gesture he replies to his former lieutenant and reminds him of his past ! Chamberlain listens calmly with finger at chin, watching for any chink in the veteran's armour. No vulnerable point is neglected and the retort comes as quick as a flash. Truly, like Alan Breck, a bonnie fighter!

The eight years in which he was a member of Unionist Governments, serving as Colonial Secretary under Lord Salisbury and Mr. Balfour, were for Chamberlain years of heavy responsibility and high authority. His power was almost equal to that of a Prime Minister, and for considerable periods, indeed, he was more conspicuous than his Conservative chief. His development as an Imperial statesman and orator was observed with mocking antipathy by the party from which he had cut himself off and his policy in respect of the Transvaal, his treatment of the South African War issues and his conduct of the " khaki election " of 1900 drew upon him onslaughts as vehement and violent as any he encountered at any stage of his career, the keenest among the younger section of his assailants being the Welshman who, with courage equal to his own, faced him from a corner seat below the Opposition gangway. With undiminished force he replied to attacks, teaching that young Welshman how to turn the defensive into the offensive, and in his Imperialist appeals he displayed a lofty eloquence which aroused the enthusiasm of his audiences.

It was easy to quote Chamberlain on both sides of many questions. He changed so completely in his environment and point of view and his statements were always so clear and emphatic that I was able to compile a little volume of apparent inconsistencies between, I will not say his Radical days, because he claimed to be in a sense always a Radical, but his days as Radical leader and his days as the ally and colleague of Conservatives. Charges of inconsistency are a familiar part of the political armoury. They are levelled at many statesmen. Some against whom they are brought try to show there is no inconsistency, others justify it by change of conditions, a few attempt neither denial nor excuse. Chamberlain was never distressed by the contrast of his present with his past. The past was dead. His mind was in the present, full of vigour and resource.

The greatest sensation of his life was caused in 1903 when after his visit to the " illimitable veld " he raised the fiscal question with the cry of Imperial Preference. His sudden and unexpected advocacy of a tariff stirred as much commotion as Peel's decision in favour of the repeal of the corn duty or Gladstone's adoption of Home Rule, and it had as rapid effects on political fortunes. It embarrassed Mr. Balfour as head of the Government, it produced discord in the Unionist party, it gave the Liberals a new weapon which all could use. Chamberlain took his own course and took it with characteristic boldness and energy. In order to pursue it he resigned office, as he did on Home Rule in 1886, and returned to a seat below the Ministerial gangway, where he continued to be the most conspicuous figure in the House. Taking little part in debate, while the authority of the Government steadily declined, he waited for a freer Parliamentary opportunity of promoting his new policy for which he conducted a " raging, tearing propaganda " in the country. After the Unionist rout of January, 1906, he sat with Unionist colleagues on the front Opposition bench, arriving at a fiscal agreement with Mr. Balfour and looking undismayed at the huge army of triumphant Liberals.

Political history might in the domestic domain have taken a very different course from that of the pre-war years if good health had continued to bless Joseph Chamberlain, but at the age of seventy he was struck down by the infirmity which made his remaining eight years those of a recluse. After the summer of 1906 he was never seen in the House of Commons except when he came at the opening of two new Parliaments to take the oath and when, assisted to the table, he touched the pen with which his son wrote his famous name in the Roll. His fame endures. It is cherished by all parties. All have joined in the decision to erect a statue to his memory in the precincts of the House where he was so outstanding a figure. Most of the animosities of his time are fading away; there remains the reputation of a very great Parliamentarian.

# CHAPTER V

## LATE VICTORIANS

" MOST people," as Bagehot remarks in an essay on
Peel, " have looked over old letters. They have
been struck with the change of life, with the doubt
on things now certain, the belief in things now
incredible, the oblivion of what now seems most
important, the strained attention to departed
detail, which characterize the mouldering leaves."
One receives a similar impression on looking over
the records of late-Victorian statesmen. Their
day is not long past and yet it seems very far off.
Were people, the present generation asks, ever
excited by the things now certain or now incredible
those statesmen dealt with in full-dress debates ?
Could the passion of Parliament have been excited,
the fate of Governments affected by their controversies ? Yes, in the time of the late Victorians
the pulse beat as quickly as it beats now and so
it may be worth while to turn over the old fading
leaves and try to catch their spirit and see what
manner of men they were.

In the careers reviewed in this chapter may be
found an epitome of the political life of an era of
constitutional development and democratic growth.
They present notable examples of the statesmen
who in the last quarter of the nineteenth century
still acted with the sometimes uncomfortable con-

sciousness that the eye of the Sovereign was upon them, but who looked more and more to the division lobby as the supreme arbiter of their fate and acquired the modern habit of direct appeal to the people from the platform. The Queen, as Lord Morley states, never relished Gladstone's oratorical crusaaes, but in reply to a letter from Balmoral in 1886, the crusader pointed out that since 1880 the Conservative leaders had established a rule of addressing public meetings at places with which they were not connected. That practice grew rapidly in the late-Victorian era. It was an era when statesmen, although still nominally the servants of the Crown, became more avowedly the servants of the people.

Two of the extraordinary men described in the preceding chapter, Randolph Churchill and Chamberlain, had their eye—as their contemporaries believed—on the top of what Disraeli with gay cynicism called the greasy pole. For a time they were the most promising climbers. Yet fortune favoured neither. The present chapter exhibits others who were near the top of the political pole— the Duke of Devonshire who, if guided by personal ambition, would have been at the head of Government; Mr. Goschen, who by equipment and experience was fit for the highest place; Sir William Harcourt, who had claims as well as hopes which were never realized; Mr. W. H. Smith, who was amply satisfied with the leadership of the House of Commons; and Sir Michael Hicks Beach, who at more than one crisis was mentioned as a possible Prime Minister. All had a high sense of duty to the State.

## SIR MICHAEL HICKS BEACH

" A constitutional statesman," according to a well-known dictum, " is in general a man of common opinions and uncommon abilities." To this type Sir Michael Hicks Beach belonged. Very tall and very thin, a baronet of long descent, with a sharp tongue and reserved manner, a strong departmental chief, a tactful Parliamentarian, a champion of the Church of England and the Landed interest, a Conservative open in the last resort to compromise, Sir Michael, with common opinions and uncommon abilities, was for thirty years a conspicuous figure in the political world, trusted especially in the Country House which Mr. Galsworthy has described.

A link between Disraeli and the European war, he distinguished himself in 1880–1885 as one of the few forceful personalities of the front Opposition bench. Although he assisted in averting a constitutional struggle over the Franchise Bill in 1884 by opening communications with Hartington which led to meetings of the leaders of the two great parties, he was a severe critic of Gladstonianism and, as a rule, a dour and dogged combatant. More friendly than some of his front bench colleagues to the aggressive tactics of the group below the gangway, Hicks Beach co-operated occasionally with Churchill. It was he who moved the amendment to the Budget of 1885, on which the Liberal Government fell. The amendment had been drawn up at Mr. Balfour's house at a meeting with the Fourth party.

On account of Randolph Churchill's refusal to join Salisbury's first Government if Sir Stafford Northcote were leader of the House of Commons, this post, after being accepted by Northcote, who had previously hoped to be Prime Minister, was transferred with the Chancellorship of the Exchequer to Sir Michael. It could not have been agreeable for a sensitive man to acquiesce in pushing aside his former Parliamentary chief, but he was influenced by the consideration that Churchill was indispensable to the success of the new Administration. He did not hold the post long. Although an efficient and dignified, if not inspiring, leader first of the House and later of the Opposition in 1885–1886, he was overshadowed by the most popular member of the Conservative party, and when Salisbury returned to office, Hicks Beach gave way to Churchill, holding that the man who was leader in fact should be leader also in name. "I thought it," said fine old Sir John Mowbray, "the most magnanimous thing I had ever known in public life."

This magnanimity was of little service to the party seeing that Lord Randolph soon threw up his great place. It did not revert to Sir Michael. He went for a short time to the Irish Office, where he had been under Disraeli, and after a retirement due to an acute affection of the eyes, he became President of the Board of Trade, a post which was not in those days considered so important as it is now. Mr. W. H. Smith succeeded Lord Randolph as leader of the House and by the time of that good man's death, in 1891, Mr. Balfour had won the affection and admiration of the Conservatives. The Chancellorship of the Exchequer was held by Sir Michael from the formation of the Unionist Coalition Government in 1895 till Salisbury's retirement in 1902, but he did not exercise so much influence as in 1885–1886, greater prestige

being possessed in his later years, not only by
Mr. Balfour, but also by his not altogether congenial
colleague, Chamberlain.

" Black Michael," as he was called by a familiar
Press, became a sort of legendary figure. His
austere-looking face, dry manner and sharp sayings
provided the materials out of which it was con-
structed. It is probable that he was more accommodating in council than many a man less rigid
in popular repute and that his temperament was
not so hard as it seemed to the observer who did
not look for the lights and shades, but the tartness
with which he gave expression to his feelings
contributed largely to the legend of a fearsome
character. " Who the devil is this ? " he was
heard to ask a colleague as one of his Budgets was
criticized by a Liberal who, however, was rather
flattered than frightened by the whispered inquiry.
" Go and tell him he is a pig," said Sir Michael
to his private secretary when provoked by a member
behind him. Naturally the secretary, who himself
rose to be a Cabinet minister, softened the message
on delivery. A Conservative who went to his
room to see him on some subject returned to the
Lobby indignantly complaining of his reception.
" Never before," moaned the visitor, " was I
called a damned canting attorney."

Although a strong party man, Hicks Beach
sought and obtained the good-will of the House
as a whole, and although a hard hitter he never
hit a foul blow. He was very angry, when after
voting in a snap division taken by Conservatives
during a Liberal Administration, Harcourt exclaimed in an aside intended to be heard : " A
dirty trick ! " To be accused of unfairness in the
great game was intolerable to the proud player.

He had a correct Parliamentary manner and in his conduct as a Minister he was conciliatory. His Budget statements, although lacking the glow and suggestiveness of more brilliant Chancellors, were clear and competent, with passages of that rather artificial jocosity which is enjoyed by an easily amused House. " Who drinks rum ? " he inquired, in 1896, as he raised to his lips a glass of tawny liquor. There had been a notable increase in the consumption of rum and members wondered if the Chancellor himself was tasting it. What he drank, as his private secretary has recorded, was port. "As a rule he brought down some of his own in a flask. This time he forgot it and I procured him some at the refreshment bar—a light wine from the wood, of a tawny hue." *

With his instinct for public affairs and his faculty of forcible, persuasive speech, Hicks Beach won a solid Parliamentary reputation excelled by few of his contemporaries. What he lacked was the power of popular appeal. Even in the House of Commons he inspired little personal devotion. In private life, according to the testimony of friends, he was one of the most gracious of men, but a colleague admitted that he was not always easy to approach ; and his aloof, moody habit prevented him from attracting a large number of adherents. Yet he had the honest, downright hard-headed qualities which secure the trust of Englishmen. Like James Elia, " determined by his own sense in everything," he commended *you* to the guidance of common-sense on all occasions. He remained long enough in the House of Commons to be its father, and after he crossed to the other place among the Elder Statesmen, the eyes of cautious Conservatives

* *Fourteen Years in Parliament* :  Griffith-Boscawen.

followed Lord St. Aldwyn as a man who appreciated the true interests of the country with a prudent, dispassionate judgment. On the crimson benches he did not associate closely and regularly with the official leaders of his party. He brooded over his own thoughts with a far-away look in his eyes, not always acting with friends, seldom agreeing with opponents. He died during the war, a week after his son was killed in action.

## MR. W. H. SMITH

It is a remarkable fact that Mr. W. H. Smith was one of the most successful leaders the House of Commons has ever had. Macaulay wrote of another leader, Lord Althorp :—" I doubt whether any person has ever lived in England who, with no eloquence, no brilliant talents, no profound information, with nothing in short but plain good sense and an excellent heart, possessed so much influence both in and out of Parliament." Mr. Smith was no better equipped than Althorp and was not, like him, the son of an Earl. He possessed no brilliant Parliamentary talents ; his personality was not magnetic ; he was neither a clever debater nor an interesting speaker. A successful business man, God-fearing, jealous of his country's honour, he had the middle-class character called mid-Victorian. He might have figured in the pages of Thackeray as a type of the irreproachable, rather solemn merchant who did his duty in every sphere of life and observed all its proprieties. The smart men of the younger generation were apt to smile if not to sneer at him and his side-whiskers. But he distinguished himself in one of the highest positions in the State.

Early in life W. H. Smith was ready to stand on principles " politically and religiously liberal," but a distributor of newspapers was not good enough for the haughty Whigs of the Reform Club ; when he came up for election there the tradesman was blackballed. This, as his biographer says, was a rebuff sharp enough to have discouraged a much less sensitive nature than Smith's. The rejected of the Reform lived to be honoured at the Carlton.

In 1865 he stood for Westminster as an Independent and was beaten by two other candidates, but in 1868, when he appeared as a Liberal-Conservative, he was at the head of the poll and John Stuart Mill was at the foot. Appointed Financial Secretary to the Treasury in 1874 by Disraeli, who was impressed by his business aptitude, Smith rose three years later to be First Lord of the Admiralty. " It must," he observed to a caller at that great department, " be funny enough to you, who remember me working in my shirt sleeves, to see me installed here." * Nobody except the modest man himself thought his official success funny.

An intimate, helpful colleague of Northcote in opposition between 1880 and 1885, Smith shared the gibes thrown across the gangway by Randolph Churchill at bourgeois mediocrities. A reference he made to Irish peasants who lived in mud-cabins provoked a jeer at " the lords of suburban villas, the owners of vineries and pineries," but even the brilliant son of a duke learned to respect a man so shrewd, steadfast and sincere. On his refusing as War Minister to make the reduction in the estimates which Churchill, from the Treasury, demanded, Salisbury sided with a Secretary of State " so little imaginative as Smith." Great was the surprise when he succeeded Churchill as leader of the House of Commons.

The success of the experiment was creditable to the House itself. For half a century it had been led by men of high political capacity and oratorical or debating power. Not for the first time, however, did a leader succeed without gift of speech. Grenville says of Castlereagh that " as a speaker he was prolix, monotonous and never eloquent except,

* *Life and Times of W. H. Smith* : Sir Herbert Maxwell.

perhaps, for a few minutes when provoked into a passion." Nevertheless he " was considered one of the best managers of the House of Commons who ever sat in it." There was also the case I have mentioned of Lord Althorp whose fine temper assisted the passage of the Reform Bill of 1832. Bagehot quotes a remark that a man who speaks seldom and who speaks ill is the best leader of the House. " And no doubt," he continues, " the slow-speeched English gentleman rather sympathizes with slow speech in others. Besides, a quick and brilliant leader is apt to be always speaking, whereas a leader should interfere only when necessary, and be therefore felt as a higher force when he does so. His mind ought to be like a reserve fund—not invested in showy securities, but sure to be come at when wanted, and always of staple value. And this Lord Althorp's mind was ; there was not an epigram in the whole of it ; everything was solid and ordinary." *

Everything in Smith's mind was solid and ordinary, but he was a better leader than Gladstone. That great man was " apt to be always speaking," and by speech he, too often, provoked controversy. There was no provocation in Smith. He was content to be business manager of the theatre of St. Stephen's without assuming a prominent acting rôle. The leading parts in debate on behalf of the Government were taken by Mr. Goschen and Mr. Balfour and it had powerful support from the Liberal Unionists on the other side of the table.

By strict attention to business Smith succeeded where a more brilliant man might have failed. Unpretentious in manner and simple in words he steered the House through years of dangerous

* *Biographical Studies:* Walter Bagehot.

debate. His homilies on duty to Queen and Parliament and country won for him in the genial banter of Sir Henry Lucy the title of "Old Morality." He said very little that was remembered, but one phrase which he used in his unimaginative way was often quoted in sarcasm. It became known that while the question of *The Times* charges against Parnellism, which subsequently formed the subject of judicial inquiry, was under the consideration of the Cabinet, the leader of the House was visited by the chief proprietor of the great newspaper and on being challenged on the event he explained that he received Mr. Walter as "an old friend." A long time passed before "an old friend" vanished from Parliamentary controversy. The House, however, was not unkind. It had a thorough liking and respect for "Old Morality."

Mr. Smith was one of the last of the leaders who spent many hours every evening on the Treasury bench. His freedom from departmental cares and the responsibilities of a Prime Minister enabled him to do this, and his diligent attention contributed to his success, for the House of Commons is a jealous mistress and does not endure avoidable neglect. A leader who took a severe view of obstruction and disorder and anything that interfered with business was called the headmaster, but on hearing himself so described Smith rejoined that he was "only one of the big boys." He was indeed easy in his relations with the rank and file of his party. So constant was his attendance and close his control that as a rule for several sessions, instead of going home for dinner, he had the meal served in his room behind the Speaker's chair. Every one appreciated the devotion with which he remained at his post in the Government while suffering personal discomfort in the last year or two of his life.  A sense of loyalty to colleagues and fidelity to the State kept him at public duty long after he had received a warning from his doctor.  He endured the torments of eczema and gout.  At last he used to sit on the Treasury bench with a rug spread over his knees—a spectacle of patient, conscientious, self-denying service which appealed to all parties.   He died on the same day as Parnell—October 6, 1891.

## SIR WILLIAM HARCOURT

" Ah, but a man's reach should exceed his grasp,
Or what's a heaven for."

When the highest office in the State seemed almost within Sir William Harcourt's grasp it fell into the hands of a younger if not a better man. His reach exceeded his grasp. Missing the prize he secured a degree of sympathy which increased with his years and ere he died he gained in apparent failure more respect for courage and sincerity in opinion than he enjoyed in days of apparent success.

During a large part of his life Harcourt was supposed to be a Liberal from opportunism rather than conviction. He sacrificed, as he told Mr. Arthur Elliot,* a professional income at the Parliamentary bar of £10,000 a year to enter the House of Commons, but the world did not till near the close of his career allow him credit for disinterestedness or deep-rooted political principle. An old colleague and friend who became an opponent likened him to Dugald Dalgetty. Even on his own side a certain distrust of Harcourt was maintained for a long period on account of his friendship with Disraeli and his intimate association with other Conservatives. It was his fortune, as he himself said, to live much among political opponents. Men of little faith, judging him by themselves, assumed that his aristocratic instincts, his family connections, his ties with the Church and the Land,

* *Life of Lord Goschen.*

would naturally incline him to the Conservative side in the movement of democracy.

His speeches as Home Secretary in the Government of 1880–1885 did not prepare the country for his support of Home Rule in 1886. An Irish member asserted that he was " of all the Ministers, with scarcely the exception even of Mr. Forster, the bitterest and most rancorous enemy of Mr. Parnell and his followers." The principal responsibility for the passage of the Arms Bill, the Crimes Bill, and the Explosives Bill fell upon the Home Secretary, and his denunciation of Irish agitators who sought to attain their ends by violence was certainly not lacking in vehemence. When in 1886 he took a new course with Gladstone and tried conciliation where coercion had failed, Unionists laughed at, and doubted the honesty of, his conversion. Chamberlain, whose tone was that of scornful amusement, jeered at " the chameleon " and " the swordsman whose sword was always at the service of the strongest faction." Others cynically suggested that he adhered to Gladstone because by so doing he had the better chance of realizing his personal ambition. When Hartington and Chamberlain allied themselves with the Conservatives, he stood second to the old leader in the House of Commons. This was a consideration which was supposed to be in his mind.

A more generous view of Harcourt was taken in the years following the first defeat of Home Rule. He won the gratitude of sympathetic Liberals by his devotion to the beaten chief, and by his staunch adherence to the cause which the country had rejected he showed in their eyes that he was no time server. Lord Morley has described him " holding stoutly in fair weather and in foul to the party ship "—a quality highly appreciated in days when the steering was risky—and has declared that in his powerful composition loyalty to party and conviction of the value of party were ever indestructible instincts. This feature of his composition was more generally recognized the longer he lived. His services to chief and party were specially conspicuous and valuable during Gladstone's last Premiership. As deputy leader of the House of Commons he did his utmost to lighten the labours of the aged man. There was, as Mr. Justice Darling—then a member—remarked, "The greater light to rule the day and the lesser light to rule the night."

Tall and portly in figure and massive in features, Harcourt was nick-named Jumbo by an irreverent Lobby. His voice was loud, and people who disliked him considered his manners overbearing. Critics called him the Bombastes Furioso of political debate. Sometimes his speech was ponderous and then they would recall the learned letters—powerful letters they were—that he wrote over the name of Historicus to *The Times* to uphold the policy of non-intervention in the American Civil War. His efforts at playfulness reminded a listener of the scene where

"the unwieldy elephant,
To make them mirth, used all his might, and wreathed
His lithe proboscis."

He was a formidable controversialist. With an extensive knowledge of men and affairs he combined a remarkable power of repartee and sarcasm. His satirical quotations, particularly from writers of the eighteenth century, were very effective. Many of his sallies, although they may seem now to be rather strained, were in the heat of debate extremely enjoyed. Goschen as Chancellor of the Exchequer remarked in 1891 that he would have had a nice surplus had he not been despoiled by his colleagues. " Yes," retorted Harcourt, " but you are a member of the same ' long firm ' and practically an accomplice of the burglar ; for like an accommodating maid-servant you left the door open and yourself carried the bag." On many an occasion by prepared oration or impromptu reply he scattered the enemy and revived the fainting spirit of friends. He loved to trounce an opponent, especially a Liberal Unionist. Nobody trounced harder, and he took his own share of blows with a manly equanimity.

" I count among my political opponents," as he once said, " many friends and, as far as I know, no enemies." Between himself and Mr. Balfour, and not least when they were opposing leaders, there was a warm regard, and his friendship with Chamberlain, as I have pointed out in a previous chapter, stood the severest test. " I would love Harcourt more," one of his colleagues declared, " if he loved Joe less." If Harcourt had any enemies they were on his own side. A big-hearted, generous man, he was quick to praise and encourage young men of promise such as Mr. Lloyd George and Mr. Henry Dalziel. After an eloquent speech by a new member he invited him to dinner. " I live at a distance and I have not my dress suit with me," pleaded the modest orator. " After such a speech," said Harcourt, " I would take you without any clothes." On the other hand, he was not considerate of the feelings of blundering, self-important colleagues, and in his impatience, by blunt words, he sowed the seeds of resentment.

It was natural that Harcourt should suffer disappointment when, on Gladstone's retirement, Queen Victoria sent for Lord Rosebery. The world at large assumed that it was for personal reasons that the disappointed Minister received little sympathy from the Cabinet. Although some private members protested against the appointment of a peer to be head of a Liberal Government Her Majesty's choice was agreeable to his colleagues as a rule. Influenced by a sense of duty to his party as well as to the State, Harcourt remained in office under the new chief, accepting the leadership of the House of Commons. In this position he knew he could exercise almost as great power as he desired. On one occasion, while Lord Rosebery was Prime Minister, he referred to him as leader of the Government in the House of Lords. That limited description was significant of his view and attitude. How far he was responsible for the lack of harmony which enfeebled Liberalism it is difficult even yet to say.

Disappointed although he was, the sixteen months of his leadership of the House endeared him to it and enhanced his personal reputation. He left a permanent mark on finance as Chancellor of the Exchequer by his democratic Budget revolutionizing the death duties. The graduated estate duty on real and personal property was strenuously resisted. Yet Harcourt carried it without the closure; he prevailed by persuasion and courteous, conciliatory persistence. As leader, indeed, he proved unexpectedly successful. It had been feared that he would display a domineering temper, whereas nobody could have been more deferential. The leadership of the Commons, he said, on laying it down, he had always regarded as a position of greater responsibility and higher obligation even than any office under the Crown. The whole House now held him in honour; he was, as Mr. Balfour said, one of its greatest ornaments.

As leader of Opposition, from 1895, Harcourt was neither fortunate nor happy. The differences among Liberals, between persons and between principles, were openly manifested when the party was out of office, and even after Lord Rosebery withdrew to his tent discord continued, his friends remaining in the field to champion his cause. " A disputed leadership beset by distracted sections and conflicting interests " was Harcourt's wretched lot, and at the end of 1898 he abandoned it. With Morley, then in sympathy with his views, he retired to the gangway end of the front Opposition Bench, divided on Imperial policy from Rosebery's friends, Asquith and Grey, while Campbell-Bannerman took the vacant post. By and by, loyally playing a secondary rôle, Harcourt moved to the side of the new leader, acting with him in a stout opposition to Chamberlain's Transvaal policy. In resistance to Tariff Reform he made his last great effort. His blows were well aimed. But his strength was failing.

The heart of the House went out to the veteran in his final months. The dwindling figure, formerly so massive, and the narrowing shoulders, once so broad and straight, told a tale which could be read also in the struggling sentences of the orator who had been so ready and vigorous. He had the gratification of seeing his elder son in the House, but he never heard his voice in debate. Although elected early in 1904, it was not until the Liberals were in office in 1906 that Mr. Lewis Harcourt— from the Treasury Bench—delivered his maiden speech. Sir William did not live till then.

## MR. GOSCHEN

Although he was distinguished among peers, it is difficult for one familiar with Goschen's career to write of him as Viscount. He was a great House of Commons man. With a harsh voice, short sight, and awkward gestures, he lacked the graces of the orator, yet, through force of intellect and character, he played a powerful and at a crisis an almost decisive part in the political world. A thinker himself, he induced others to think. He was a leader not of parties, but of opinion. For popular leadership he was unfitted, his mind was too critical. Beginning his career as a Liberal and closing it nominally as a Conservative, Goschen was ever a moderate. In the Liberal party he tried to restrain the more ardent advocates of change; in the Conservative party he resisted the fiscal doctrines which the large majority of its members were eager to carry out at the bidding of Chamberlain. He was really to the end, like Granville, Harcourt, and the Duke of Devonshire, a Whig.

His career was closely linked with the Duke's. Early a partner in the city house of Frühling and Goschen, and elected in 1863 to Parliament, where he quickly distinguished himself in the cause of the abolition of University tests, he entered Lord Russell's Cabinet at the same time as Lord Hartington. He was a member of Gladstone's first Government, but his opposition to the extension of the household franchise to the counties prevented him from returning to office in 1880. He declined the vice-royalty of India and the embassy at

Constantinople, but accepted a temporary mission to Turkey.

It was from his resumption of Parliamentary duties that my observation of him dates. A somewhat uncertain element in the party of Whigs and Radicals which was held together by Gladstone's prestige, he was the most conspicuous figure on the benches behind the Liberal Government. The Speakership, his acceptance of which would have relieved the Ministers from a possibly dangerous critic, was offered to Goschen in 1883, but he found he could not take it on account of his short-sightedness. From a back bench, while declining to give Lord Salisbury a blank cheque, he watched with uneasiness the vacillating Irish and Egyptian policy of Gladstone and his discordant colleagues.

By public argument and, as his biography * shows, by private exhortation, Goschen did his utmost to encourage and strengthen the moderate section of the Government to resist Radical pressure. Between Chamberlain and himself in the final years of their membership of the Liberal party there was resolute antagonism. It was he who first described Chamberlain's advanced proposals as the " unauthorized programme." His trenchant criticism of that programme brought upon him the derision of its author. He was " the candid friend," the " skeleton at the Egyptian feast."

The blank cheque which in 1884 Goschen refused to entrust to the Conservative leader, he signed a few years later, when he was in a position to influence the use to which it was put. Associating himself whole-heartedly with Hartington in opposition to

* *Life of Lord Goschen* : The Hon. Arthur D. Elliot.

Home Rule, he contributed much to the defeat of the bill of 1886. According to Gladstone he supplied " in the main, soul, brains and movement to the dissentient body " of Liberals. His accession to the Conservative Government as Chancellor of the Exchequer on Randolph Churchill's sudden resignation saved its chief from a great and even dangerous embarrassment. Those cautious politicians who, although they had rejected Home Rule, did not yet fully trust Salisbury, were reassured by the appointment of a man so sound and safe as Goschen. Not only his financial authority, but his powers as a debater were invaluable to his new colleagues. Frequently from 1887 till 1892 he was chosen to reply for the Government to the Liberal leader, and he enjoyed the intellectual exercise and caused others to enjoy it. As his new chief testified, his finance shed lustre over the Administration. It shed lustre over his own name, which became associated with the conversion of Consols.

Formal leadership never fell to Goschen, although he was of the rank from which leaders are drawn. On Gladstone's first resignation of the Liberal leadership in 1875 he had been named by friends as a possible successor, but he supported the choice of Hartington, and although, in 1891, on the death of W. H. Smith, he had clear claims to the leadership of the House of Commons, he readily acquiesced in Salisbury's appointment of Mr. Balfour. Naturally the Conservatives preferred —as they preferred after the Great War—to be led by a member of their own party, and Goschen had not then become a member of the Carlton Club, although he joined it in 1893. In the Unionist Coalition Government of 1895 he returned to the office of First Lord of the Admiralty, which he occupied more than twenty years previously. Surprise was expressed at his taking one of the great spending departments instead of resuming the position of Chancellor of the Exchequer. His reply was that he did not like paying other people's bills. While maintaining the strength of the Navy at the period of what he called our " splendid isolation," his influence was used in support of Salisbury's efforts to maintain the peace of Europe.

With massive head, intellectual brow and expressive mouth, Goschen gave the impression of high and virile character. He was trusted and respected. Whatever might be thought of his opinions every one recognized that they were carefully formed and sincerely held. There was no doubt of his integrity of mind. His speeches had the force of clear conviction and the interest of good literary quality. He held his notes close to his face when referring to them, and occasionally he groped on his breast with his hands as if searching for the eye-glass which had fallen there, but the keenness and vigour of his argument overcame the clumsiness of his gestures. He rivalled Chamberlain in the effectiveness with which he met interruptions. These he courted, for he could tear a weak argument to tatters.

In the House of Lords, after retiring from office in 1900, Viscount Goschen was a notable and picturesque figure. Age did not abate his mental vigour. The spirit of the old fighter was aroused by Chamberlain's fiscal proposals. With much force and vivacity he denounced a " gamble with the food of the people." This phrase became one of the battle cries. It was quoted on a thousand platforms. Another catch-word was contributed by its author to the tariff controversy when he spoke of those who were prepared to " go the whole hog " with Chamberlain.  Having helped to save Free Trade, he died a year after the Liberals obtained their huge majority.

## THE MARQUIS OF HARTINGTON

Just as it is difficult for one whose memory of statesmen goes back over the last twenty years of the last century to write of Viscount, instead of Mr. Goschen, so it is more natural to write of the Marquis of Hartington than of the Duke of Devonshire. In old age he was pre-eminently *the* Duke, but the national confidence and respect which he then possessed he had won before he succeeded to the peerage. It was in the House of Commons that he revealed his cool, sage, and steadfast qualities. There he sat for thirty-four years. The generation which knew him only as "the Duke," the ally and colleague of Salisbury, could scarcely realize how deeply attached the Liberal party was to him as its temporary leader, and as the lieutenant of Gladstone.

Of few men can it be said that they "might have been" Prime Minister. It can be said of Hartington. In 1880, after the Liberal victory at the polls, Queen Victoria asked him to form a Government. Seeing that he had for several years acted as leader of the Opposition—a function which he reluctantly undertook and faithfully discharged—it was natural that he should, on Beaconsfield's defeat, be sent for by the Sovereign. Her Majesty insisted strongly on his duty to accept the commission, and important colleagues wished that, if possible, he might do so. But as Gladstone, who had resumed an active part in political life, would take no position except that of Prime Minister, Hartington, sacrificing in the public interest any personal ambition that he might have felt, declined to form an Administration which would have divided the party.

Twice in 1886 the prize was held out to the ungrasping hand. On the rejection of Home Rule by the country, and the resignation of Gladstone's third Government, Salisbury proposed to advise the Queen to send for the Liberal Unionist statesman whose action had largely determined the course of events, and who was then the most influential figure in the House of Commons, but he thought he could be of more use in an independent position. Again, at the end of the year, when disturbed by Churchill's resignation, the Prime Minister suggested that Hartington should either form a Coalition Government or join his Administration as leader of the Commons, and " the desire of the Queen again coincided with that of Lord Salisbury." * Still, however, he preferred to stand aside, believing that his acceptance of either post might not be agreeable to the whole of the Conservative party, while it would probably alienate the Radical Unionists who were not yet ready for amalgamation.

Between 1880 and 1886 he had given proof of his staunch fidelity to party, a characteristic which in those days was not accounted for weakness or lack of patriotism. Although from 1875 he performed the uncongenial duties of Liberal leader in Opposition, he did not yield to resentment at Gladstone's resumption of the first place in 1880, but took office under him. Needless to say, he was a faithful colleague. Disloyalty by a lieutenant to a chief is rare in public life, and it is an offence of which Hartington was never accused or suspected.

A terrible strain was placed upon him by the assassination of his brother, Lord Frederick Cavendish, newly appointed as Irish Secretary, in Phœnix Park, Dublin, in 1882. One can imagine the shock

* *Life of the Duke of Devonshire* : Bernard Holland.

suffered by a member of an affectionate family
when the news of that tragic event, which reached
Harcourt, the Home Secretary, at a party at the
Admiralty, was communicated to Hartington by
their host, Lord Northbrook. Deep as was his
grief, he did not allow personal feeling to affect his
political conduct. And in spite of disagreements
with colleagues on various matters of policy and
all the vexations of life in a divided Cabinet, he
maintained a position which to him was peculiarly
irksome. His Whig friends feared that if he withdrew the cohesion of the Liberal party would be
destroyed and that its control would pass to the
Radicals. It was, among other reasons, with the
object of keeping Gladstone at the head of the party
and thus preserving a moderating influence over
the extreme section that, although " terribly sick
of office," Hartington remained in the Government
of 1880 as long as it lasted.

Till the struggle arose on Home Rule his powers
of mind and speech were not fully displayed to the
public. He had been known as a calm and cautious
statesman, and the soundness of his judgment had
been recognized by those associated with him, but
there was a popular impression that he was indolent
and on most subjects apathetic, and that the
energetic Radicals might elbow him out of political
life. Often he slumbered and nodded in the House
of Commons. Even his own speeches bored him.
While delivering his Indian Budget statement to a
sparsely occupied House, in 1882, he turned to Mr.
Porter, an Irish law officer, the only occupant of
the Treasury bench, and putting his hand over his
mouth to suppress a yawn, whispered with extreme
gravity : " This is damned dull." Mr. Porter,
telling the story, added that the speech went on

to its conclusion, clear, convincing, and logical. Certainly, by his manner, Hartington did himself injustice.   When, in the autumn of 1885, he engaged in a platform contest with his colleague, the Radical leader, many observers were, like Salisbury, disposed to put their money on active and alert Mr. Chamberlain, who sneered at the Whig Marquis as Rip van Winkle.

A generation whose interest in politics awakened with the present century may have difficulty in realizing the strength of the feeling against any form of Home Rule, however restricted, when Gladstone suddenly proposed it.   Between 1886 and the Sinn Fein rising, the Irish movement, under Liberal restraint, took a constitutional course, alarm about separation was abated, land legislation removed one of the most feared dangers, and Ulster supplied the chief motive of resistance.   A prediction that Unionists would join in the promotion of Home Rule, as they did in 1920, would have been treated at the end of last century as the vision of a madman. The project, when Gladstone took it up, excited a vague, but all the more terrible terror.   It appeared in the aspect of a frightful monster, the product of obstruction and outrage, seeking to devour property and to destroy the Empire.

In resistance to this monster Hartington appeared as a new, unknown man.   He did not yawn, nor did others yawn, during his speeches against Home Rule.   The Press had not then obtained its present widespread power, Parliament and the Platform were still the principal instruments in the instruction of the country, and it listened to Hartington when he flung off apathy and addressed it with vigour and earnestness.   I have never heard a more powerful speech than that which he delivered on the introduction of the first bill for Irish self-government. It was full of solid argument arranged with skill and presented with animation and force. And there were the same qualities in all his contributions to the controversy. Lord James of Hereford testified in later years that he "saved the country from Home Rule." Certainly many Liberals, relying on his sagacity, followed when and where he led.

I recollect the Marquis standing at the bar of the House of Commons, shy and rather dour in aspect, tall in figure, with thoughtful, candid forehead, grave, clear eyes, heavy lips and a full beard; he glances at his bench to see if there is a convenient, vacant place; slowly he lounges to it. I see him sleeping in his seat, mouth slightly open, head jerking back, hat in danger of falling off. A dull, indifferent man, you think! But rouse him by a call to duty! He is awake at the critical moment. See him rising from the bench behind the Gladstone Government of 1886 or from the front Opposition bench in after years! Hear his speeches then! His handkerchief clenched in his hand, determination in word and gesture, he turns on old colleagues and Nationalists and hits at their policy shrewd, strong, stunning blows. His blows on such an occasion, as Mr. Bryan, the distinguished American, observed, were like "the driving in of piles."

While personal ambition and pique were attributed to Chamberlain by men from whom he had parted, nobody accused Hartington of any selfish motive. The worst said of him by Liberals was that even if the Home Rule issue had not been raised, he would have fallen out of the army of Progress. He treated his old chief with marked respect. When groans and hisses followed the mention of Gladstone's name at the Opera House meeting in April, 1886, at which the Whig leader stood for the first time on the same political platform as the Conservative chief, he deplored this display of animosity with regard to " one whom I shall always admire and revere as the leader of a great party," and whose feelings were " as noble and honest as any that have ever inspired the conduct of an English statesman." Hartington spoke plainly and bluntly enough of the action of opponents, but never made imputations against their character. He did not attempt personal scores. For the artifices of debate he had neither talent nor inclination. It was the consciousness by the public of his disinterested, dispassionate judgment which enabled him at a crisis to gain its ear.

The association of men of conflicting views on the same bench is apt to prove embarrassing. During the Great War political opponents could easily tolerate each other's company, but the case was different in the time of stiff party contention. When the Conservatives took office in 1886, with the support of Liberal Unionists, a question was raised as to where Gladstone's former colleagues, who were at issue with him on Home Rule, should sit. Still claiming to belong to the Liberal party they asserted the right to the same position as its other members. Hartington asked Gladstone whether he saw any objection to their sitting with him on the front Opposition bench, and as he politely, though coldly, acquiesced in their doing so, the opposing sections of Liberal statesmen remained for six years side by side. The arrangement emphasized, instead of removing, discord. Probably it gave more satisfaction to Chamberlain than to Hartington. It may have been distasteful to the latter to stand beside an old chief while attacking his policy. His attacks, however, had increased significance in coming from that position.

At the age of fifty-eight Hartington in 1891 passed from the House of Commons to the other place as the eighth Duke of Devonshire. The political life of the Duke, although very distinguished, was calmer and less conspicuous than that of the Marquis. In 1895 he and his colleagues did what he refused to do in 1886 : they joined the Conservatives in a Coalition Government. The Duke relapsed into his early quiescence, refusing to be agitated by affairs which disturbed others. As Lord President of the Council he was responsible for education, but he did not share the Church enthusiasm of the Cecils. Just as he " never could understand Mr. Gladstone in conversation," he was " incapable even of understanding the apprehensions of the advocates of denominational education." It was interesting to see the Duke of Devonshire and the Marquis of Salisbury side by side. Old opponents, they had become close and tried allies, and now they were comrades in office. Yet there was not much in common between them. Their tastes were different. They had little conversation as they sat on the crimson bench.

Once more the Duke asserted himself in his own slow, dogged way. He was modestly serving as leader of the House of Lords in Mr. Balfour's Administration when the peace of his old age was rudely disturbed by Chamberlain's fiscal propaganda and by appeals from old comrades to save Free Trade. Loyalty to the Prime Minister and the Coalition induced him to tolerate Mr. Balfour's tactics longer than some of his colleagues. But, at last, when the head of the Government openly renounced the doctrine that duties should never be imposed except for revenue purposes, the Duke came out of the Cabinet, as Lord Rosebery observed, with slow, reluctant, but dignified steps. Again, as in the pre-Unionist era, he proved " a drag on the wheel " of the rushing Chamberlain, and although the more pushful politician was confident of ultimate victory, the fiscal question was settled by the election of January, 1906, for the remainder of the pre-war period.

By the death of the Duke, in 1908, the country lost, as Mr. Asquith said, " almost the last survivor of our heroic age." The new generation looks upon that as a heroic age in the sense in which the age of the knightly tournament was heroic. The war, with its countless heroes of another field, has given an almost mediæval aspect to what occurred before August, 1914. Yet in their time those Victorian statesmen grandly did their duty by the country and the Empire. They deserve to be remembered.

# CHAPTER VI

## KING EDWARD'S MINISTERS

SINCE the death of Queen Victoria till the present year (1921) there have been five Prime Ministers. The Marquis of Salisbury, essentially of the Victorian age, was still at the head of affairs when the Queen's son came to the throne. King Edward, during his brief reign, sent for three statesmen to fill the highest office in the State—Mr. Balfour, who succeeded his uncle in 1902, and resigned at the end of 1905; Sir Henry Campbell-Bannerman, who held the office thenceforth till he lay on his death-bed in 1908, and Mr. Asquith, whose tenure of it lasted long into the present reign.

In choosing Mr. Balfour rather than Mr. Joseph Chamberlain, whom a section of Unionists would have preferred, or the Duke of Devonshire, whose friends were surprised that he had not been consulted by the outgoing Premier, Lord Salisbury, before communications were made to the Sovereign, King Edward acted upon his own judgment.* Sir Henry Campbell-Bannerman and Mr. Asquith were, in turn, unmistakably marked for the highest place. Whether King George, on Mr. Asquith's resignation, acted upon his own judgment in sending first for the Unionist leader in the House of Commons, and whether it was on Mr. Bonar Law's advice

* *Life of the Duke of Devonshire.*

119

that he commissioned Mr. Lloyd George to form an Administration, we may not surely know till the authoritative memoirs are published. Popular sentiment pointed to the ultimate choice, although it had not been prompted by any precise Parliamentary event.

The Prime Ministers of the twentieth century represent a variety of classes and types. Mr. Balfour, a landed aristocrat, whose mother was a Cecil, belongs to the traditional ruling caste whose prestige was shaken if not destroyed by the war; Campbell-Bannerman came from the wealthy merchant class, which was a growing factor in the State last century and had produced two of its greatest Prime Ministers; Mr. Asquith, a landless barrister of the middle class, adorns a profession which has for centuries exercised powerful influence in national affairs, but has usually looked to the woolsack as the goal of its ambition; Mr. Lloyd George came of a still humbler stock than any which had previously given the First Minister to the Crown.

In this chapter I deal with the two statesmen, Mr. Balfour and Sir Henry Campbell-Bannerman, whose tenure of the highest office lay entirely within King Edward's reign.

## MR. BALFOUR

A wide period is covered by Mr. Arthur Balfour's career. Entering the House of Commons while Disraeli was still a member and remaining in it after the war, he has wandered between two worlds, one dead, the other struggling—if not (as in Arnold's words) powerless—to be born. Private secretary to Lord Salisbury at the Berlin Congress, an in-and-out member of the Fourth party, Irish Secretary during Parnell's strongest stage, leader of the Conservative party in the House of Commons for twenty years, leader of the House for a full decade at a single stretch and Prime Minister for three and a half years, he sought relief in 1911 from the " continuous and unceasing " strain of leadership, but as Mr. Asquith then prophesied, there were many chapters of his life " still to be written by the pen of history." The added chapters were the strangest of all. Not even the most daring visionary could have imagined that the Conservative ex-Prime Minister, the champion of the Lords, the Church and the Land, would serve under Mr. Asquith, the author of the Parliament Act, and Mr. Lloyd George, the Radical and Nonconformist.

Elected in 1874 for Hertford, which was almost a Cecil borough, Mr. Balfour, whose father died when he was quite young and who was brought up under the influence of his mother's family, came conspicuously into view in the early 'eighties with his long legs outstretched from the front bench below the Opposition gangway. It was, according to his whimsical explanation, for the convenience of his limbs that he took his seat there with the Fourth party. Evidently at the opening of his career he did not give indication of political talent. Lady Randolph Churchill pictures the young man "æsthetic with long hair and huge spats," and according to her son, who was six at the time, the Arthur Balfour of 1880 was " an affable and rather idle young gentleman who had delicately toyed with philosophy and diplomacy, was earnest in the cause of popular concerts, and brought to the House of Commons something of Lord Melbourne's air of languid and well-bred indifference." * In the 1880–1885 Parliament he delivered caustic speeches and was specially severe in criticism of Joseph Chamberlain, but he continued to be regarded by superficial observers as a trifler with politics. What was then chiefly said about him was that he had written *A Defence of Philosophic Doubt*, a book the title of which, as he himself asserted in his sarcastic way, "attracted more interest than the contents." Many of the gibes flung at the Tory aristocrat were in the form of allusions to Philosophic Doubt.

I do not recall any political appointment which caused greater surprise than the selection of Mr. Balfour as Chief Secretary for Ireland at a time when the post required a very strong man. He was President of the Local Government Board in 1885 and Secretary for Scotland in 1886, but he had done nothing to let the world know what sort of man he really was. Lively critics gave picturesque descriptions of a *malade imaginaire* and a " pampered darling of a perfumed drawing-room." How the facile wits of the Lobby in 1887 joked at his acceptance of the most difficult and dangerous post in the State, a post which had been the grave of

---

* *Lord Randolph Churchill* : W. S. Churchill.

great reputations ! Ireland was in disorder, the
law was flouted. Nationalists led by Parnell were
flushed with hopes excited by Liberal support,
Gladstone was devoting all his political resources
to the promotion of Home Rule. And here came
an elegant and languid trifler, " Miss Nancy,"
" Miss Clara," " the supercilious young person "
to rule the defiant country and confront the most
experienced statesman and some of the ablest and
least merciful debaters who ever sat in Parliament !

A thrilling chapter was contributed to political
history by the bound into fame and popularity of
the man who was the subject of these derisive
epithets. The post which had broken careers and
cancelled reputations was for Mr. Balfour the
stepping-stone to the highest places in the State.
In 1887 he counted for little in the Conservative
party except that he was the Prime Minister's
nephew; at the end of 1891 he was hailed with
enthusiasm as its leader in the House of Commons.
This marvellous success he achieved by the steady,
unflinching application of " resolute government "
in Ireland and by dazzling dexterity in debate.
Early in his rule the Nationalists poured light-
hearted sarcasm on the " tiger lily " and the
" plaster of Paris Cromwell " ; at the end of it they
respected a foeman worthy of their steel. He dared
to ridicule the histrionic elements of their agitation,
he made fun of the lamentations over Mr. William
O'Brien's prison breeches. His public letters were
masterpieces of raillery, his speeches were aggressive,
vivacious and trenchant. " In the dialectic of
senate and platform," testified Lord Morley, "Mr.
Balfour displayed a strength of wrist, a rapidity,
an instant readiness for combat, that took his foes
by surprise, and roused in his friends a delight

hardly surpassed in the politics of our day." *

During the years of his Chief Secretaryship he fought in the front of the Parliamentary battle. For a short time at first his manner in debate was flurried and fumbling, but rapidly his speeches improved until they became deadly in their invective and irony. He amazed the Nationalists by carrying the war into their camp. It was said by Justin McCarthy in a retrospect that Mr. Balfour was never actually unpopular with the Irish party. Sometimes, however, they showed violent resentment. An irritated Nationalist on an occasion which I recall left his seat with the object apparently of physically assaulting the provocative Minister and was with difficulty restrained by calmer colleagues. On another occasion Mr. Healy declared that if he were put in gaol and treated like Mr. O'Brien, he would save up a bucket of slops and carry it across the floor of the House and fling it into the Chief Secretary's face. The Chief Secretary laughed and went fearlessly on his way.

Perhaps he was happier in those days of growing prestige than at any later period. Frequently I saw him walking home from the House late at night. With him was his brother, Gerald, or his cousin, Lord Cranborne, or his brilliant private secretary, George Wyndham. Occasionally all three were his companions; and how gaily they chatted— the world before them—as they crossed Palace Yard, with detectives in guard of the Minister at a respectful distance! Mr. Balfour became not only the Conservative favourite, but a popular celebrity. All his ways and manners, little and great, were watched and recorded. His habit of reclining,

* *Life of Gladstone.*

with body low down, on the bench and placing his
feet against the table was caricatured in countless
cartoons. "Dinna put yer feet on the table"
was one of the hints in etiquette given by Jess at
*The Window in Thrums* to her husband when she
expected the genteel wife of the Tilliedrum bill-
sticker to tea. "Why does Mr. Balfour put his
feet on the table?" asked the genteel lady in the
Gallery. If he himself had been asked he would
have said: "Dear me! Do I put my feet on the
table? I suppose I do so because my legs are so
long."

The modern golf craze in England was due largely
to Mr. Balfour's example when the eye of Press and
People was fixed so curiously on all his doings.
Although a Scotsman, he took up golf, as he said,
" at an age when other people are leaving off the
games they learned in their youth." He took it
up with enthusiasm. At the end of a week of
political strife he strode over the links or the inland
course, with head bare, exulting in the fresh air,
as keen on winning as a professional. A good stroke
out of a bunker was as fine a joy as a successful
stroke in debate. Mr. Balfour was boyish in his
pleasure at winning a match. Like Sarah Battle
at whist, he loved a determined enemy and insisted
on the rigour of the game. He was not among
those " who affirm that they have no pleasure in
winning ; that they like to win one game and lose
another." As medicine for the mind he gave a
high place to golf. "Care may sit," he said,
" behind the horseman ; she never presumes to
walk with the caddie." Thus he set the fashion.

His charm of manner was felt on both sides
while he was leader of the House, a position which
he held for a longer consecutive period than any one

else since the passing of the Reform Act of 1832.
As Chief Secretary his iron hand was conspicuous.
When leader he hid—except on rare occasions—
the iron hand in the velvet glove. " The base,
bloody and brutal Balfour " of Irish alliteration
was changed in the public view to " a verray
perfight gentil knight." Although he could drive
the House hard, sternly suppressing insubordination
on his own side and ruthlessly using his superior
numbers against the Opposition, he was conciliatory
in ordinary arrangements and gracious to individuals.
Liberals, as a rule, liked him personally, and rarely
has a leader secured such affection as went out to
Arthur Balfour from his own party. Mr. Lecky
noted as a slight but characteristic fact that no
other public man was so often called by his Christian
name. (He was, by the way, named Arthur after
the Duke of Wellington, his mother's mother
having been a personal friend of the Duke.)

As a speaker Mr. Balfour was more effective in
criticism than in exposition. He made a jumble
of figures and details. These he could not or would
not master. His cousin, Lord Hugh Cecil, went so
far as to reproach him with an " indolent attention
to fact." One of his important speeches was
described by a friend as " almost ramshackle "
and it was not singular in that respect. He provided
himself with very few notes. Those for a speech
in the course of a debate he made on a long envelope
(with a fountain pen) as he reclined on his bench.
It was as a controversialist that he shone. He
had extraordinary skill in directing attack at the
weak point of an opponent's case and he was quick
in rejoinder. His mind, as an admiring opponent used to say, was the most critical in the
House.

"He was in logic a great critic,
  Profoundly skilled in analytic ;
  He could distinguish, and divide
  A hair 'twixt south, and south-west side."

Impatient politicians were sometimes irritated by the manner in which, as they thought, he trifled with the House.  Campbell-Bannerman noted disdainfully his airy graces, his subtle dialectics, his light and frivolous way of dealing with great questions.  As a rule, however, his graces and dialectics were enjoyed.

One of his peculiarities was his dislike of political lawyers as a class.  He has had many friends among them, such as Mr. Alfred Lyttelton, Lord Finlay and Mr. Asquith, but frequently they irritated him.  Chatham did not love gentlemen of the long robe.  Henry Fox was the sworn enemy of lawyers in Parliament.  " He loved disputing as much as they did," wrote Horace Walpole, " but he loved sense, which they made a trade of perplexing." The same might be written of Mr. Balfour's view. He once observed with bitter sarcasm that he always found that the expert opinion of lawyers coincided with the opinion held by their political colleagues.  Finlay, nettled by his friend's tone, suggested that Mr. Balfour himself would have made a very great lawyer and that the levity with which he treated their profession was due to regret that circumstances had debarred him from this field of intellectual activity.

His appearance has been in his favour.  The tall, thin figure, with distinguished, meditative face and shapely head, as he stands at the box grasping the lapels of his coat or stooping to look at his notes, makes a favourable appeal to the eye, and his expression—sometimes animated as when he asks,

" Am I to be told ? " sometimes whimsical as he adjusts his pince-nez and glances at an interrupter —sustains the general interest. Those who watched Mr. Balfour in his long leadership saw his hair gradually grow silvern. The first sign of the abhorred approach of old age appeared in the curl behind the ear. Slowly it spread until an added dignity was given to the head by the beautiful grey hair. No change has been made by Mr. Balfour in his mode of attire. Except when he dons a blue lounge suit, he wears a frock-coat, with handkerchief peeping from outside breast pocket, and he has always a black bow tie under a turn-down collar. To gaiters he has remained faithful.

Although in his leadership of the House he did not spend so much time on the Treasury bench as his predecessors, he not only attended at question time and during the delivery of important speeches, but as a rule was present late in the sitting, when he wrote the nightly report to the Sovereign. Sometimes documents and cheques would be brought in a despatch box for him to sign. But we always knew when he was writing the letter for the royal eye or the royal ear. He would select the notepaper carefully and see that his fountain pen was running properly. Then, with his feet set against the table, he would make a desk of his knees. Never was Gladstone so informal and at home in his attitudes, but never, I am sure, did Gladstone write more dutifully. Perhaps Mr. Balfour's letters, if they are published, will bear comparison even with Disraeli's.

" I am as a child in these matters," Mr. Balfour said on more than one occasion. He expressed surprise at the fuss made over this or that question, pretending, like Richard the Third, to be " too childish-foolish for this world." Inspector Bucket's advice apropos of Harold Skimpole was that : " Whenever a person proclaims to you ' In worldly matters I'm a child,' you consider that that person is only a-crying off from being held accountable, and that you have got that person's number and it's Number One." But the inspector was professionally suspicious. Mr. Balfour's simplicity was not entirely affectation. His thoughts ran apart from ordinary channels ; what was important to others was to him really trivial. With all his simplicity, however, he was a subtle political strategist. For over two years in his Prime Ministership he evaded a direct issue on Tariff Reform, placating Chamberlain on the one hand and Free Trade Unionists on the other and at the same time holding off the menacing Liberals. Perhaps no other Parliamentarian could have maintained such tactics so long. Yet when they failed they were followed by disaster.

No part of Mr. Balfour's career was more creditable than the period subsequent to the Unionist rout of January, 1906. At no stage did he display greater courage or win a larger measure of respect. When he obtained an easy seat for the City of London, after being thrust from Manchester, he entered an unsympathetic House. In front of him and to left of him was an overpowering force of triumphant opponents, resolved to undo much of what he had done. He found a strange new party, the Labour party, in addition to Liberals and Nationalists. At first, in this unfamiliar assembly, the statesman who for ten years had led the House was viewed rather scornfully. " Your day is ended," the eager, sanguine, combative reformers seemed to say ; " this is no longer a

theatre for your gifts and graces." But, as Mr.
Bonar Law said, in words applied to Cromwell in
his darkest hour, hope shone in him like a pillar of
fire when it had gone out in all the others. Gradually,
in spite of its prejudice, he gained the ear of the
House. Calm, courteous, conciliatory, attentive
he became again a dominating factor and even those
who had the most disliked his policy recognized
his intellectual power and his personal charm.

For six years and in two general elections he led
the Opposition. Dissensions, however, continued
among his followers on the fiscal question and there
were differences on the degree of resistance which
should be offered to the proposals of the Government dealing with the House of Lords. At last,
weary of the strain and worry, he laid down the
leadership. " I have not, I am confident," he declared, " the vigour again to conduct a Ministry."

Fortunately he had vigour to take a distinguished
share in Government during the war. " I wonder,"
he wrote in 1900, " if I live till seventy-two, whether
I shall still wish to be a Cabinet Minister. I like
it so very little at fifty-two that I can hardly
believe it." Whether he liked it or not—and one
is usually sceptical of protests by men in power
that they do not care for office—he was a Minister
at seventy-two. As First Lord of the Admiralty
in the Asquith Coalition and Foreign Secretary
in its successor, he worthily and unostentatiously
did his bit. " An Ex-Premier," says Lord Rosebery
in his volume on Pitt, " is usually found, in any
Cabinet in which he may serve as an ordinary
member, to be a fleeting and dangerous luxury."
Mr. Balfour proved an exception to the rule.

What his share was in the transactions which
substituted Mr. Lloyd George for Mr. Asquith at

the head of the Government the world does not yet know, but there is no reason to think he was influenced at any stage of the war by personal or party motives. He appeared seldom in the House of Commons. Perhaps he did not feel quite the same full sense of responsibility for all the actions of the Coalitions which he felt in the case of other Governments. But he did loyally and capably what was entrusted to him to do. And when duty called him into the House, he showed all his old skill in debate. His hand had lost none of its swiftness or subtlety. His mission to the United States was of great service to the Empire and as a member of the Peace Conference his talents found congenial play. And after he resigned the Foreign Secretaryship he continued to adorn the Government and did what a veteran trained in the old diplomacy could do for the new and troubled world on the League of Nations.

## SIR HENRY CAMPBELL-BANNERMAN

If the frequent calling of Arthur Balfour by his Christian name has been, as Mr. Lecky suggested, a sign of affection, there was significance also in the reduction of his successor's long double-barrel to an intimate C.B. There was no disrespect in the initials. The first time I heard them they were used in the Lobby by a distinguished Liberal. " C.B.," I repeated with a puzzled air. " Campbell-Bannerman," explained my friend. *Mr.* Campbell-Bannerman was long enough for tongue or pen. *Sir Henry* Campbell-Bannerman, as he became in 1895, was intolerable for everyday use. So the genial, homely Scot was called C.B. Only the most conventional spoke of "Sir Henry." He was C.B. in the smoking-room, in the street and in the Press.

" It has not been by my seeking that I am where I am," he said when Prime Minister, " but simply because I have gone straight forward, and I find myself here without knowing very well how I came here." Superior persons also wondered how he got to that position. He was neither brilliant nor eloquent nor had he a magnetic personality. He shared with many lesser people shrewdness, humour, patience and tenacity, but what distinguished him was that he combined with the temper and tastes of " a cultured citizen of the world," unusual political conviction and courage. Mr. Lloyd George described him as absolutely the bravest man he ever met in politics.

Although he had been in the House of Commons since Gladstone entered on his first Premiership, the country did not become familiarly acquainted with Campbell-Bannerman until 1884, when he succeeded Sir George Trevelyan as Chief Secretary

for Ireland. At that time the Parnellites hated
Liberals more than Conservatives. They had
broken rugged Mr. Forster, and while Sir George
Trevelyan was the victim of their attacks his hair
had rapidly become grey. Against Campbell-
Bannerman they battered in vain. He was likened
by Mr. T. P. O'Connor to a sand-bag. He did not
scold or storm like Forster nor wince like Macaulay's
sensitive nephew and biographer. Under the
fiercest criticism he kept his temper ; he smiled
at violent abuse. Parnell admitted in a railway
conversation with Lord Ribblesdale that " no
impression could ever be made on him."

How he found salvation on the Irish question all
the political world learned from the gibes of 1886.
To the disappointment of Liberal Unionists Campbell-Bannerman, after " protracted and painful
deliberation," concurred in Home Rule as the
only practicable policy. When the confession that
he had " found salvation " was attributed to him
by Mr. Mundella, it was explained that he had really
applied the phrase to his colleague's mental process.
" I have come to the conclusion," Mundella had
said to him in the Lobby, " that Home Rule has
got to be accepted and that it alone can clear
everything up." " Yes ! " replied Campbell-
Bannerman, " you're just in the position of the
man who in the language of the Salvation Army
has found Jesus." It was, however, to his own
case that quizzing Unionists insisted on fitting
the metaphor. He was the sinner suddenly and
mysteriously saved.

Although he did not take a conspicuous part in
Opposition between 1886 and 1892, he grew steadily
in reputation as a sensible, tactful, reliable Parliamentarian. As leader of the Scottish Liberals he

gave proof of the qualities which later endeared him to a wider sphere. He returned in 1892 to the office of Secretary for War, which he had filled in 1886, and during the career of the Gladstone-Rosebery Administrations he was a helpful, conciliatory colleague. An admirable picture of him was drawn by the *Spectator* in 1894. He was described " creeping to the front inch by inch no one exactly knows how. . . . Whenever the coach has seemed like sticking in the mud, there has been a cheery but never garrulous Scotchman, a man who always inspires confidence and never raises envy or malice, ready to lend a hand and set things going again."

When some one in Mr. Balfour's hearing compared him to W. H. Smith, the Conservative leader said : " Yes, he was like Mr. Smith, but far cleverer." So useful was the " cheery but never garrulous " Scot that although, on Mr. Peel's retirement, he aspired—as Mr. Asquith said—to the Chair, his colleagues could not spare him from their bench. Among other notable measures, he celebrated his career at the War Office by introducing the eight hours' day in the ordnance factories and he concluded it by deposing the Duke of Cambridge from the post of Commander-in-Chief. This achievement was described as a triumph of tact. Not only did he induce the Duke to resign, but he persuaded his Royal Highness that he was his best friend.

It was by an attack on Campbell-Bannerman's department that the Unionists, after repeated efforts, brought down the Rosebery Government in June, 1895. The story of that summer sitting has been often told. Many members were on the terrace chatting over the Duke of Cambridge's retirement, which had just been announced, and Harcourt was

congratulating himself that on that day at least—
a day devoted to Army Estimates—there would be
no political crisis, when the fatal assault was opened
on the vote for ammunition. The Opposition
made the grave contention that the supply of
cordite was insufficient. The amount was what
the experts considered necessary, but an amendment
implying censure on the Government was pressed
and was carried by 132 to 125.

According to Sir Richard Temple's Conservative
testimony in *The Story of My Life*, the attack had
been planned several weeks previously. The
Liberals were taken by surprise. At the sound of
the division bells they entered the chamber without
flurry or fear, little expecting what happened.
While the Unionists were cheering in triumph, a
whisper passed between the Secretary for War and
the leader of the House; Campbell-Bannerman put
his papers back in his box and Harcourt moved to
report progress. In that moment they had realized
that all was over. A division taken without notice
in a small House was not necessarily fatal, but the
Government were so disunited that they could not
in any event have stood much longer and they
threw up the game.

The Government were beaten on a Friday
evening. At the opening of the following week
Lord Salisbury was in Lord Rosebery's place. On
Tuesday, in the precincts of the House of Commons,
Campbell-Bannerman was accosted by a young man
who, on behalf of the Prime Minister, asked if it
would be convenient for him to hand over his seals
of office to his successor in the course of the afternoon. As Lord Kimberley observed, the Prime
Minister had sent his private secretary " as he
might have sent a footman." The suggested

proceeding would have been a strange departure from practice, and after consultation with Lord Rosebery, the outgoing Secretary of State sent an answer that it would be improper for him to surrender his seals to any one except the Sovereign, from whom he received them.

It is recorded that on the dismissal of North and Fox " in order to mark emphatically the royal displeasure, they were desired to send in their seals by the Under-Secretaries, as a personal interview with them would be disagreeable to His Majesty." There was no such motive underlying the request to Campbell-Bannerman. Critics conjectured that the new Premier's haste was due to a fear that the retiring Minister might appoint Sir Redvers Buller to the Commandership-in-Chief, Lord Wolseley being the choice of the Conservatives. Salisbury's own explanation was that in view of the possible requirements of the War Office, it was desirable that there should be no interregnum. At first he pooh-poohed the indignant complaints of Campbell-Bannerman's friends, but later he expressed his extreme regret.

The man over whom the Unionists strode into office in a manner which gave him the sympathy of all Liberals maintained an unruffled temper and a constant cheerfulness amid the dissensions of his colleagues. Although he never pushed himself forward, he did not shrink from the call when, on Harcourt's resignation in 1898, he was unanimously elected leader of the Opposition in the House of Commons. It was an unattractive job, as *Punch* described it. " Well, 'Enery Bannerman," said Harcourt, the departing butler to the new man, " so you've took the place, 'ave you ! I wish you joy ! She used to be a Liberal Old Party, but now

she's that contrairy there's no living with her."
Neither Rosebery nor Harcourt could put up with
her tantrums. Could the new man ?

On his appointment to the leadership Campbell-
Bannerman was commonly regarded as a stop-gap.
It was known that he was a good conciliator and it
was supposed that when the party was re-united
he would give place to somebody else. He was
said to be fonder of French novels than of Blue
Books, he was accused of a liking for French
cookery, he was easy-going and suspected of
indolence ; it was remarked that " a few crackers
ignited under his coat-tail would do him good."
While superficial observers spoke and wrote of him
in this way, those who knew him scouted the idea
that he considered himself a stop-gap. " He will
stick to the job," prophesied a brother Scot, " till
he is Prime Minister." And he stuck to it in evil
fortune and in good, courageous and constant,
serene and smiling, living laborious days and
spending long dull nights on a front bench.

The South African War, in accentuating the
differences of Liberals, increased the new leader's
difficulties. He did not go so far as Harcourt in
attacking Chamberlain's diplomacy and policy,
nor did he go so far as the Liberal Imperialists in
supporting the Government. " It is a just war,"
said Sir Edward Grey. " It was in the last resort
forced upon us," said Mr. Asquith. Campbell-
Bannerman did not hold the Government free from
responsibility for it, but he protested against being
called a little-Englander and he made his protest
respected. On the one hand he kindled the wrath
of Unionists by his charge against the Government
of " methods of barbarism " in respect of farm
burning and concentration camps ; on the other

hand, by his support of measures for the prosecution of the war, he incurred the censure of the rising Radical below the gangway, Mr. Lloyd George. At last, when the Boer War was over, the unity of the Liberals was secured under their patient leader. They were united in opposition to the Education and Licensing Bills of the Government, to the fiscal policies both of Mr. Chamberlain and of Mr. Balfour, and, in fact, to the whole trend of Unionism.

Gradually " C.B.'s " position was established. Although Lord Rosebery made brief, picturesque excursions, the leader who fought steadily and staunchly was the leader whom the party in the end followed.   A witty Unionist onlooker described how

> " when the fight was done,
> Came there a certain lord, neat and trimly dress'd,
> Fresh as a bridegroom."

It was not thus that a campaign could be conducted to success.  The call to Lord Rosebery, as I have shown in a previous chapter, weakened as the years went on.  How could Monmouth's men fight when Monmouth stayed during the battle in his tent ? It was recognized a considerable time before the opportunity came that the leader in opposition would be the leader in office.  The first place in the State fell to him by a title which, according to Mr. Asquith, " no one disputed."

With large round head held slightly to the side, as if in a perpetually quizzing attitude, and with broad, shrewd face, a roguish twinkle in his clear eyes and a quiver of the lips under the heavy moustache, he looked—what he was—a capable, trusty, kindly, humorous man.  Hatred of humbug went with his sense of fun.  His speeches were

carefully written out and they owed nothing to their
delivery ; he read considerable portions and fluttered
the MS. as if fanning his face.   In form they were
neat and crisp, with a literary suggestiveness.
Those delivered on ceremonial occasions were
models of good taste and good feeling.

By humour in answers as well as in speeches
" C.B." entertained the House.   The Nationalists
having complained that Irish soldiers were forbidden
to wear the shamrock on St. Patrick's Day, some one
as a set-off asked him if the soldiers of his own
country were allowed to wear the thistle.   " The
Scottish emblem," he replied, " does not lend
itself with convenience to the button-hole."      A
self-praising Government he likened to a plain
woman admiring herself in a looking-glass.   " A
little *tête montée* " he said of Joseph Chamberlain
on the return of that vivacious statesman from a
triumphal tour in South Africa, and the phrase,
which he accompanied with an arch expression was
often merrily quoted.   He enjoyed a joke at
himself.   " I see you are famous," a friend said to
him.   " What have I done now ? " he asked.
" The ' C.B.' corsets," his friend explained, " are
in all the shops."   " I assure you," he retorted
with mock gravity, " that I owe my figure entirely
to nature."

The years of his Prime Ministership were few but
eventful.   Called to the highest office in December,
1905, " C.B." formed an unexpectedly strong,
broad-bottomed Government, which included Mr.
Asquith and Sir Edward Grey, as well as the anti-
Imperialists, Mr. Morley and Mr. Lloyd George ;
and obtaining at the General Election an overpowering majority, he was eager to get on with
reform.   " Enough of this foolery," he cried in

March, 1906, when time was, as he thought, wasted
by Mr. Balfour's dialectics. Even on the verge
of old age, as his successor remarked, he was not
ashamed " to see visions and to dream dreams."
Few of these were realized in his lifetime. Although
he closured opponents in the House of Commons, his
legislation was confronted in the other place with a
barrier which he could not in the span allotted to
him pull down. It was largely by administrative
measures which the Lords could not thwart that
his Government carried out a new policy.

While " C.B." was at the head of affairs, Mr.
Asquith, as Chancellor of the Exchequer, laid the
financial foundation of old age pensions, and Mr.
Haldane initiated the army reforms which proved
so valuable when the Great War broke out.    The
most memorable act of his Ministry was the granting
of responsible government to the States which had
been at war with us in South Africa—an act so
fully justified and so fruitful in 1914. Bold and
significant of his political sympathy was the phrase
in which he expressed belief in the permanence of
the Russian Duma. That body having been dissolved while several of its members were attending
an inter-Parliamentary conference in London,
" C.B." concluded a speech in the Royal Gallery
of Westminster Palace by exclaiming: " *La Duma
est morte* : *vive la Duma!* "

Great sorrow was expressed when this figure of
Standfast crossed from life to the other side.   The
strain of Lady Campbell-Bannerman's long illness,
with its call upon his care and his own nursing, told
heavily upon him, and her death in 1906 dealt
what proved to be " a fatal blow to his heart."
His health gradually failed and he passed away
in April, 1908, at No. 10, Downing Street.   It was

fitting that after his long, brave career he should, with his party in power, end his days in that historic house, although he had three weeks previously, on the urgent recommendation of his medical advisers, sent his resignation to the King at Biarritz and a new Cabinet was formed while he lay on his death-bed. His Majesty, before going abroad, had visited the patient and on his return called again at Downing Street. From the highest to the lowest the feeling of sorrow was the same. There have been greater, more brilliant Prime Ministers than " C.B.," but none better loved.

# CHAPTER VII

### THE WAR MINISTERS

IT is difficult to write of Mr. Asquith and Mr.
Lloyd George at a time when their fine comradeship
has been turned to antagonism. For eleven strenuous years they served together in office, Mr. Asquith
being for nearly nine of these years Prime Minister.
Then they parted. The parting of colleagues is
always dangerous and the breach between the two
Liberal statesmen has widened until now it seems
irreparable. Lord John Russell served under
Palmerston after being his chief. Mr. Asquith, in
different circumstances, has not taken the same
course. Mr. Lloyd George has maintained the war
Coalition in peace and the ex-Prime Minister is its
stern opponent. To write impartially of the two
is difficult, but I shall try, as I have tried in other
cases, to give my impressions without bias.

## MR. ASQUITH

" Perhaps," says Bagehot, " as long as there has been a political history in this country there have been certain men of a cool, moderate, resolute firmness, not gifted with high imagination, little prone to enthusiastic sentiment, heedless of large theories and speculations, careless of dreamy scepticism ; with a clear view of the next step, and a wise intention to take it ; a strong conviction that the elements of knowledge are true, and a steady belief that the present world can, and should be, quietly improved." Among politicians of this temperament is the man who, as he himself said, " led the British people at the most critical time of their life into the path of honour." Mr. Asquith has certain qualities traditionally trusted by the English people, and yet in the midst of the great struggle he was replaced by a Celt of high imagination.

In my vision of Mr. Asquith, as a private member in his first Parliament, I see him on the second Opposition bench leaning forward to chat with his Unionist friend, Sir Henry James, or delivering one of his rare and measured speeches while he hitches up his shoulders as if the barrister's gown were slipping off. Elected in 1886, a rising lawyer with a brilliant Oxford record, he was reserved in manner among those who did not know him and spent little time in the Lobby where it is so easy to waste an hour. Unlike the average lawyer-politician, he made no effort to advertise himself and commend his services to party managers, but although he spoke seldom, each speech, concise, lucid and emphatic, maintained the impression which he had at once produced in debate and marked him as a man of unusual power of mind and force of character. It might have been said of him even then, as of Chaucer's Clerk of Oxenford :

> " Not oo word spak he more than was neede ;
> Al that he spak it was of heye prudence,
> And schort, and quyk, and ful of gret sentence."

I have also an indelible recollection of his cross-examination of Mr. MacDonald, the manager of *The Times*, at the judicial inquiry in 1889 into the articles on Parnellism and Crime. Mr. MacDonald had purchased the notorious documents, so damaging to Parnell if they were genuine, including the letter reproduced in facsimile which purported to be an apology by the Irish leader to a confederate for having as a matter of expediency publicly condemned the Phœnix Park murders. Enveloped by the glamour of a magnate of the greatest newspaper in the world, he entered the witness-box with an air of tranquil, dignified confidence. He left it with his prestige shaken and the case of *The Times* weakened. His cross-examination by Mr. Asquith, who was with Sir Charles Russell for the defence of Parnell, was one of the sensational incidents of the inquiry. It excited all of us in court : it was so searching, so pitiless, so destructive.

The last time Mr. Asquith spoke from a back bench on which, as he has asserted, he spent the happiest period of his Parliamentary life, was in 1892 when, after the general election, he moved the vote of no-confidence in the Conservative Government. His speech was both pungent and prudent. All as they listened to it knew that the man entrusted by Gladstone with the fateful motion which was to send the Liberals to the Treasury bench would himself receive office. There was surprise, however, when by a single stride, at a time less venturesome than the present, the lawyer politician, born, as he said, in " a humble station of life " and without powerful social connections, entered the Cabinet as a Secretary of State. His Conservative predecessor at the Home Office had gone straight to it without holding a subordinate post, but whereas Henry Matthews on his appointment was sixty and a leader at the bar, Mr. Asquith was only forty and had taken silk only two years previously.

I think the chief impression produced by Mr. Asquith as Home Secretary was that of a firm, efficient administrator. He was then, as always, a quick, clean worker. He saw things clearly and when he made up his mind he held by his decision. Although the Government had only a small majority, including Nationalists, he would not give way to pressure. He was attacked in one quarter because he resisted demands for an unconditional amnesty to dynamiters and he incurred odium in extreme Labour circles by authorizing the employment of troops to aid the Local Authority in dealing with strike disorder in Yorkshire. For his staunchness in this affair, while clearly showing that the forces of the Crown were not used in the interests of employers, he was much praised by Conservatives.

One of his administrative achievements was the satisfactory settlement of the question of meetings in Trafalgar Square, a difficult question which had excited dangerous agitation and baffled his predecessor. His genuine sympathy with Labour he manifested in the most practical manner. He improved the means of dealing with sweating and other industrial evils, he adopted special rules for dangerous trades and he appointed working men inspectors and inaugurated a system of women inspectors.   Although his bill on employers' liability was sacrificed on account of changes introduced by the House of Lords, he left his legislative mark on factories and workshops.   Mr. Stead found in him an exponent of " the revival of civic religion."

Although by candour in opinion, courage in administration and distinction in speech Mr. Asquith increased in office the reputation he had won as a private member and contributed his ray of brilliance to a brilliant Cabinet, he was not yet, in 1892–1895, regarded by any section of the Liberal party as its man of the future.   The party was then well provided with leaders and lieutenants.   There were Lords Spencer and Rosebery in the Upper House ; and next to Harcourt in the House of Commons, there was Mr. Morley, who had ambitions and friends.   There were also the safe men, Campbell-Bannerman and Henry Fowler.   Even Sir Edward Grey, although only an Under Secretary, was described as a possible Prime Minister.   Mr. Asquith did not arouse enthusiasm.   He was considered to be too coldly intellectual.   Much surprise was caused by Lord Rosebery's remark that great as were his powers of head, his powers of heart were still greater.   Every one, however, recognized that the Secretary of State, who was married to Miss Margot Tennant in 1894 and at whose marriage the register was signed by Mr. Gladstone, Lord Rosebery and Mr. Balfour, the past Prime Minister, the Prime Minister of the day and a future Prime Minister, would have a career—whatever its course might be—of much lustre.

The long term during which their side was out

of office (1895–1905) put a severe strain on the
patience of Liberal lawyers who relied upon political
service for professional advancement and the differences between their leaders embarrassed those who
hoped to be on the winning side.   Such calculating
lawyers did not include men of the position and
character of Mr. Asquith.   Resuming practice at
the bar, he bided his time in Parliament, and while
refraining from avoidable, needless controversy,
proved himself a man of conviction.   On behalf of
his party he moved the rejection of several of the
Ministerial measures, notably those dealing with
voluntary schools and agricultural rates, and he
was occasionally caustic in criticism of the external
policy of the Government and the foreign excursions
of Chamberlain, whom he accused of " touting for
allies in the highways and byways of Europe," but
generally in Imperial affairs he supported Salisbury
rather than Campbell-Bannerman.   Being convinced
that the Boer War was in the last resort forced upon
us, he held we could engage in it with clean hands
and a clear conscience.

Although Mr. Asquith was associated with Lord
Rosebery in the Liberal League, which blended
Imperialism with Liberal doctrine, so suspicious
a Radical as Mr. Labouchere admitted that he
took no part in the intrigues with which some others
were charged.   While holding aloof on certain
issues from Campbell-Bannerman, who found a
lieutenant in Mr. Bryce, he acted with him whenever
possible.   No word of acrimony escaped from his
lips.   The toleration he claimed for himself he
allowed to others.   Thus when the controversies
over South Africa became faint and Imperial
questions ceased to divide the party, no personal
feeling prevented his full co-operation with old

colleagues. Tariff Reform brought him to the front with new proof of his valuable qualities. Following Mr. Chamberlain throughout the country, he assailed his fiscal theories in what Lord Rosebery described as " clinching, convincing speeches."

Here is a note I made one of those days on his Parliamentary appearances :—" He arrives between nine and ten o'clock in evening dress ; by and by he takes a small bunch of MS. from his pocket, he glances over it, makes an alteration here and there, adds a note suggested by what is said on the other side ; the benches fill up, the time for his intervention arrives, the MS. is placed on the box, he stands back a step from the table, and with head held high he sends forth in a strong voice his faultless phrases, while Mr. Balfour smiles, Mr. Chamberlain sneers and Liberals applaud."

Campbell-Bannerman's success in forming a broad-bottomed Government in December, 1905, was complete when he secured the assistance of the leader of the Liberal Imperialists in the House of Commons. There was no question of Mr. Asquith's capacity. As Chancellor of the Exchequer he obtained a place worthy of his reputation and of his position in the party and that reputation and position he strengthened in office. He was a sound if not a brilliant financier. He practised economy, reduced debt and prepared the scheme of old age pensions which he included in the Budget handed over to Mr. Lloyd George. And he was more than Chancellor ; he was deputy leader of the House. He spoke less frequently than eager followers desired, but when called upon by his chief, his blows were those of a sledge-hammer. He was generally and increasingly recognized as the second man in the Government. It was evident to the whole

political world during Campbell-Bannerman's last
illness that he would be his successor. "To-day
he is an important man," said Mr. Healy in a
sneering speech on March 30, 1908 ; "to-morrow
he may be a god." And " a god " he became nine
days later when, summoned by King Edward to
Biarritz, he kissed hands on his appointment as
Prime Minister.

Succeeding to the command of a great Parliamentary army, Mr. Asquith's career as its head was
marked by a succession of exacting anxious events.
"No man's health," said Sir Robert Peel in 1846,
" would permit him to be Prime Minister of this
country for more than five years." So wonderful
were Mr. Asquith's constitution and temperament
that he endured the ordeal for fully eight and a half
years in circumstances of strain and stress not
dreamed of by Peel. Even his six years of peace
were full of trouble and tension. In addition to
threatening incidents abroad and industrial com-
motions at home, he had to deal with grave constitutional questions, the rejection of a Budget by
the House of Lords, the consequent struggle with
the Peers, the passing of the Parliament Act, the
promotion of Home Rule, the revolt of Ulster and
the alarming Curragh incident. His Government
carried national insurance as well as old age
pensions and introduced payment of members, it
strengthened the Navy and organized an Ex-
peditionary Force, and it displayed activity in
other branches of administration, but all its achievements of reform were blotted out of the national
mind by the constitutional hurricane, and then
came the war, which changed all things.

Dilke, who had long experience and was no mean
judge, looked upon Mr. Asquith as one of the greatest

Parliamentarians he had known, much superior in that capacity to Gladstone. Few men have possessed such authority as he acquired in the House of Commons. He did not supply the driving force of Liberalism, but he gave it direction. His Government got out of one trouble to fall into another. Many times its defeat seemed imminent. There was no apparent escape for it. But a way out was found by its dexterous chief. Popular he was not in the sense that Mr. Balfour or " C.B." was popular, his reserve standing in the way of affectionate relationship with his followers, but the whole Liberal party regarded him with trust and pride until the war was far advanced and every section of the House recognized his eminent qualities.

No Government had a more tolerant chief. " I have had the honour to serve under Mr. Asquith," said Mr. Austen Chamberlain after the collapse of his Coalition, " and I know how loyal he is to colleagues." He was not jealous of any credit or popularity they might win personally. Instead of taking the centre of the stage as often as possible to himself, he gave them ample opportunity. At the same time, if they fell into scrapes, he helped them out. His fault rather was that he allowed too much liberty. It might have been said to him as Junius wrote to the Duke of Bedford : " Your friends have a privilege to play upon the easiness of your temper." A Unionist member of his Coalition Cabinet remarked that he did not hold a tight enough rein. This was one of the defects of his qualities. As for his kindness to colleagues, I may quote the tribute of Mrs. Hamilton in *The Life of Lord Wolverhampton*. Referring to the illness which soon ended her father's career, she writes : " Then it was, during a most difficult and distressing time, that the friendship and loyal affection of Mr. Asquith stood out, as it will ever stand out in our memories, in a consideration and patience and tenderness which men rarely show to each other in this working-day world."

As a Parliamentary orator he has proved unique in a certain style. He has not the eloquence of Gladstone or Lloyd George nor the incisiveness of Joseph Chamberlain, but Lord Curzon noted in 1913 that he " represented a type of public speaking carried to higher perfection than by any one in modern times. He never fell below a certain majestic level, even though he never soared above it or kindled an audience into flame. His speeches were a miracle of succinctness, the apotheosis of business-like efficiency." His succinctness has been in agreeable contrast to the verbosity which afflicts so many members, especially on the front benches. A time-limit would have no terror for him. In later years he has been much given to qualifications and parentheses which check the flow of his oratory, but certainly in his prime it could be said of him, as Ben Jonson said of Bacon : " No man ever spoke more neatly, more pressly, more weightily, or suffered less emptiness, less idleness in what he uttered." His voice is sonorous and his language dignified. He excels in

" Choice word and measured phrase, above the reach
    Of ordinary men."

It is true that he has hardly ever, in Lord Curzon's words, " kindled an audience into flame." This incapacity, notable at public meetings, has been felt also in the House of Commons. Sometimes his followers have been disappointed by the coldness of his speeches.

Only on rare occasions has he aroused party enthusiasm. One of these occasions was when he sounded the note of battle with the Lords on their rejection of the Budget. His followers then rose in his honour as he entered the House and his speech appealed to their militant instincts. It abounded in strong, thrilling phrases, denunciatory of the Peers' "most arrogant usurpation" and was delivered with extraordinary energy and animation. The cold Mr. Asquith was then invisible. That, however, was not his characteristic vein.

A lawyer and politician prophesied, on his appointment as Prime Minister, that he would not prove a fighting leader. "I have often been against him in the courts," the lawyer who was against him also in politics said, "and sometimes when he might have had a chance of winning he agreed to a compromise." Probably his critic was generalizing too much, but in public affairs, at any rate, Mr. Asquith has shown the compromise temper —the temper which has done so much to smooth the working of the English Constitution.

Personal attacks and small debating scores at his expense are unnoticed by Mr. Asquith except with a shrug of the shoulders or a pursing of the lips. He has described recriminative comparison as "the idlest and most unpatriotic of all diversions." His own avoidance of recrimination when retort was tempting has proved his coldness of temper as well as sense of proportion. He has never indulged in the personal thrusts which excite the Parliamentary passions. "During more than twenty years," wrote Lord Rowallan, "we sat on opposite sides of the House, but I cannot recall an occasion on which it seemed to me even in the heat of party warfare that Mr. Asquith did a dishonourable thing or used a dishonest argument."

Like Mr. Balfour, Mr. Asquith found it impossible with the heavy duties and responsibilities of Prime Minister to spend a great deal of time on the Treasury bench. He arrived at the proper moment to answer questions, scanning the prepared answers as he came in; and having given his replies, he went to his room, reappearing only when his intervention in debate was required. With an adroitness never surpassed he replied to questions intended to embarrass him, but his answers in many cases were so brief that they conveyed the impression of curtness. They appeared to have the character of a snub, although that was not intended by the most courteous of Ministers. He had a stock of serviceable phrases, such as " if and when," " there will be no avoidable delay," and " all relevant matters will be taken into consideration." " Over a hundred questions," Mr. Asquith boasted to a colleague one day when acting both as Prime Minister and as Secretary for War, " and not once caught out ! "

The Great War, which changed the course of the world, completely changed the course of Mr. Asquith's career. Prime Minister, master of the House of Commons and honoured leader of the Liberal party when it broke out, it left him broken in reputation, forsaken by many to whom he had given office, followed in ill-fortune by only a fragment of his once great Parliamentary force. Some tears were shed for him, but they were few compared with the gibes of which he was the target. History will in time pronounce its final judgment. Whether it will modify the sentence of the Contemporary Court who can say ?

In the early stage of the war Mr. Asquith encountered few difficulties in Parliament. Under
the stress of strong emotion it was practically united
in support of the Minister who had led the country
into the path of honour and on whom was laid an
enormous responsibility. His speeches, resolute
and dignified, expressed the national spirit and
exhibited to the world the greatness of the issue
in which we took up arms ; and the initial measures
of the Government, prompt and energetic, were
approved. Leading Unionists co-operated with
Ministers and set an example in restraint. But
as months of anxiety and disappointment succeeded
each other the temper of the House of Commons
changed. There were increasing signs of distrust
and after the sensational report of the shortage of
shells these became ominous. As usual, Mr. Asquith
was too little responsive to Press and popular
criticism and he gave members the briefest of
answers. But when he found at last from the
attitude of the Front Opposition Bench that a
party Government such as he led could no longer
be trusted as an efficient instrument for the prosecution of the war, he formed in May, 1915, the
Coalition, embracing Unionist and Labour representatives.

Unity seemed to be secured when Mr. Bonar Law,
instead of walking to the left of the Speaker, took
a seat beside Mr. Asquith. If there had been any
personal bitterness in their relations in peace time,
it was removed by the comradeship of the common
danger and the minds of both were concentrated on
the common purpose. The Coalition excited little
enthusiasm in any quarter. Many Liberals
regretted its formation, Nationalists hated it,
Unionists thought their side had too few of the

important places.  It survived longer than doubters
expected.  Lord Curzon, after it had undergone a
considerable trial, expressed the belief that it was a
very efficient Administration.  Parties were, he
said, united under a Prime Minister whom " we
regard with profound respect and whose services
to the Government and the country in the prosecution of the war appear to be in danger of
receiving insufficient recognition."  The Government had, he added, retrieved the fortunes of the
war and had paved the way for the triumph which
would ultimately be obtained.

Gradually, however, it shared the fate of its
predecessor.  In peace time such a Coalition would
have had an ideal chief in Mr. Asquith, with his
Parliamentary talents, personal magnanimity and
powers of compromise.  In war neither its system
nor its leadership maintained confidence.  There
were differences and discords in the Cabinet, not
entirely following party lines, and the very efforts
of the Prime Minister to secure agreement conveyed
to critics the appearance of irresolution and
vacillation.

Amid criticism from " ginger groups " in the
House and attacks in the Press Mr. Asquith pre-
served his equanimity.  But equanimity was not
counted to him for strength.  On the contrary, it
was regarded as evidence that he did not realize the
gravity of the situation.  Probably no Prime
Minister could have retained the confidence of the
country from the beginning to the end of a struggle
so long and so trying to its temper.  Mr. Asquith's
presence at the head of the Government was for
a certain period believed to be essential to national
unity.  It was supposed that he alone could win
the support of the working classes to compulsory

measures.  But 1916 saw the decline of his prestige. There was an increasing, most disturbing suspicion that he was not displaying in the conduct of the war the necessary energy or impetus.  Even if the belief was unjustified, its prevalence was fatal.  It is recorded that a conversation in which Pitt joined took place on the qualities most required in a Prime Minister.  While one said Eloquence, another Knowledge, and another Toil, Pitt said Patience. Mr. Asquith, in the opinion of critics, had too much Patience in war.

A phrase contributed to the undoing of the master of phrases.  " Wait and See " was the curt advice he gave to an inquirer on a domestic issue in peace time.  In war the phrase was remembered by those whom it had irritated.  It was repeated until its author became known as Wait and See. Members of Parliament taunted him with it as if it represented his policy or temperament in the greatest emergency in our modern history. Masses of people outside were led to believe that he had actually applied the phrase to the war.

The transactions of December, 1916, when Mr. Asquith resigned the office which he had held for a longer continuous period than anybody for the last hundred years and was replaced by Mr. Lloyd George, did not spring from any decision of the House of Commons.  Parliament was almost as perplexed as the country at large by events to which I shall return in later chapters, but although it had not been consulted, it did not complain.  If the step Mr. Asquith took in laying down his great office was taken in the expectation, held at any rate by some of his friends, that he was indispensable and would be recalled, he made a miscalculation

strange in a man so prudent and cool-minded.
The more generous view, and the view consistent
with his record, was that he acted in the interests
of the State. His place was filled with no loss of
time and with little difficulty.

Although his overthrow was resented by adherents
who attributed it to an intrigue, Mr. Asquith himself did not display his wounds. " I never heard
him express bitter feeling against any one," said
an intimate friend who saw him regularly. For
magnanimity he was praised even by those who
had lost faith in his leadership. He continued to
appeal for national unity and from the Front
Opposition Bench, to which he returned after eleven
years in office, he gave, except on a few occasions—
important occasions it is true—support to the
Government formed by his lieutenant. There
were observers who imagined for a time that its
existence depended on his sufferance. When the
trial of strength came, it was seen that his authority
in Parliament had departed. It had passed to
Mr. Lloyd George.

Near the close of the War Parliament Mr. Asquith
quoted from James Shirley the lines :

> " The glories of our blood and state
>   Are shadows, not substantial things ;
>   There is no armour against fate."

His own fate, against which he found no armour
except in patience, was as hard to bear as that of
any man who had crashed from a high position.
On evil days he fell and evil tongues. These
pursued him after the Armistice. When Mr. Lloyd
George, with Mr. Bonar Law as co-leader, appealed
to the country for confidence in the Government,

Mr. Asquith and most of the independent Liberals who, now that hostilities were over, refused to take the pledge to the Coalition, sustained such a defeat as left his successor complete master of the State.

For fully a year the ex-Prime Minister was out of Parliament and by the new men he was not missed. They had, as they said, no use for Wait and See. As 1919 passed without any effort being made by him to obtain a seat, his followers feared that, the world forgetting, he might be by the world forgot. Lively was the excitement early in 1920 when, at last, as candidate for Paisley, he set out on " a dark and difficult adventure," opposed by a Government candidate as well as by one in the Labour interest. The spectacle of the veteran who for many years led the House of Commons, fighting for admission to it as he never fought before, appealed to the chivalry of some even of those who rejoiced at his defeat at the general election and a few old Unionist friends openly wished him success, but the predominant feeling was entirely unsympathetic.

On the first of March, 1920, at the age of sixty-seven, Mr. Asquith presented himself at the bar of the House to take his seat for Paisley and confront a new career. Although his hair was white and his face deeply carved, he looked almost as vigorous as when he stood there announcing a message from the King. Not now did he see an assembly ready to carry out his will. Many of the members had never heard his voice, many looked at him coldly, sourly. In the place he had so long occupied sat Mr. Lloyd George, and on the other side of the table, beside Sir Donald Maclean, chairman of the independent Liberals, lounged Mr. Adamson, claiming on behalf of the Labour party the rights of His Majesty's Opposition.

"Welcome Home!" whispered the Speaker to him when, after signing the roll, he was presented by the Clerk to the Chair. A graceful salutation, it must have been dear to the heart of the returned exile, but from most of the inhabitants of his old home he received a chilling welcome. The cheers which greeted him were slighter than hailed many an unknown man who had won a party victory. It was not he but another who was the hero of the House. When Mr. Lloyd George, after witnessing the ceremony, passed out from the Treasury Bench, the huge Coalition host raised in *his* honour a shout which by comparison made the cheers for his former chief insignificant. Meeting behind the Speaker's chair the two statesmen shook hands, but the political breach between them was complete. Not since the days of Fox and Burke was there so painful a severance of friends.

In the early weeks after his return Mr. Asquith frequently took *Dod's Parliamentary Companion* from the table and studied the biographies of members. Most of them were strangers to him and strangers they remained. His spirit was not theirs. "It is to me," said Mr. Bonar Law when he spoke for the first time, "a great pleasure to hear my right honourable friend again." But although he was treated by Ministers with the deference that was his due, little pleasure was taken by the "hard-faced men" in his voice. With Labour rivals at his side and leaving the everyday work to the chairman of his party, he contributed distinction to any debate in which he intervened, but he found the House irresponsive. He did not make the headway made by Mr. Balfour in the hostile Parliament of

1906.  His followers were very few and they were
not as Mr. Balfour's had been, the largest party in
Opposition.  The antagonism of the great majority
of the House was maintained.

## MR. LLOYD GEORGE

What is genius ? The poet or painter, the soldier or scientist of genius throws lustre on his generation. Equally rare is the statesman with what Carlyle has described as " the inspired gift of God." To Mr. Lloyd George it has been attributed by admiring friends and conceded with an ironic shrug by enemies. Of what, then, does it consist ? Mr. Lloyd George is an eloquent orator, an astute political tactician, a man of imagination and humour, of boundless ambition and intense vitality. Yet these qualities do not make up genius. Something indefinable, Mr. Lloyd George has it, in addition to the driving power and indomitable will which do not always go with it and to the astuteness and eloquence which often go without it. It does not in his case consist of an infinite capacity for taking pains—for that quality, indeed, he is not so distinguished as countless common men : it is a light which illuminates his vision, a fire which animates his force.

" One of the children of the people," as he said of himself, " the cottage-bred man," the son of a schoolmaster brought up by a village boot-maker, the young Welsh solicitor who had practised in Petty Sessions and the County Court and had early championed the cause of the humble folk and Nonconformists, Mr. Lloyd George entered the House of Commons in 1890, at the age of twenty-seven, without any University or social advantage. In his maiden speech in his first session, discussing a proposal to compensate the drink trade for abolished licences, he dared to attack not only Randolph Churchill, but also Joseph Chamberlain, the dreaded Goliath, describing them as political

contortionists who could set their feet in one
direction and their faces in another. Quickly he
gave proof of his debating capacity by criticism
of the Tithe Bill of 1891. In 1892 he fought
Gladstone himself over the Clergy Discipline Bill
both in the House and in Grand Committee, and
during the Liberal regime he took part in a revolt
against the delay of the Welsh Disestablishment
Bill.

The young man with the slight figure, the thin
face, with bright eyes and dark moustache, was
sneered at as a Welsh Tim Healy, but competent
veterans recognized the qualities which promised a
great career. As early as 1896, on account of his
brilliant fight against the relief of agricultural rates
in the course of which he was suspended for defying
the authority of the Chair and refusing to leave the
House (as was then necessary) on a division, he
won the commendation of Harcourt, who advised
him to prepare for a responsible position. Some
observers thought he disregarded that advice. A
Unionist who lived to be a member of his Cabinet
recorded in a book that in hostility to the Voluntary
Schools Bill of 1897 he took among Welsh members
the palm for violence of language. " Indeed,"
wrote Sir Arthur Griffith-Boscawen, " many of his
friends who recognized his remarkable Parliamentary gifts and admired the pluck and grit
which he had displayed since he entered the House,
often deplored his language, which they feared
would militate against his future success." Gradually, however, in the long term of Opposition he
made his way to a foremost place. There were
other young men of promise on the same side but
the member for the Carnarvon Boroughs out-
distanced them by his political instinct, his scathing

speech, his humour and his eloquence. Yet if he thought of a responsible position, he did not prepare for it by subservience to any leader.

Whatever was said of Mr. Lloyd George's opposition to the South African War, nobody saw in it a bid for place or popularity. In denouncing its policy and the Ministerial conduct of the campaign, he encountered hostile audiences, suffering much opprobrium and running personal risk. Friends again warned him that he was destroying his prospects, but he could not be silenced or subdued by admonition on his own side or abuse on the other. When a motion was submitted with Campbell-Bannerman's authority prefacing dissent from the Ministerial view of a settlement with an undertaking to support all proper measures for the effective prosecution of the war, he turned on the Liberal leader and taunted him with having been captured, stripped of his principles and left on the veldt. " C.B." replied that he " might have expressed his difference from his friends quite as effectively with more respect to them." Respect for superiors was not among the independent Radical's qualities. He took his own course in his own way.

> " He either fears his fate too much,
>     Or his deserts are small,
>   That dares not put it to the touch
>     To gain or lose it all."

That is the key to Mr. Lloyd George's career. He has dared to put his fate to the touch. Courage has marked the decisive steps of his life, audacity has attended some of them. Before he entered office I asked him for a message to young men, to accompany a biographical sketch, and he wrote on a scrap of paper : " Never shirk duties, difficulties or responsibilities." How far he himself has followed that precept all the world knows.

By the ingenuity and suggestiveness of his criticism of the Education Bill of 1902 he extorted the respect of the Minister whose name was linked with it. The fight he led against it was inspired by his deepest feeling. " This has been in my blood," he privately said. " He owed everything," as he proudly confessed, " to the little Bethel." His brilliant, unceasing fight was distinguished by extraordinary resource. While he was on his feet Mr. Balfour would peer at him with a wondering, curiously scrutinizing but not unkindly expression, appreciating, no doubt, his mental fertility and, perhaps, wishing it were at his command in his own party. During the fight they had several private conversations in the House and also at a Welsh dinner. From the Unionist leader, a shrewd judge of the calibre of opponents, as well as from Harcourt Mr. Lloyd George received encouragement in his career for which he was grateful and he returned it with personal esteem. But of course this feeling did not affect his political conduct. He was the most vivacious assailant of Mr. Balfour's Government and became the orator most desired by Liberal audiences. Even as late in his Opposition career as 1904 he came again—as in 1896—into conflict with the Chair, refusing to leave his seat for a division on a closure motion, but this occurred in Committee, and when the Chairman reported the fact to himself as Deputy-Speaker, the whole of the Liberals, on the suggestion of Mr. Asquith, walked out as a protest, and thus Mr. Lloyd George avoided a second suspension.

His seat in the House then was at the corner of

he second bench below the Opposition gangway—
he seat occupied in after years by Mr. Healy. It
vas a convenient point from which to face the
Ministers, and the elbow of the bench was used by
he orator as a desk for his notes, while he could
keep his hands and arms free. Members of all
parties came in to hear him—his attacks were so
pungent and his humour so entertaining. Friends
vere delighted with the raillery he poured on the
Treasury bench and occasionally he thrilled the
House with a passage of eloquence.

" What will Lloyd George be ? " the placemen
asked each other when Campbell-Bannerman was
orming his Government. Prophets who saw in
his neglect to answer letters evidence of his unfitness
for practical administration, assigned to him a post
hat would leave him free for the platform on
vhich he was so effective. Others thought he might
manage as an Under Secretary—if only he were a
ittle duller ! Taper and Tadpole were vastly
surprised—and imagined he himself must have
been tremendously gratified—when he received a
place in the Cabinet. At the Board of Trade he
would, they declared, as they lifted the eyebrows
of amazement, be a square peg in a round hole. A
short time brought them another surprise when the
man of the platform proved himself the man of
business, with initiative, aptitude and a conciliatory
temper. Already possessing the sympathy of the
workers, he gained the good-will of the commercial
classes by consulting them where their interests
were affected, and his treatment of the railway
strike in 1907 revealed his possession of talents
with which he had not hitherto been credited.

There was no long pause in his career. Those
who thought his ambition might have been amply

satisfied were again amazed—some, indeed, were startled—when in 1908, on Mr. Asquith's appointment as Prime Minister, he received the high office of Chancellor of the Exchequer. By this recognition of the ablest of his colleagues Mr. Asquith avoided the mistake made by Gladstone in the case of Joseph Chamberlain.

In the six pre-war years of his Chancellorship Mr. Lloyd George was, as Chamberlain had long been, the stormy petrel of politics. Those were stirring years in Parliament, and he was seldom for any considerable period out of view. Now and again his figure disappeared, but it soon re-emerged to disturb the equanimity of those who loved a quiet, old-fashioned world. When Disraeli was appointed Chancellor of the Exchequer in 1852, Lyndhurst wrote to him :—" You will, I am sure, evince to the world that addition and subtraction are not the only qualifications for a Chancellor." * Mr. Lloyd George knew and cared as little about addition and subtraction as Disraeli. At the Treasury he regarded himself as the protagonist of the poor and he worked out his sums in the figures of social reform, basing the schemes of his busy brain on the belief that

> " To make a happy fire-side clime
> To weans and wife,
> That's the true pathos and sublime
> Of human life."

The Budget of 1909, by which he " robbed the hen-roosts," produced a greater Parliamentary turmoil than any measure in my recollection except the first Home Rule Bill. It was a Budget, as its author said, not for " building gigantic flotillas to

* *Life of Disraeli* : Monypenny and Buckle.

encounter mythical Armadas," not for "building navies against nightmares," but "for raising money to wage implacable warfare against poverty and squalidness." Having carried, with a zeal that endeared him to countless homes, the scheme of old age pensions, introduced by Mr. Asquith, the Chancellor of the Exchequer sought to provide for these and other social necessities, including insurance against ill-health and unemployment, by the super-tax upon large incomes, increased death duties, increased duties on licences and spirits, and land value duties which were intended also as a lever in constructive reform. His proposals, and still more his manner of advocating them, aroused among Conservatives an alarm and antagonism, and among advanced men on the Liberal side an enthusiasm, unequalled since Chamberlain's unauthorized Radical programme.

The speech in which he submitted the notorious Budget was not one of his oratorical successes. Although a consistent design ran through its texture, yet as it dealt with a vast variety of subjects, it was full of intricate detail. It was extremely long. After speaking for nearly three hours, the Chancellor's voice sounded faint and his strength almost failed. He retired for a brief interval while the sitting was suspended, and on his return to the Treasury Bench he went on fully an hour and a half longer. After the labour of preparation the submission of so elaborate a policy, affecting the structure of society and involving a mass of facts and figures, was naturally a severe strain on one who had not Gladstone's mastery or love of detail. He had only a glass of water to sustain him till near the end of his task, when a friend brought in a glass of milk.

Many elements of that established order of society which considered itself essential to the stability of the State turned in wrath on the revolutionist. The land taxes excited the most powerful hostility. They were attacked, as their author recorded, with " a concentrated and sustained ferocity." His Limehouse speech in July, 1909, with its championship of the million against the few and its gibes at ducal landowners, and other appeals of a popular character, brought upon him such denunciation as few public men have had to endure. Unionist leaders accused him of preaching a class war. Sir Edward Carson called him an " unscrupulous demagogue"; *The Times* scolded him for " coarse personalities " and " pitiful clap-trap." He was not turned from his path. In the House of Commons and out of it, amid the encouraging applause of Radicals, he replied to angry assailants with jaunty defiance. His retort to Lord Curzon, for instance, was greatly enjoyed. He " did not mind Lord Curzon as long as he kept to his bombastic commonplaces which had been his stock-in-trade through life, but if he were going to try here that arrogance which was too much even for the gentle Hindu, they would just tell him they would have none of his Oriental manners."

By his programme the Chancellor gave impulse to the constitutional movement directed by Mr. Asquith. The hero and hope of all who desired change in the social order, he spent strenuous months in carrying his Budget. One evening he came into a club and told a friend it had been decided that the Lords were to throw it out. His manner showed neither fear nor exultation, but a quiet sense of the gravity of the event. When the Budget had been endorsed by the country, and a second general election had clipped the powers of the peers, the Chancellor proceeded with his next great project of State insurance against sickness and unemployment. This, in turn, was pelted with criticism, one of its chief critics being Sir Laming Worthington Evans, whose ability he acknowledged at the time, and who received office from him. The sanguine hopes he founded on his scheme were merrily ridiculed by countless tongues and pens. But by his ardour and tenacity he prevailed again.

Meantime, at the Mansion House, in 1911, by a warning to Germany in connection with the Agadir incident, he revealed what was regarded as a new development on his part similar to that of the man whose career his own was so closely resembling. If Britain were to be treated where her interests were vitally affected as if she were of no account in the Cabinet of Nations, then emphatically, said Mr. Lloyd George, " peace at that price would be a humiliation intolerable for a great country like ours to endure." Here was no little-Englander such as ten years previously he had been supposed to be ; here was no anti-Imperialist ! Like Chamberlain, the advocate of reform at home was prepared, if need arose, to fight for the interests of the Empire. What was surprising was not that the warning should be given by the Government to Germany, but that it should be uttered by Mr. Lloyd George. From him it was specially effective, but his words, disclosing him in a new character, drew reproaches from Radical friends.

After he had carried his insurance bill we wondered what he would attempt next. Our wonder did not last long. To the fresh alarm of the Conservative classes he opened a campaign against the land system. This system, the most strongly entrenched and most resolutely defended in the State, the last bulwark of the old order of things, he attacked with a fervour which excited everybody interested in politics. His antagonism to it, as some of his words suggested, may have had root in his own early experience. Perhaps, like Devenish in Mr. Mason's novel, *The Turnstile*, he was as a boy " chased out of the woods and off the grass " ; it may have been his case that he was " forced to walk in the road and the dust of it was still bitter in his mouth."

His speeches of 1912 and 1913, vibrating with sympathy for the landless toilers of the country, produced a very great commotion. The orator, with the sins of his terrible Budget heavy upon him, was attacked more severely than ever. He was accused of political spleen, prejudice and reck-lessness, he was jeered at on account of his ignorance of pheasants, every effort was made to discredit the inquiry which—in deference probably to reluc-tant colleagues—he initiated as a preliminary to legislation. On a noisy occasion in the House he was hooted and boo-ed at by Conservatives with a discourtesy unique in modern annals. Just as Chamberlain had been, he was dreaded and de-nounced as a new Jack Cade.

Hope of revenge was kindled in Mr. Lloyd George's opponents—if ever opponents could be called enemies, these were enemies—by the dis-closure of his dealings in American Marconi shares. The outcry over this matter forms a painful chapter of Parliamentary history. In ordinary circum-stances politicians are generous in their view of the personal conduct of leading public men, but in the heat and fury of abnormal conflict the Marconi affair was used in an effort to destroy a formidable

Minister's reputation and end his career. He was exposed, as he said, to calumnies, slanders, insults, and poisoned shafts. Two other members of the Government were concerned, but it was against the Chancellor of the Exchequer that the hue and cry was raised.

A roaming inquiry by a Committee, not an ideal body for the purpose, fostered party passion. Even its report, acquitting Ministers on the charge of corruption, which had been loosely and recklessly made by the lesser politicians and by certain journalists, did not at once subdue the agitation. Mr. Lloyd George admitted that in view of after events, which showed how his conduct lent itself to misconstruction, he had acted thoughtlessly, carelessly, mistakenly although innocently, openly, honestly; and to that extent regret was expressed by himself and a colleague. Unionist leaders, while repudiating the idea of corruption, insisted that the transactions were of a speculative character and put forward what was really a vote of censure, but the majority of the House accepted the explanations of the Ministers and recorded its reprobation of charges which were proved to be wholly false.

Although he proved adroit in administration and potent in legislation, these notes have shown that it was as a speaker that one of the greatest men of action first won fame. Few men have exercised so much influence over an audience as Mr. Lloyd George. It is true he is not a perfect orator. His speeches seldom have a sustained sweep. Portions of them may be loose and ragged. As a rule, however, they are racy, forceful, and vivid; their language is simple, pure and direct; many of them are lit up by humour, almost all contain passages of moving eloquence. Mr. Lloyd George,

as his friends report, has read the classics—mainly
in translation, and has read much fiction and other
modern literature, but it is less from books that he
draws his illustrations than from nature. The
landscape of Wales appeals to his poetic fancy. His
voice touches all the notes of emotion and the effect
of his words is heightened by his gestures—the
play of the features, the gleam of the eyes, the
swing of the arm this way and that way, the
clinched fist, the hands closed and pressed together
at the knuckles with thumbs held up, the pointing,
challenging, mocking, derisive finger.

When he is deeply in earnest, when he has to win
a battle with an adversary, no man now living can
approach Mr. Lloyd George in art of speech. He
is one of the few Parliamentary orators of any time
who have made listeners forget themselves. He
casts a spell over his audience. A Liberal member
who entered Parliament in 1906, and who was of a
rather critical temperament, remarked to me, after
being a short time in the House : " I cannot understand why you have always praised Lloyd George
so much as an orator." A little later he said :
" You were right ; he is an orator." The spell had
been cast.

The change wrought by the world war in Mr.
Lloyd George's life and fame is one of the most
wonderful transformations in our political history.
Only such a supreme test could have produced such
a change. The man most distrusted and feared by
the Conservatives, by the people of property, by
those who claimed the title of Imperialists, became
their hero ; the divider of the people became for a
time the leader of the whole nation.

Of all that he did in the war it is not for me to
write. I keep my pen as much as possible for

Parliament, and with the revolution there I deal
more fully in the later chapters, as the biographical
system which I have adopted is not appropriate to
a connected story. Here I may say that Mr.
Lloyd George's concentration on the one great
object, his determination, swiftness and energy,
his insistence that every matter " must be look'd
to speedily and strongly "—in short, his " do it
now," his extraordinary success as Mr. Asquith's
colleague in organizing an adequate supply of
munitions, and at the same time his efforts to
maintain the high spirit of the country, turned
domestic foes into grateful friends and followers.
A section of Liberal members also put their faith
in him in the dark days. It was at first a small
section. " If he sets himself up against Asquith,"
some observers used to say, " he will not carry
a dozen Liberal votes." As the war went on
and disappointment deepened, a steadily growing
number looked to him for leadership.

The historian in the future who desires to throw
light on the events of December, 1916, on the
personal elements of the situation, on what took
place below the surface seen by the public, which
saw only a dispute with regard to the formation
and constitution of a War Council of Ministers, will
have more materials than are available now. It
was obvious that Mr. Lloyd George, before he took
the helm, must have come to an understanding
with Mr. Bonar Law. How and when that understanding was arrived at and what other negotiations
occurred will be definitely known when the private
memoirs of any of those engaged in them are
published. Mr. Lloyd George's own motive for
his action was explained by him three years later.
" I felt," he said, " in my heart, that unless we

quickened our action and imparted new energy into the struggle, the cause of the Allies, which was to me the cause of humanity, might be doomed, and I had no alternative but to take the course I did." In the hope of new energy Parliament and the country acquiesced in the Ministerial revolution.

Party barriers were more completely thrown down by Mr. Lloyd George than they had been during Mr. Asquith's Coalition. In that Government Liberals held among other great posts the Chancellorship of the Exchequer, the Foreign Secretaryship, and the Lord Chancellorship. All these passed under the new Premier to Unionists. The revolution in political arrangements carried out by the war attained its picturesque climax when the famous Radical headed a Ministry, in which his chief colleagues were Mr. Bonar Law, Lord Curzon, Lord Milner, Mr. Balfour, and Sir Edward Carson. His main support was from his former opponents, and he had no front rank Liberal in a Government which included Labour members and business men until he gave office to Mr. Churchill half-a-year after its formation. Some old friends, seeing the breach with former associates, were sad and reproachful. Others stood by him.

" He thought of nothing, and aimed at nothing, and hoped for nothing," as Mr. Bonar Law testified in 1920, " except the successful end of the war. That was his life and he had no other life. In good report and evil they saw what courage meant. It was not merely the courage of dogged determination, but was accompanied by a brilliant hopefulness which was an example and inspiration to every one who worked with him." There were unfriendly critics among those from whom he was separated who said he gave part of his thoughts and aims and hopes to the winning of a personal victory over displaced Liberal colleagues, but the view expressed by the Unionist leader was the view popularly accepted. Thus he obtained mastery of the War Parliament, received the approbation of the country at the Armistice Election, and secured ascendancy in the Parliament of Reconstruction.

His appearance was now very striking—with the massive head, long, grey hair, chin formidably square, moustache drooping over the mouth, the eye very searching and as bright as ever. Will and force emanated from his aspect, voice and gesture. Yet his face relaxed quickly in humour, and he had a ready smile and familiar nod for those who knew him in less exalted days. No Minister of the Crown was easier to approach or assumed fewer airs. Complaint has been made from generation to generation of the aloofness of the great men in Government. Only a few Prime Ministers, such as Melbourne, Palmerston, and " C.B." have escaped the reproach. The ordinary member did not dare to approach Gladstone, and Salisbury did not know the ordinary member. Mr. Asquith, like Peel and Russell, suffered from reserve. Mr. Lloyd George, on the other hand, has benefited by his free and friendly ways. No Minister was less aloof.

Nor was any Minister less conventional. When he was Chancellor of the Exchequer it used to be whispered that older-fashioned colleagues were shocked by his methods. It was said of Bright that he had " a great distaste and almost an incapacity for wading through a bundle of official papers." Mr. Lloyd George had a similar distaste. Much of the information he required was obtained by him at personal interviews with officials and experts—for instance, at the Downing Street breakfasts, which became celebrated—instead of by the perusal of documents. His way of doing business has been described by Sir Edward Carson. " He begins getting information at breakfast in the morning, where he invites a particular colleague whose department he wants at the moment to severely criticize. He goes on from that time until midnight seeing one person after another—any person at all whom he thinks can give him information, and although it may be a wearying process for himself, I cannot," said Sir Edward, " conceive anything more likely to give him the fullest information, not only with regard to expert opinion, but even with regard to the man in the street who is sometimes a very important individual." There is no reason to suspect sarcasm in this account. In his time Mr. Lloyd George must have read an immeasurable quantity of official papers, but these, as he once remarked, he cannot cross-examine. In personal conference his quickness of mind is as invaluable as his magnetic temperament.

What Carlyle wrote of Mirabeau may be written of Mr. Lloyd George :—" This is no man of system, then ; he is only a man of instincts and insights. A man, nevertheless, who will glare fiercely on any object ; and see through it, and conquer it ; for he has intellect, he has will, force beyond other men. A man not with *logic spectacles*, but with an eye ! "

One of the men whose names are landmarks in history, the Welsh solicitor, who had practised in Petty Sessions, became after the war one of the three dominating figures of the world, the three who re-made the map of Europe and re-settled the fate of nations so far as it could be re-settled by human agency. And in the end he towered above all in power and fame. " Our friend " (the Prime Minister), wrote Mr. Balfour to Mr. Bonar Law, just after the Armistice, " is, I think, the most remarkable political figure produced by the Great War." And two years later Mr. Law, as he left Westminster Abbey after the burial of the Unknown Soldier, said to one of his colleagues : " One hundred years hence will Lloyd George occupy in the minds of our descendants the position William Pitt holds to-day ? " His colleague replied : " I cannot tell, but it is quite possible." " It is quite possible," repeated the Unionist leader at a dinner at which Mr. Lloyd George was entertained by the Constitutional Club, and the prediction was cheered by those who had been his political opponents, but who now honoured him for what, like Pitt, he had done to save the nation.

# CHAPTER VIII

## OTHER MEN AND MEMORIES

### I

### THE GLADSTONE ERA

" Ah ! I hear that shout again. Hear ! Hear !
What a life it was ! " said Wilberforce when Hannah
Macaulay (Lady Trevelyan), speechless with excitement, showed him Lord Lansdowne's letter, offering
her brother a seat in Parliament. Ah ! that shout
of Parliamentary battle. Can any one who has
heard it ever forget it ? It rings in the ear of all
who have shared or watched the life of the House of
Commons. There are many dull nights in the
House, nights when it may be described as

> " A theatre magnificently lit
> For sorry acting, undeserved applause."

But it is never dull for long. The happening of
the unexpected sustains its interest. Its conflict
of personalities, parties and policies provides it
with a never-ending, always changing, fascinating
drama. It is extraordinarily quick and vehement
in the expression of feeling. Its " Hear ! Hear ! "
has a sound and a thrill which the same shout does
not possess anywhere else.

As my memory retraces the period during which
I have heard it I recall the long struggle of the
Conservatives with Gladstone, when he was last

178

at the head of an unbroken party in office—their
controversies on the Transvaal, on Irish land
legislation, on Bradlaugh, on coercion, on Parliamentary procedure, on Egypt, and on franchise
and redistribution. The great Whig families had
not yet left the Liberal leader. They were more
frightened by Chamberlain than by Gladstone, who
still counted dukes among his satellites. Then
came the Home Rule transformation of the political
scene, the Parnellites allying themselves with the
Liberals, whom they had previously turned out of
office, and the arch-Radical, acting with the
Conservatives, to whom he had been as a bogey.
I think again of Parnell and Randolph Churchill,
two of the most challenging and remarkable figures
ever seen in Parliament, and I recall how Mr.
Balfour gradually took the place rashly left vacant
by Lord Randolph, and how the Irish leader who
had mastered his country and almost mastered
the House of Commons, was ruined because he
could not master himself. After six years of Conservative rule, tempered by the Radicalism of the
seceders from the Gladstone ranks, there was the
interregnum during which the Liberals held office
without full power and submitted to the rejection
of the second Home Rule Bill by the House of
Lords without an appeal to the country. Then
were revealed the differences within their party
which crippled it for a decade.

Last century closed with the coalition of Conservatives and Liberal Unionists in government,
and it handed down to its successor the controversies on the South African War. The Marquis
of Salisbury, regarded in early years by opponents
and by many on his own side as rash and reckless,
was in old age trusted in foreign affairs by the

whole country and universally respected. It was Chamberlain whom the Liberals now most dreaded and disliked. His ascendancy reached its height at the opening of the twentieth century. But soon the political scene was changed again by his fiscal propaganda, the re-union and recovery of the Liberals and the decline and fall of Mr. Balfour. From that time we have had scarcely a quiet, dull month in Parliament. There came the tenacious contest between the triumphant Liberals and the Unionists, whose long spell of office was followed by a long period in aggressive opposition —a period of social reform and constitutional turmoil. Finally, the Great War swept away the old world.

Now that the perspective is so completely changed we may wonder if that old world was a world in which we ever really lived. As we think of the heated debates, the ambitions and intrigues, the snap divisions, the sniping and bombarding, we may ask in a cynical mood what has been the result.

> " For what avail'd it, all the noise
> And outcry of the former men ?—
> Say, have their sons achieved more joys,
> Say, is life lighter now than then ? "

Whatever may be the answer to the latter of these lines, the answer to the first two, written in the record of the time, refutes the cynic. Old plays at St. Stephen's give place to new, and many of the old players are forgotten, but in their day they played great parts, moulding and expressing the sentiment of their generation.

Everywhere in our vision of the past we see,

as the result of Parliamentary discussion, a gradual ascertainment of, and submission to, the national will and temper : we see modification, compromise, acquiescence, understanding.   A victory is obtained by one party amid a loud flourish of trumpets, the turn of another comes, but there is rarely a sharp reversal of policy.   " Between the noble lord who goes out and the right honourable gentleman who comes in, where," asked Disraeli in *Sybil*, " is the distinctive principle ?   A shadowy difference may be simulated in opposition to serve a cry and stimulate the hustings ;   but the mask is not worn, even in Downing Street ;   and the conscientious Conservative seeks, in the pigeon-holes of a Whig bureau, for the measures against which for ten years he has been sanctioning, by the speaking silence of an approving nod, a general wail of frenzied alarm."   That means, in short, that there has usually been in the end a shaping of national will and decision to a common standard.

While the Moving Finger, having writ, moves on, the writing endures, and it is interesting to reflect on those who have held the pen.   Nothing I confess, impresses me more as I look back than the change which time effects in the reputation of political celebrities.   It is often said that great men are like mountains : we cannot appreciate their height until we are at a distance.   Bulwer Lytton writes in *St. Stephen's*—

> " And men now living might as tall appear
>    Judged by our sons, not us—*we* stand too near."

That may be consoling to some of our contemporaries.   On the other hand, many men who loom large in the eye of their own generation seem to the next very small. Recently I looked through three volumes of political portraits, published between 1866 and 1873. Several of the celebrities, whose characters are drawn by eminent writers, have long since passed into oblivion. Who now knows anything about the " solid virtues " of the Right Honourable John Wilson-Patten ? Who remembers the points in which Mr. Henley resembled Squire Western ? And what has become of Mr. Ayrton's supposed character as a bore ?

In their estimates of some of the most distinguished men the writers of those volumes were proved to be mistaken. Gathorne Hardy was half-a-century ago described as the future leader of the Conservative party, " the sure successor of Mr. Disraeli." On Lord Salisbury the portrait-painters were not agreed. Hutton, writing of him while still Lord Cranborne, said, " if he should remain long enough in the House of Commons " there was no man more likely to succeed Disraeli, and after he had succeeded to the peerage, Wemyss Reid wrote that he was destined to take even the highest rank in the service of the Crown, but another publicist was confident that he could never become leader of the Conservative party, or the instrument of the convictions of his countrymen. Even so keen an observer as Reid failed to recognize the ability of Hartington when a member of Gladstone's first Government. It was only upon the ground that he was the eldest son of a duke that the critic could account for his presence in the Cabinet, although " much more unlikely things have come to pass than that this languid young man should be called to the helm of affairs."

Contemporary estimates of certain statesmen, even since the time of Disraeli, are already being modified. While a few stand out with increased distinctness, others are fading. The war has hastened the decaying process, and my task is to try to show their lineaments as I saw them.

## 1880–1885

### GLADSTONE IN POWER

In previous chapters I have given impressions of several of the great Parliamentarians. A few notes on others may now be set down, with recollections of famous scenes and incidents.

JOHN BRIGHT.—It was delightful to me to observe the serene, beautiful face of the Tribune of the People beside the grave, strong face of his friend and chief as they sat together on the Treasury Bench. Both seemed to belong to the past, although Gladstone had not yet begun the greatest of his battles. Never was there a more affectionate official farewell than that of the two veterans when Bright, leaving the Government in 1882 on account of the bombardment of Alexandria, delivered his resignation speech from the corner of the second bench below the Ministerial gangway. He and his honoured chief differed on the moral law—or rather, as the latter characteristically pointed out, on the application of that law, but the Prime Minister, turning round and glancing at his old friend, assured him of the unbroken esteem of his colleagues.

In Lord Salisbury's opinion Mr. Bright was the greatest master of English oratory that his generation had seen. His oratory was purer, more chastened than Gladstone's. Gladstone could speak every day and on any subject without preparation. Bright spoke seldom and he carefully rehearsed his speeches, although writing out in full only the peroration. Gladstone had the advantage of a striking figure and employed many dramatic gestures. Bright's figure, clothed in black, was short and stout, and he rarely moved as he stood; his gestures were few and simple, such as the slight raising of the hand. But there was force as well as dignity in the face, with the expressive eyes, the ample forehead and the combative mouth. No man of the time, not even Spurgeon, had a better command of the noble English of our Bible and of Milton. Every word he uttered was measured, every tone appropriate. I was thrilled when he spoke. His voice had music in it.

An old friend of Ireland, Bright's indignation was aroused by the obstruction of the Parnellites and the outrages of the Land League. With habitual directness he spoke of the Irish " rebel " party and accused it of boundless sympathy with criminals and murderers. His language was warmly resented. Justin McCarthy repudiated a personal friendship of which he had been proud, and Thomas Sexton who himself, as Gladstone said, was little short of a master in oratory, taunted Bright with his age and suggested that his powers were not what they had been. Annoyance to all sections of Englishmen was caused by such offensive allusions to one who was held in honour. He had been a leader in a bitter and protracted struggle, but now his personality was regarded as a national possession.

JUSTIN McCARTHY.—The journalist, novelist, historian, and Parliamentarian, whoe renunciation of Bright's friendship could not have been uttered without sorrow, was one of the mildest-mannered men who ever figured in violent political agitation. With head tilted back and eyes gleaming amiably through glasses while he fingered his beard, Justin McCarthy delivered speeches in which the harshest criticism of English rule in Ireland was presented as if it were part of a historical survey before an academic society. It was difficult for any one to feel animosity for this kindly man of letters and the giving of pain to anybody must have been painful to himself. His speeches, as a rule, of the character of essays were adorned with a great many literary allusions. They were listened to with interest even when they had little influence on debate. While one of the leader-writers for the *Daily News*, McCarthy used to write his article at the House and bring it with a smile and a nod to the Press Gallery attendant. Frequently I met him in the corridor between the committee rooms and the entrance to the ladies' gallery walking with Mr. Frank Hill, the editor of the *Daily News*, and I have seen him there also with Mr. Hutton of the *Spectator*.

WILLIAM EDWARD FORSTER.—William Edward Forster was a conspicuous figure during my early experience of Parliament. He had left a mark on legislation by the Education Act of 1870, which supplemented the voluntary system by the introduction of School Boards, but which, by its concessions to Church schools, produced intense disappointment and soreness among Nonconformists. He was suggested for the Liberal leadership in the House of Commons when Gladstone resigned in 1875. Hartington was in his favour, but he could not have united the party. A big, rugged Yorkshireman, fearless and large-hearted, with a rough yet forcible style of speech, rather clumsy in his methods, Forster had a stormy experience in the 1880 Government as Irish Secretary. Sops and stripes were the mixed regimen of the Liberals for the troublesome country. The Nationalists returned no gratitude for the sops and the Conservatives thought the stripes were not systematic enough, while the Radicals wanted a policy of conciliation.

A prominent part in the politics of the time was played by the *Pall Mall Gazette* under the editorship of John Morley, with whom Chamberlain and Dilke, the Radical leaders in the Government, were in close alliance. According to Dilke, Chamberlain gave the editor information on domestic policy. Those who knew of their relations attached special significance to an article which appeared in the *Pall Mall* in April, 1882, urging the Chief Secretary's dismissal or resignation. On account of the weakening of his authority by this article and the view taken of it by Irish newspapers, Forster offered to retire. Gladstone set aside the idea, but a few weeks later the baffled Minister threw up his office in consequence of the release of Parnell and other political prisoners under the " Kilmainham Treaty " which was arranged through Captain O'Shea. This he denounced as a surrender to the law-breakers.

From the second bench on the Ministerial side Forster, after his resignation, played the rôle of a candid critic. Not only did he exchange hard blows with Parnell, who hated him more than anybody else, but as an Imperialist he criticized the vacillating policy of the Government on Egypt and the Soudan. Standing behind his former chief, he aimed at him some shrewd thrusts. I recall the anger he excited among those around him when in debate on the Soudan, in 1884, he said sarcastically of Gladstone that " he can persuade most people of most things and above all he can persuade himself of almost anything." This taunt became a classic in controversy. It was cherished by Conservatives.

Liberals resented the gibe at their leader from one
who had been a colleague, and Hartington was
greatly applauded when he rebuked him for making
" a bitter and personal and evidently highly
prepared and long reflected-over attack " upon
the man " by means of whose support he had been
assisted in acquiring some part of the position which
he so deservedly occupies." Forster felt the rebuke,
but attributed its severity to Hartington's consciousness of a bad case.

SIR CHARLES DILKE.—It was only between 1880
and 1885 that Dilke, with all his gifts of statesmanship, held office, and it was then that his influence
was greatest. The first feature of his career
which interested me was his comradeship with
Chamberlain. It was one of the finest things in a
world of rivalries and ambitions. For the ten years
from Chamberlain's entrance to the House of
Commons till the Home Rule split it was very close
and intimate. On hearing of Dilke's engagement
to Mrs. Mark Pattison, Chamberlain wrote : " I
prize his friendship as the best gift of my political
life." * The one was the complement to the other.
They made a compact that neither would enter
the Government in 1880 unless one had a seat in
the Cabinet. What was remarkable in this was
that each was willing to see the other in the higher
position. Gladstone resisted, but had to give way,
and took Chamberlain into the Cabinet, while his
friend became Under-Secretary for Foreign Affairs.
With the support of Morley in the Press they were a
formidable pair.

The two leaders of the Radical section of the
Liberal party were frequently shoulder to shoulder

* *The Life of Sir Charles W. Dilke* : Gwynn and Tuckwell.

on the Treasury Bench and late at night they would drive away in the same cab full of energy and enterprise. They might have said :

"Whereso'er we went, like Juno's swans,
    Still we went coupled and inseparable."

I have already mentioned the sneer that Chamberlain got his information from his friend. Dilke certainly had more than he himself could use. He was tremendously industrious and, like George Eliot's Casaubon, was ever amassing notes. He had little personal magnetism and did not appeal to the country so effectively as Chamberlain, but conventional members preferred him because he had the old Parliamentary style, and to the advanced men he was none the less acceptable because he was long in disfavour at Court on account of his early Republican speeches and his demand for inquiry into the Civil List. The Queen had made a difficulty about him at the formation of the Government of 1880 and probably her prejudice was an obstacle to his promotion, although he was on terms of friendship with the Prince of Wales, whom he kept informed on foreign affairs. At last, in 1882, his position in Parliament was so powerful that he had to be admitted to the Cabinet.

I heard the speech which Dilke delivered at Kensington on the occasion of his promotion. Sarcastic comment was made in the Press on the fact that one who had expressed Republican principles should "kiss hands." Conservatives inquired if he was still of the same opinion and practical Republicans taunted him with inconsistency. An allusion to the subject in his Kensington speech provoked a significant smile at the meeting and attracted amused attention else-

where. " There were," Dilke said, " opinions of
political infancy which, as one grew older, one
might regard as unwise, or might prefer not to have
uttered," and he added a reference to the years
when he was " rather scatter-brained." Although
the passage was vague, all knew what it meant and
all assumed that it was intended for the eyes of the
Queen. " There is every reason to believe," say
Dilke's biographers, " that it was taken as satisfactory."

His speeches, although crammed with facts and
arguments, rarely had a popular form. They
lacked light and shade; they were without grace
or humour. A widely read man, Dilke sometimes
gave an interesting historical reference, but his
solid matter was seldom relieved by literary
quotation. I remember, however, that when talking
of pauperism on his appointment to the Local
Government Board, he thrilled a meeting by the
emotion with which he spoke of those who indulge
in " yet a little sleep, a little slumber, a little
folding of the hands to sleep." Not often has a
Biblical quotation in a political speech been so
effective and impressive.

Dilke's prospects in 1885 have, I think, been
rather exaggerated by his biographers. It is said
that Disraeli prophesied he would be Prime Minister
and that from 1882 Gladstone seemed to look to
him as his ultimate successor in the House of
Commons. Gladstone's mistake was that he did
not truly appreciate Chamberlain's powers. There
is no saying what position Dilke might have reached
if the career from which Beaconsfield, as he admitted,
borrowed traits for *Endymion,* had pursued a
fortunate course, but in the early 'eighties the
section of Liberal opinion which had not attached

itself to Hartington was steadily inclining to Chamberlain. At the same time, it is true that Dilke, when the catastrophe of his life occurred, was in the front rank of statesmen. He had shown a rare knowledge both of foreign affairs and of local administration, he had distinguished himself by his services in connection with the redistribution of seats, Parliament recognized his industry and competence and his mastery of its procedure, he was trusted generally by friends and respected by opponents, and he had a European reputation.

No other personal event in my time caused such a painful sensation in the House of Commons as the divorce case in which Dilke was co-respondent. Not only Liberals, but high-minded Conservatives, who found no satisfaction in the ruin of an opponent, spoke and looked as if they had heard of a national calamity. All proud of the fair fame of England's public men were truly grieved at the stain on one of the most distinguished politicians. Dilke never recovered his position. After being out of Parliament for six years, he returned in 1892, and remained till his death in 1911. His industry in this latter period was as great as ever, he was regular in attendance, he took deep interest in foreign affairs, and in army, navy and labour questions, he delivered elaborate speeches full of information, methodically dropping into his hat each piece of note-paper after he had used it, he made frequent entries in his diary, he clipped extracts from the Parliamentary papers with pocket scissors, he was always first in and through the division lobby in order to avoid waste of time, he hurried along the corridors with coat tails flying out behind him, he gave interviews, organized committees and was the busiest of members, but although a few friends stood staunchly

by him and time lessened the feeling excited by the
divorce case and sympathy went out to him on
account of his devotion to public duty, he was
never restored to the Treasury Bench.

SIR GEORGE TREVELYAN.—Another interesting
figure in the early 'eighties was Sir George Trevelyan.
He was then in his most promising political period,
standing beside Dilke and Chamberlain in the van
of Liberalism.  He was a more interesting speaker
than Dilke and was better informed than Chamberlain.  Celebrated as the biographer of his uncle,
Macaulay, and the author of *The Early History of
Charles James Fox*, a man of culture and conviction,
he had shown reforming zeal by his advocacy of
the abolition of purchase in the Army and the
extension of household suffrage to the counties, and
in middle age he still excited high expectations.
The great chance came to him when he was appointed
Chief Secretary for Ireland.  He displayed patriotic
courage in accepting the post after the murder of
Lord Frederick Cavendish and he entered on its
duties with the loftiest, most enlightened motives.
It broke his sensitive spirit.  He shared with the
Lord Lieutenant the gross personal attacks of the
Parnellites and under these he quivered.  " Lord
Spencer and I " was a frequent phrase on his lips,
and Lord Spencer and he were subjected to asper-
sions very hard for men of honour to endure.
Touched to the quick, Trevelyan reminded his
assailants that, although Irish Secretary, he was an
English gentleman.  But there was nothing too ill
for them to say of the English gentleman who ruled
at Dublin Castle.  They drove him from it.
Succeeded after two years by phlegmatic " C.B.,"
Trevelyan withdrew into the calm haven of the

Duchy of Lancaster and his troubles in later Cabinets were with Scots, he being twice Secretary for Scotland. By his vacillation on Home Rule he was exposed to attack first by one section of Liberals and then by the other. Opposing Gladstone's proposals, he retired with Chamberlain from the Government of 1886, but soon he refused to follow the Conservatives in the path of coercion and declared in an arresting phrase, which irritated the Unionists, that "the game is up." Elected as a Gladstonian in 1887, there was effusive rejoicing among the faithful at the return of the much-esteemed wanderer. After he had taken the oath, Mr. Bryce led him up to the Liberal chief on the front Opposition bench and the reconciliation was publicly consummated. This was a pretty incident, but Liberal Unionists ever after poured scorn on the colleague who had so quickly left them, Chamberlain describing him as the most perfect specimen of the political weathercock.

As he revealed in debate on Parliamentary habits and hours, Sir George Trevelyan's heart panted for the garden and library, for art and travel. Instead of passing the best months of the year in a hot lobby, he wished to spend July in fishing and sailing, in driving over Alpine passes and walking on Alpine pastures. The true politician cannot afford to let his fancy thus roam. Parliament is a jealous mistress. She is never content with a half-heart. Although an earnest constitutional reformer, Trevelyan was in truth a man of letters among politicians. This was shown in his oratory. He strained after literary form in speeches, adorned with learned allusions. Much was lost by Parliament when he abandoned it, but more was gained by literature. To his release from the exacting demands of the rough world of politics we owe the volumes on the American Revolution, which formed the " tranquil and pleasant occupation " of his later years.

CONSERVATIVE FRONT BENCH.—Turning to the Front Opposition Bench as it was in 1880–85, I think of meek Sir Stafford Northcote, with his arms folded and his hands almost hidden up the sleeves of his coat ; Sir Michael Hicks Beach, so dark and dour ; Mr. W. H. Smith, the shrewd, steadfast model of the political proprieties ; Sir Richard Cross, the Lancashire lawyer and man of business who had been Home Secretary ; Lord George Hamilton, one of Disraeli's young men of promise, who spoke as if he had a pebble in his mouth ; Mr. Gibson, afterwards Lord Ashbourne, the handsome Irishman, with ruddy face and abundant white hair, loud-voiced in denunciation of the Government ; Lord John Manners, afterwards Duke of Rutland, the model of Lord Henry Sydney in *Coningsby* and *Tancred*, tall and stately with single eye-glass, a severe censor of the Radicals who often twitted him with his celebrated couplet, published in a volume of poems entitled *England's Trust* :

" Let wealth and commerce, laws and learning die,
    But leave us still our old nobility."

All have gone except Lord George Hamilton, who entered office under Disraeli, was a member of Lord Salisbury's Governments and served in Mr. Balfour's Cabinet until his Free Trade principles led to his resignation, proving himself a man of principle as well as a good Parliamentarian and a capable administrator.

BRADLAUGH SCENES.—Passion and prejudice were displayed in the proceedings which gave Bradlaugh something of the celebrity of Wilkes. Bradlaugh lived to extort the respect of Parliament by the propriety of his conduct as a member and the moderation of his political sentiments, but at his election in 1880 he was loathed by large sections on account of his atheism, his *Impeachment of the House of Brunswick,* which Randolph Churchill flung on the floor and stamped upon, and his re-issue of an American pamphlet on the question of population. His claim to make an affirmation of allegiance instead of taking the oath was rejected, and then, in consequence of his declared views, he was not allowed, when he offered, to " swear by Almighty God." His persistent assertion of the right to a seat, his speeches from the bar of the House, his struggles with the officers, his contests in the Law Courts formed an exciting chapter of history.

When the House decided in June, 1880, that Bradlaugh could not be permitted either to make an affirmation or to take the oath, he presented himself at the table to challenge the decision. He was led back below the bar by the Sergeant-at-Arms, but shouting, " I claim my right as a member," he again advanced, and as Gladstone informed the Queen, " entered into what was almost a corporal struggle with the Sergeant." He strove to break away from the officer of the House, and it was only when several attendants were called in that he was induced to retire. He was taken into custody, but was next day discharged from the Clock Tower. Without going through the formal preliminaries which were denied to him, he spoke several times in debate and voted in divisions, thereby raising the question of penalties. In May, 1881, when he again went to the table and claimed to take the oath, the Sergeant conducted him once more below the bar and he was ordered to be removed from the House until he should engage not further to disturb its proceedings. He tried in August to force an entrance, but his path was blocked by attendants. A number of police laid hold of him and being a man of powerful physique he offered formidable resistance. His coat was torn in the struggle.

What was considered to be his most unseemly and outrageous proceeding occurred in 1882. At the opening of the session he appeared in the House, but obeyed an order to withdraw. A fortnight later he hurried up to the table, took from his pocket a copy of the New Testament, recited the oath from a paper in his hand, and kissed the book. For this conduct he was expelled and his seat was vacated, but he was re-elected for Northampton. In the end Bradlaugh, with a constituency behind him, prevailed. After his return at the general election of 1885 he was allowed at last to take the oath. A few years later he secured the passing of an affirmation law. Gradually, by his anti-Socialist speeches, he won the cheers of Conservatives, his correct conduct as a colleague removed early prejudice, and in 1891, while he lay on his death-bed and had just passed into final unconsciousness, the House expunged from its records the resolution by which eleven years previously it refused him permission to swear or affirm.

DRAWING THE BADGER.—Piquant personalities and politics were involved in the struggle in 1884 between Randolph Churchill, the champion of the militant Conservatives, and Chamberlain, the champion of the Radicals, over the Aston Park riot by which Northcote and Churchill himself were prevented from addressing a demonstration in support of the action of the Peers on the Franchise Bill. As the political " boss " of Birmingham, Chamberlain was accused of complicity in the riot. Drummond Wolff, on behalf of the Conservative fighter, tried to draw the badger—" the wariest, toughest and most powerful badger ever known," said Mr. Morley—but Chamberlain waited for the dangerous assailant. Churchill's attack was made with animation and force and was encouraged by the cheers and cries of the Tories, who hoped to see the dreaded Radical severely wounded in reputation. Chamberlain retaliated with one of his most vivacious and brilliant efforts. Not content with defence, he turned on his enemies and, as a friend recorded, proved that the badger had very powerful claws. The majority in his favour did not represent the full party strength, but so far as the Radicals were concerned, their delight at the encounter was unbounded. How they cheered their pugnacious leader and how they laughed at the discomfiture of those who had challenged him !

BLANK CHEQUE.—The " blank cheque " current in Parliamentary exchange was introduced in debate in 1884 when the fate of the Government depended to some extent on Goschen. Their Egyptian policy was the object of determined attack by the Opposition, and Goschen, who had influence over the uneasy Whigs, was out of sympathy with the Liberal Ministers behind whom he sat. There was keen excitement when he rose at a late hour in a crowded House. Ministers waited anxiously on his words, several of them turning round to watch him. Their faithful followers were suspicious of his attitude, while the Conservatives based upon him their hopes of success. These hopes were sustained by the critical character of his speech. But then came the decisive declaration. " I am asked," said Goschen, " to have the courage of my opinions and vote to-night against Her Majesty's Government because I do not agree with them on some points. I *have* the courage of my opinions ; but I *have not* the temerity to give a political blank cheque to Lord Salisbury." Seldom has a phrase been so dramatic. Applauded by the relieved Liberals, it was received with chagrin by the Opposition. A " blank cheque " struck the public imagination. It was quoted everywhere and it has become one of the standard terms in a Parliamentary vocabulary which is neither rich nor varied.

GLADSTONE'S FALL.—It may be hard now to realize the antipathy with which the Conservatives regarded Gladstone in those far-off days. His imperial policy was distrusted on account of his ardent sympathy with peoples " struggling to be free " and what was thought to be his extreme love of peace ; he aroused the alarm of many interests at home, his courtship of the common people excited jealousy, he was considered a danger to the institutions of the country ; it was said that he would sacrifice anything for the sake of power. Session after session his opponents hoped to destroy his Government ; session after session, notwithstanding disagreements in his Cabinet, the wonderful man baffled their attacks. At last, after five years of unrelenting effort, they succeeded in June, 1885.

I have witnessed the downfall of several Administrations, but on none other of these occasions have

I seen such frantic jubilation as on the night when Hicks Beach's motion against the Budget was carried. The event was acclaimed with specially fervent demonstrations of delight by Randolph Churchill. He more than any one else had pulled down the giant; to him the victory opened a splendid vista. When the figures were announced he sprang upon his seat and standing there led the cheers. Many other Conservatives, as well as their Nationalist allies, rose and flourished their hats— for hats were worn then—and shouted till they were hoarse. For several minutes they continued their exultant cries as they looked across at the fallen Minister. He calmly wrote his letter to the Queen.

## 1886–1895

### GLADSTONE'S LAST CAMPAIGNS

From the strict party warfare between Liberals and Conservatives which had been carried on since the Peelites were merged with either side, the story proceeds to the ten years' conflict on the new Irish policy which Gladstone adopted in valiant old age and which permanently altered the Parliamentary battle array. Other important questions were raised in that decade, but Ireland was the determining, dividing issue. The fear of Home Rule finally scattered from the adventurous leader's side most of the Whig patricians who had hitherto with hesitating steps followed him and it provoked the creation of a new party, including many Radicals, with a new name. Those who broke away from Gladstone resented their being called dissentient Liberals. They claimed to be the true upholders of the principles of their party. But separated from its official leader on the decisive issue of the time, the Liberal Unionists, as they styled themselves, gradually linked their fate with that of their hereditary opponents.

The year 1886 is memorable in Parliamentary annals. When it opened Salisbury's first Government, which had been formed in the previous summer to carry on till the general election at the end of 1885, was in existence, waiting the verdict of the new House of Commons. I recall the defeat of the " Government of Caretakers," as Chamberlain had called it, on Jesse Collings's three-acres-and-a-cow amendment ; the entrance of the " Grand Old Man " on the hardest of his campaigns ; the refusal of Hartington to accompany him ; the early withdrawal of Chamberlain from his Administration; the crowded House, with chairs between the bar and the table, when he introduced the Home Rule Bill; his encounters with his former lieutenants, the Whig sitting behind him, the Radical below the gangway; the pleasure taken in their quarrel by the Front Opposition Bench; the enthusiasm aroused by Gladstone among the Nationalists who formerly denounced him and now rose in his honour; the violence of their contentions with Chamberlain; the appearance in the official hierarchy of John Morley as Gladstone's closest colleague in the Irish cause; the excitement of the division which resulted in the defeat of the bill.

A FATEFUL DIVISION.—Few events are more exciting than a doubtful division on which the existence of a Government may hang. Party passion is inflamed red-hot, personal ambitions as well as high policies are at stake, the possessors of power and patronage dread their dismissal from the seats of the mighty, their opponents are thrilled by the vision of the Treasury bench. There was in the division in the summer of 1886 more complexity and more significance than in the usual trial of strength between Ins and Outs. It marked the first formal stage in the revolt of the Liberal Unionists. Three times within a year a vital division had been taken in the House of Commons. In June, 1885, Gladstone had been defeated by the combination of Parnellites with Conservatives; in January, 1886, after the General Election, he recaptured office with the assistance of the Irish; and now in June he was confronted by a section of his own party in alliance with the Conservatives. How many of his old followers would vote against him on the Home Rule Bill ? That was the question which had been asked for weeks.

There had seemed to be a possibility that a section of the Radicals acting with Chamberlain would in the end shrink from a hostile vote. This possibility was shaken by a letter from John Bright. Out of consideration for his former chief, Bright did not take a prominently active part in the new struggle; he was seldom in the House during its progress. But his advice was sought. In a letter read at a meeting of the Chamberlain group, he wrote that his own intention was to vote against the second reading of the Home Rule Bill. He added that if others could content themselves with abstention he would be glad, but they preferred his practice to his precept and were as a rule resolved to follow his own course. Almost to the last, however, the issue was in some doubt. Gladstone's influence was still magical. And who could say what might not be the effect of his oratory ? At a quarter past one on the morning of June 8 he concluded the debate with an appeal to the conscience such as in former years sustained his power. "Think, I beseech you," said the orator in his most solemn, impressive tone, "think well, think wisely, think not for the moment but for the years that are to come before you reject this bill."

When at the close of the division the Liberal Unionist Whips, Mr. Brand and Mr. Caine, who were acting respectively for Hartington and Chamberlain, took the places of the victorious tellers at the table, such a hubbub arose as delayed the announcement of the figures for several minutes. The defeat of the bill was celebrated with rapturous cheers by its opponents. From the Irish quarter came ferocious taunts at those Liberals who had, according to bitterly disappointed men, betrayed their leader. " The Brand of Cain," shouted Nationalists in bitter play on the names of the Whips. " Judas ! Judas ! Judas ! " one of them cried as he glared at Chamberlain.

PARNELL DETHRONED.—In the six years of Conservative Administration following the rejection of Home Rule there were many dramatic debates in which Chamberlain and Hartington, rising from the bench where Gladstone, Harcourt and Morley sat, defended the Government against their attacks, while Smith led the House and Goschen acted as Chancellor of the Exchequer in place of Churchill, who ate his heart out on a seat behind the Ministers, and Mr. Balfour won favour and fame by his Irish regime and his encounters with the Nationalists. The hopes of the Liberals, while their leader's courage was steadfast, rose and fell with the vicissitudes in the history of their allies. Exposure of the forgery of the infamous letter attributed to Parnell produced a sentiment in his favour which assisted the cause of Home Rule. It was prejudiced and the " union of hearts " of Liberals and Nationalists was weakened by the divorce case in which he was co-respondent and by the consequent dissensions in his party.

Committee Room No. 15 was for many years pointed out to visitors to the House of Commons as the scene of the struggle in which the " uncrowned king of Ireland " was at the end of 1890 dethroned by a majority of his colleagues. Among them were eloquent orators and brilliant debaters, who had played popular parts in the Irish movement, and the conflict of prickly individualities was marked by a passion and a histrionic vividness which gave it a conspicuous place in Parliamentary annals.

Unionists looked on with amusement in the House while the now divided Nationalists denounced one another, the majority continuing to act with Gladstone and the minority standing by Parnell as he turned on the man whose prompting had led to his overthrow. At old colleagues he flung derisive epithets. One was a gutter-sparrow, a second was a cock-sparrow, Michael Davitt was a jackdaw, Justin McCarthy, who had been chosen to succeed him, was " a nice old gentleman for a quiet tea party." There could have been no greater contrast than that between Parnell and the new chairman of the party, but McCarthy, who was in sincere sympathy with the Liberals, was respected by the House for his courteous and dignified ways.

GLADSTONE'S LAST FIGHT.—During Gladstone's last term of office the attendance in the House of Commons was very large. The Government had so small a majority and the Unionists were so keen in their efforts to destroy it, that members on both sides mustered as a rule in unusual force. Putting on his Ministerial armour at the age of eighty-three, the desperate struggle of the veteran was worthy of the attention it received. His personality with all its prestige and splendour and the cause in which he was engaged excited the very liveliest emotions. The scene at his introduction of the second Home Rule Bill of 1893 recalled the similar event in 1886. So inadequate was the accommodation that chairs had to be placed in front of the bar and also at the upper end of the House. Members assembled in the lobby for hours before the doors were opened, and when admitted they rushed forward, elbowing and jostling each other. They strode over benches in order to secure seats and took whatever vacant place they could reach, perspiring and panting. Such was the eagerness to hear the great old leader unfolding his last great plan.

Important changes had occurred in the personnel of the House. Parnell and W. H. Smith were dead and Hartington had gone to the other place. Among the occupants of the Treasury bench new to Government was a future Prime Minister—Mr. Asquith; another sat below the gangway—Mr. Lloyd George. A third member destined to fill a leading rôle in the world drama was Under-Secretary for Foreign Affairs—Sir Edward Grey, a young man, of grave manners and high character, noted for tennis and fishing, a Radical and an Imperialist. Mr. Lloyd George was as yet known only as one of a group of young Welshmen impatient for dis-establishment; Mr. Asquith, although a Secretary of State, did not take a leading share in the Home Rule fight. It was carried on chiefly by those who had been conspicuous in it since 1886. The "Grand Old Man" himself conducted the campaign with unabated fire, courage and resource, and with him as his chief lieutenants were Harcourt and Morley.

JOHN MORLEY.—Although later occupying higher rank in the Ministerial hierarchy, Mr. Morley stood at the most conspicuous point of his Parliamentary career in the period of the second Home Rule Bill. The active stage of that career, beginning while Joseph Chamberlain was a Liberal minister, ex-tended over thirty years to the opening of the war, but it was as the colleague, friend and disciple of Gladstone that his biographer was most honoured by Liberals and exercised the greatest influence.

Sir Algernon West has quoted Morley as saying

many years ago : " I wonder if I should not have been happier writing obscure philosophical works, which nobody would read, on the Hog's Back, than leading a political life." There is no reason to suppose that he was much disturbed by any such doubt while engaged in the business of Westminster and Whitehall. He has observed that a French philosopher rated liteiature, " *as it ought to be rated,*" below action, and he set his own action in State affairs above his achievements, great as these were, in literature. Few men of letters have risen to such a pinnacle in the political world as Viscount Morley, Secretary of State.

Ere he entered Parliament he had become a force in the movement of public affairs by his editorship of the *Fortnightly Review* and the *Pall Mall Gazette.* Gifted as he was with a fine intellect, clear-cut principles and rare felicity of expression, general interest was excited by his election. I saw him taking his seat, in 1883, when his friends Bryce and Trevelyan moved to his side to chat with him, and I heard his maiden speech on the Transvaal and native races : a speech consisting largely of references to Blue Books. Many years afterwards, meeting him at a luncheon party, I recalled those events. " Ah ! " he said, " that was in another world."

Voltaire, as Morley has observed, " is supposed to have hinted to Cardinal Fleury that to have written epic and drama does not disqualify a man for serving his king and country on the busy fields of affairs." His own leader did not hold him disqualified for high service by the fact that he had written many books and he may have included himself among those men, like Burke, who " showed that books are a better preparation for statesmanship than early training in the subordinate posts and among

the permanent officials of a public department."
A great opportunity came to him in 1886, when,
without apprenticeship in subordinate posts and
with brief Parliamentary experience, he was
appointed Chief Secretary for Ireland, with a seat
in the Cabinet.  His devotion to Gladstone and his
intimate association with the Home Rule policy
which the majority of Liberals adopted with the
fervour of believers in a new gospel, gave him a
warm place in the heart of the party.  To him as a
man of the future many who had put their faith in
Chamberlain now turned.  And their confidence
in him grew during their years of opposition.  The
sincerity of the Home Rule convictions of some
others might be doubted ; his were not.  He was
unsparing in his denunciation of Mr. Balfour's Irish
policy of " manacles or Manitoba " and untiring
in his efforts to preserve the alliance of Nationalists
and Liberals.

It was natural that in the Government of 1892
he should again be Irish Secretary.  Throughout
the last Parliament in which Gladstone sat he
maintained high authority and influence as a
Minister, standing almost on a level with Harcourt,
Rosebery and Spencer.  Whoever might be Gladstone's immediate successor, there were many
Liberals who regarded Morley as his true political
heir.  He had inherited from him and Bright and
Cobden the doctrines of peace, free trade and reform
and he could be trusted more than any other
statesman with the cause of Home Rule.  The
India Office, which he occupied in a later era under
another chief, was offered to Morley when Rosebery
became Prime Minister, but he declined then to take
any post which would separate him from Ireland.

As a speaker Morley was animated and attractive

until in his later years he suffered from an affection of the vocal chords. He was seldom so effective in Parliament as before a sympathetic, popular audience, but however the House of Commons might be constituted it always heard him with respect and with an intellectual pleasure. Mr. Chamberlain once accused him of talking " literary nonsense— the worst of all." That was the last accusation to which he would have pleaded guilty, but whether listeners considered what he said to be sense or nonsense, his richness of vocabulary, purity of language, and suggestiveness of phrase, his literary, historical lore and quaint byways of thought gave charm to all his speeches for the fastidious ear. One of the best he delivered was on Oliver Cromwell. A vote of £500 for the erection of the statue of the Protector within the precincts of Parliament was on the motion of Rosebery's Government carried by a small majority, but the project was so vehemently opposed by the Irish, as well as by Mr. Balfour, that the Ministers allowed the vote to be rescinded. Their retreat was covered by Morley with an impassioned and eloquent speech in eulogy of the ruler whom he, like Mr. S. R. Gardiner, may have regarded as being " in the world of action what Shakespeare was in the world of thought, the greatest because the most typical Englishman of all time." A few years later, while the Unionists were in power, he had the satisfaction of seeing the statue erected by the side of Westminster Hall, the cost being defrayed by Lord Rosebery.

Aloofness of manner may have been one of the obstacles in the way of Morley attaining the leadership which his friends designed for him and to which possibly he aspired. He did not suffer bores gladly—and they are very numerous in the House of Commons.   There are, as he has said, subjects " which the wise take care only to discuss with the wise," and the range of those subjects in his view was large.   A popular Liberal who sat in the House for a score of years told me that Morley never exchanged a word with him.   They had been in the same division lobby countless times and they remained strangers.   Occasionally a member on the second bench behind Morley would lean forward and whisper to him ; he would turn stiffly and answer perhaps by the raising of the eyebrows.   Belonging to the aristocracy of the intellect, he had the reserve of the aristocracy.   The delightful companion of those whose society he valued and a man of sincere sympathy with the lot of the humble, he practised —unconsciously and undesignedly—a frigid aloofness among the common mortals of St. Stephen's.

FISTICUFFS.—In the protracted struggle on the second Home Rule Bill feeling was excited to an excessive and reckless degree when the fame of the Mother of Parliaments was sullied by members raising their hands against each other.   I was a witness of that lamentable scene on a July night in 1893.   I recall the vehement invective of Chamberlain on the eve of the guillotining of the committee stage of the Bill, his taunting of the Gladstonians with adulation of their leader, the retorting cry of " Judas " from the Irish quarter, the recriminations of members as they passed to the division lobbies ; I recall Radical Mr. Logan defiantly taking a seat among Conservatives on the front Opposition bench, Mr. Hayes Fisher from behind pushing him off, the Nationalists rushing across the gangway and engaging in a scrimmage with their adversaries, the noise and confusion while those who had gone to vote hurried back; I recall the hissing by horrified strangers, Michael Davitt looking down from the gallery, Mr. Ashmead-Bartlett, a bellicose Tory, standing at the table and shouting across at the aged, sad Premier; I recall the dramatic entry of Mr. Speaker Peel on being sent for by the Chairman of Committee, his stern aspect as his eye swept over the scene, his calm " Order ! Order ! ", the immediate stilling of the storm and the shamed looks of the offenders.

Peel had an extraordinary mastery over the House. From the day that he cast a spell over it by the dignity of his speech from the steps of the chair as Speaker-Elect it regarded him with a respect which developed into awe; it became, in fact, afraid of him. Members quailed at his angry glance; a formal rebuke from him was terrible. The effect was not due entirely to his figure and manner, although their stateliness was impressive. It was due in part to his lofty, austere character. No Speaker's authority was put to a severer test than Peel's on that night of disorder when members for a time lost their self-control. Fortunately for the House it submitted to him like a school to the headmaster.

GLADSTONE'S EXIT.—Although all who listened on the first of March, 1894, to Gladstone's attack on the House of Lords, which had rejected the Home Rule Bill and mutilated other measures, did not know that this was to be his last speech in Parliament, there was a general consciousness that his official career was at its close. In the gallery of the Commons were Lord Rosebery, for whom the Queen was soon to send, and Lord Spencer, whom the retiring Minister would, if asked, have advised

Her Majesty to choose as his successor. His manner was unusually solemn, and so was that of the colleagues to whom he had bidden farewell in Cabinet. There was no special demonstration at the end of the sitting on that eventful day; there was no dramatic exit by the veteran whose coffined body was four years later passed by mourning multitudes as it lay in Westminster Hall and was followed to the Abbey by princes and by statesmen of both parties.

It was amazing that the last Government of Gladstone and the only Government of Lord Rosebery should have lived for nearly three years with a highly contentious programme, and with a majority, including Nationalists, of only about forty. There were dissensions in the Cabinet; there were Radical revolts; yet the party held better together than when it was in greater force, and it had a loyal ally in Justin McCarthy, the leader of the main body of the Irish, while the Parnellites were led with discretion by John Redmond. When the Government was at last blown up by cordite the Unionists rejoiced exceedingly, for they saw their way to a long lease of power. Since that evening, over a quarter of a century ago, when Campbell-Bannerman, Secretary for War, closed his despatch box and Harcourt moved to report progress on their defeat on an Army Estimate, no Ministry has resigned in consequence of a vote in the House of Commons.

# CHAPTER IX

## II

### A NEW ERA

AN era ended when Gladstone left the House of Commons. Although there were followers who for years afterwards cherished his name and principles, the tide of affairs swept on through new channels to an uncharted sea. Some of the old problems, such as Home Rule and the House of Lords, remained, but any one who compares the controversies of the period from the formation of Gladstone's second Government in 1880 till his final retirement in 1894 with those of the succeeding twenty years, will see how the world and its outlook had changed even before the Great War. Labour had realized its power, and industrial questions had begun to challenge an attention which they did not previously receive.

1895–1905

## THE UNIONIST REGIME

In the political life of the ten and a half years of Unionist rule, which began in the summer of 1895, Chamberlain was the most picturesque and potent figure. Mr. Balfour was leader of the House of Commons during the whole period and Prime Minister for the last third of it. Behind these two, until the end of the South African War and the eve of King Edward's coronation, stood the massive figure of the Marquis of Salisbury, with a steady hand on foreign policy, and beside him was " the Duke," the man of plain sense and calm temper, who for a short time in Mr. Balfour's Administration led the House of Lords. For the first five years Goschen was still in office, and Hicks Beach remained till Salisbury went.

As the careers of the great Victorians were drawing to a close there appeared below the gangway the son of a Presbyterian minister in Canada, formerly an iron merchant in Glasgow. Two young men of the governing class, Lord Hugh Cecil and Mr. Winston Churchill, inspired high hopes by their talents and activities. It was, however, to the Presbyterian minister's son that leadership came.

Meantime the Liberals wandered in the wilderness. Burdened by their heritage of dissension they were dejected and hopeless. In " C.B." they discovered a leader with courage and patience, but on the bench, where Mr. Bryce was his closest colleague, Harcourt and Morley were on imperial affairs, as I have shown, sharply divided from Asquith and Grey, whose reputations steadily grew, and who were intimately associated with Lord Rosebery. Notable among the members behind the Liberal leader was Mr. Haldane, whose intellectual power was recognized by men on both sides, and who was listened to with special respect by Mr. Balfour, and below the Opposition gangway stood out more and more distinctly the vivacious figure of the Radical Nonconformist, the opponent of doles to church schools and squires, the so-called "little-Englander," Mr. Lloyd George.

SIR EDWARD GREY.—The steady growth of Sir Edward Grey's reputation to which I have referred cannot be accounted for by any conspicuous event. There had been nothing brilliant in his career. Elected in 1885 at the age of twenty-three, the grand-nephew of Earl Grey, who carried the Reform Act of 1832, and grandson of Sir George Grey, who was Home Secretary as late as 1866, he took silently the side of Home Rule in 1886 and spoke seldom in Opposition in the next six years. What he said was marked by reflection. He said in a plain way what he thought, and it could be recorded of him then, as always, as was recorded of his grandfather, whom he succeeded, that he was "moderate in speech, never attempting to be smart nor speaking with bitterness." He was never self-assertive.

Under-Secretary for Foreign Affairs in the 1892–95 Administration, the young man was described by a cynic as the "gravest of Lord Rosebery's indiscretions." Grave he always was, but if his Departmental chief was responsible for his appointment, Lord Rosebery had reason to congratulate himself on the choice he made for a most difficult office. It was a post which, in view of the critical character of our international relations and Liberal differences on Empire responsibilities, tested the qualities of its occupant. He had to make the delicate declaration that the advance of a French expedition under secret instructions from the other side of Africa into the Nile Valley would be viewed by England as an unfriendly act. His position was peculiarly trying when Harcourt became leader of the House. It was Grey's duty on more than one occasion to express views, for instance on Uganda, which were distasteful to that statesman. He discharged his task not only with discretion, but with a courage rare in an Under-Secretary, and with a single-mindedness which won general respect.

" There is the man with the real Parliamentary gift," Gladstone is reported to have said of Grey in 1895. About that time, in an article written for an illustrated weekly, I spoke of him as a future Prime Minister, and the editor in the following issue put his money on Morley. I mention this to show what was then imagined by observers. A high sense of duty rather than political ambition dominated Grey. His face, with what is called the aristocratic nose, the grave, searching eye, the mobile mouth, and the dark hair lying on the forehead arrested the attention of strangers. Health shone in it, the health of the open air. It reflected a spirit " free from mists and sane and clear." In the ten weary years of Opposition Grey displayed not only the Parliamentary gift, but the higher gift of statesmanship. Staunch in Imperialism and staunch in Liberalism, a firm friend of Lord Rosebery and a straightforward colleague of the leader of the party in the House of Commons, differing from those colleagues who opposed the South African policy of the Government, but never taking part in personal altercations, he gained almost imperceptibly an increasing hold on the confidence of the country.

His success was the success of character. Mr. Churchill has said of him in the language of the craft he loves so well that he baits his hook with good taste, good sense and good courage. Truly these are among his qualities. But are they so rare as to give their possessor an honoured place among public men? There is something beyond them in Grey's case which has always impressed his contemporaries, and that is his sincere, simple-minded, sagacious care for the interests of the State. By his conduct in Opposition all saw that these interests would be safe in his keeping.

THE RAID INQUIRY.—How remote the Parliamentary inquiry into the Jameson raid seems now! In its time it was regarded as a historic event of the first importance, resembling in significance the trial of Warren Hastings. The Prince of Wales was among the visitors to the committee room in Westminster Hall, to which society flocked. There was the liveliest interest in Mr. Rhodes, who ate sandwiches and drank beer during his examination, but Mr. Chamberlain, the Colonial Secretary, himself was on trial almost as much as the promoters of the raid. Many persons suspected that the Colonial Office knew of its being planned. This suspicion was strengthened by the disclosure of telegrams which had passed between Mr. Rhodes and a lady journalist, Miss Flora Shaw (afterwards the wife of Sir Frederick Lugard), who had access to the Department, and by rumours with regard to other cables between the Empire-builder and the Secretary to the Chartered South Africa Company which were not produced to the Committee. Weird speculations turned on these missing messages, although when published a few years later they were found to contain nothing not otherwise known.

Radicals who had hoped to drag down their most doughty antagonist were unconvinced when the Colonial Secretary and his Department were exonerated from complicity with the raiders, and their doubts were revived when he testified to the personal honour of Mr. Rhodes after the latter had been censured by the Committee for subsidizing, organizing and stimulating the armed insurrection against the Boer Republic. Great was the sensation caused by such a tribute in such circumstances. Rumour buzzed in the Lobby. It was suggested that this was the price Chamberlain was paying for Mr. Rhodes's silence on his own knowledge of the raid, but the suggestion was accepted only by those who thought the most fearless of men capable of double-dealing.

THE KHAKI ELECTION.—The khaki election of 1900 and the partisan use made of indiscreet letters from certain Liberals found in the Pretoria archives, drew upon the Minister chiefly responsible for South African policy the concentrated fury of opponents of the Government. Year after year Chamberlain kept in the forefront of the Parliamentary battle. The keener it was the more he exulted. It was his sword which flashed most frequently ; it was he who most surely aroused the applause of the Commons. After the surrender of the Boers and his tour of the illimitable veld he was at the zenith of his fame.

Till Salisbury's retirement in 1902 almost everything went well with the Unionists. They seemed

to have the prospect of office for a generation.
They had strengthened our position on the Nile
and annexed the Transvaal, and by carrying out
portions of Chamberlain's social programme they
had made an appeal to the working classes, who
were beginning to use their political power. The
two sections of Unionists had drawn closer together
in office while their opponents were still divided.
From 1902 the tide turned. Futile Army plans,
education policy, Chinese " slavery " in Transvaal
mines, and, above all, Chamberlain's fiscal proposals provided objects of effective attack, and
when the Liberals at last closed their ranks
dissension broke out in turn on the side of the
Government.

THE YOUNG UNIONISTS.—Debate during the
South African War had been, so far as Unionists
were concerned, left mainly to the old and middle-
aged, and they were not troublesome. Some of the
younger men were at the front. Others, in languid
attitudes and dress of newest cut, were content to
act as a Parliamentary chorus. Soon after the
war the smooth waters were ruffled. Young Conservatives, dissatisfied with the conduct of affairs,
asserted their individuality and claimed a right to
be heard. Ambition, wholesome and profitable,
combined with patriotism to give them daring
and energy. Older members shrugged shoulders
and muttered scornfully, but the men with faces
towards the future pressed forward hopefully.
It was, as one of them said, a sign of the times that
young men were taking a larger interest and a
wider share in public life. Their activities were
inconvenient to Mr. Balfour, who respected opponents but had a natural dislike of rebels.

LORD HUGH CECIL.—The revolt of those two
scions of Conservative families, Lord Hugh Cecil
and Mr. Winston Churchill, was specially interesting. They were conspicuous in a group which
dared to ridicule Mr. Brodrick's " paper army
corps," and to oppose the fiscal proposals which
were causing so much searching of political con-
sciences. Lord Hugh Cecil entered Parliament
ten years before his elder brother, Lord Robert, and
he soon showed some of the characteristics of the
Lord Robert of the previous generation. The
Marquis of Salisbury never heard his son speaking
in the House of Commons. Not even to witness
Lord Hugh's success would he look down on the
scene where he himself had revived the fame of
the Cecils. But he lived long enough to know that
the distinction of his name would not die with him.
The tall, thin, long-limbed young man, with pale,
ascetic face, quickly seized the attention and won
the ear of the House. Before rising he would lean
forward, evidently rehearsing what he intended to
say as he clutched his handkerchief in his hands.
Then when he intervened, bobbing up and down,
twisting and twining his fingers, he would speak
rapidly and incisively with ingenious dialectic and
irony.

The hope of the Church Tories, just as Gladstone
had been, Lord Hugh struck a high, rare note by
his idealism, touched with religious emotion. It
was strange amid the party clatter to hear a young
man declaring that the root of national strength
and power was deep planted in the religious faith
we held, and drew its sustenance from our abiding fear of God. So great was his zeal for the
Church that he was described as *L'Eminence grise*
behind the ministerial authors of legislation in

aid of voluntary schools. The House is quick to detect cant, but treats genuine religious feeling with respect, and Lord Hugh's sincerity was unmistakable. " Not only elevated but elevating in tone," observed Campbell-Bannerman in comment on one of his orations, and Morley found in him a natural gift of stirring and moving speech.

Even in resistance to the new fiscal proposals he adopted a tone which was not that of the ordinary controversialist. He poured scorn on the arguments of some of those around him when he said he despised the Imperialism " which thinks of nothing but trade returns." With all his elevated fervour he could be very biting and bitter. He had a waspish faculty for stinging. Scarcely any one irritated Chamberlain more than the Cecil who, standing in front of him below the gangway, jeered at his policy and who, while Mr. Balfour was manœuvring, kept the Free Trade flag flying in the Conservative ranks.

It seemed possible at this time that Lord Hugh might take, as he took many years later, an independent position. His cousin refrained from any word which would drive him out. When directly challenged on the point, Mr. Balfour recognized him as a true member of the party that he led. Many observers thought that Lord Hugh would in due course succeed to its leadership. One of its ablest men who shared that belief counselled him to have patience. Defeated, however, as a Unionist Free Trader, he was out of Parliament from 1906 till 1910, and when he returned to new conditions his opportunity had passed.

MR. CHURCHILL.—While the caustic Cecil, in conformity with his traditions and principles, remained in the Conservative party, his early colleague and friend, less firmly attached to it by inherited or personal sentiment, broke away. The son of Lord Randolph Churchill received a warm welcome from the House on entering it in 1900 and in his speeches from the bench behind the Unionist ministers he proved himself worthy of his father. " I am, I know," he said, in 1901, " a very young man, but——" There was much virtue in " but."

> " His years but young, but his experience old ;
> His head unmellow'd, but his judgment ripe."

His speeches had a stateliness of form and a breadth of view as well as a self-assurance rare in a novice. As the Boers had stated in a description of their escaped prisoner, he could not pronounce the letter " S " properly. He sounded it " sh." But this was soon forgotten. The literary form, the massed argument, and the careful delivery of his speeches made them effective.

To his father's memory Mr. Churchill was loyal. He turned on his finger while addressing the House a plain gold signet ring which Lord Randolph had worn. Those who sat with the father were startled by the repetition of his mannerisms and attitudes, his gifts and extravagances, in the son on whom his mantle had fallen. The young man had the same stoop, the same gait ; he lurched forward in his walk and kept his elbows out, and when he spoke he kicked his heel on the ground or grasped the lapels of his coat just as his father did. Even in the frock-coat and the large bow tie and in the shape of the collars, the young man carried out the resemblance.

Soon it was seen by colleagues with no little annoyance that Winston Churchill had one of

his father's inconvenient qualities. " Randy over
again," muttered Mr. Pliable and Mr. Placeman
when he struck the note of independence. " A
future Liberal Prime Minister," predicted the
discerning journalist, Mr. Massingham. His audacity
was displayed in attacks on Government policy
in the South African War and in ridicule of
their " phantom army " schemes ; he espoused
his father's cause and irritated the Prime Minister
by persistent advocacy of retrenchment, and he
took a spirited part in the defence of Free Trade.
In 1903 he moved below the gangway. By 1904
he was a declared opponent of Mr. Balfour's
Government.

Resentment at his conduct was expressed by
the members among whom he sat. His father's
experience, they thought, should have taught him
a lesson. They let him know that they would
value his room better than his company. Mr.
Balfour set the fashion by walking out when he
rose, and on more than one occasion, while he was
speaking, almost the whole of the Government
supporters left the House. Boycotted by his
father's friends, he crossed the floor in 1904 to the
Liberal side, and was welcomed with open arms by
the arch-Radical, Mr. Lloyd George, beside whom
he sat when possible. Thereupon the Unionists
called him " rat."

A fellow-guest in a week-end party in a country
house came upon him gazing intently upon a
portrait of Pitt. " Have you ever wondered," he
asked, " how Pitt managed to persuade the King
to make him Prime Minister at twenty-four ? "
" It is probable," said Grey of Churchill himself, at
a literary club dinner in 1905, " he will one day
be Prime Minister." How long, then, I wonder,

ve`

did he think he would have to wait? He was thirty when he looked at that portrait.

THE YOUNG LIBERALS.—" I know no life," says Mr. Arabin in *Barchester Towers*, " that must be so delicious as that of a writer for newspapers or a leading member of the Opposition—to thunder forth accusations against men in power; show up the worst side of everything that is produced; to pick holes in every coat; to be indignant, sarcastic, jocose, moral, or supercilious; to damn with faint praise, or crush with open calumny." These delights, or most of them, were enjoyed by a set of able young Liberals who made their mark in the early years of this century. Fortunate are the ambitious Parliamentarians who begin their career in Opposition! They find many opportunities for practice in debate and for the cultivation and display of their political talents. Among such at this period were Mr. M'Kenna, Mr. Runciman and Mr. (now Sir) Herbert Samuel. Able, keen, industrious and persistent, they had an ample field for adventure.

Eager Liberals were never happier than in those days when, after long wandering, they drew near to the land of office and power. United by the issues raised after the South African War and excited by their prospects, they pressed hard on the party which, weakened by prosperity and divided in opinion, was drifting to disaster. With the clash of debate and the snap division, the closing in of the pursuers upon the elusive Prime Minister thrilled the spectator.

MR. BALFOUR AT BAY.—Never were pursuers more astutely held off than the aggressive, sanguine

Liberals were by Mr. Balfour. His ablest colleagues had gone. Goschen had resigned and moved to the other place in 1900, Hicks Beach had retired to a back bench in 1902, Chamberlain had relinquished office in 1903 in order with greater freedom to advocate Tariff Reform. Without lieutenants of their capacity or authority the Prime Minister displayed an ingenuity and a courage which won the admiration even of assailants. Attacked relentlessly by Free Traders, Nonconformists and Nationalists, while a section of his own party viewed his tactics with disfavour, he kept his pursuers at bay much longer than it had been considered possible for any one in such circumstances to hold out. Loving power and hating Liberalism, and, as has been suggested, anxious to develop his Entente policy, he continued his manœuvres month after month, and session after session, in the hope that something might happen to save him. At last he resigned, when it seemed that Lord Rosebery's refusal to fight under an Irish flag might divide the Liberals at the general election. His hopes in that respect were doomed to disappointment. Liberals taught by adversity did not fling away the opportunity of victory. Led to the country by " C.B.," they put an end for ever to Mr. Balfour's rule.

## 1906–1914

### THE LIBERAL REGIME

I have never at any other time seen such a House of high expectations as was elected in January, 1906. It contained a great many earnest, eager, sanguine reformers elated by victory. For twenty years, with a brief interval, the Unionists had been in office. Now the Liberals were in overwhelming strength, and with them were the Nationalists, and, as a rule, also the Labour members, who for the first time in our history formed a substantial party. Reformers dreamed dreams of a political millennium. Elected to do great deeds, they intended and hoped to democratize the institutions of the country, break the privileges of the aristocracy, destroy the land monopoly and bring comfort and happiness to the manual workers and the poor. When the world war intervened they had not realized all their ambitions and aspirations, but vast social and constitutional changes had been carried out.

The period from the Liberal triumph to the war, one of the most disturbed epochs in our domestic annals, may be divided into three stages. The first culminated in the holding up of the Budget of 1909 by the House of Lords, the struggle with the peers occupied the second, Ulster dominated the third. Throughout the whole period staunch and reliable support was given to the Government by the Nationalists, who hoped for their reward in Home Rule. Mr. Dillon had succeeded Justin McCarthy as leader of the anti-Parnellite majority in 1896, but in 1900 the two sections were re-united under John Redmond, who had given proof of his Parliamentary talents as leader of the Parnellites.

The Labour party also was an important although self-assertive ally with some of the impatience of youth. There had been working men members in the previous generation—Alexander Macdonald, Thomas Burt and Henry Broadhurst. Broadhurst and Burt, stonemason and miner, had held office. They were, however, Liberals by principle and party, and so were Charles Fenwick and John Wilson, ex-colliers, who kept their old Radical connection even till the reign of King George. Keir Hardie introduced a new type and laid the foundation of the Parliamentary Labour party, independently of what were called the two great parties in the State. Besides some thirty members returned on its " ticket " in 1906, there were over a score of Liberal-Labour members, most of whom acted with it and gradually joined it. It had its own Chairman and its own Whips. Hardie, its first leader, was succeeded by Mr. Arthur Henderson, Mr. George Barnes and Mr. Ramsay Macdonald. While giving a general support to the Liberal Government in reform legislation, it took its sectional point of view and exacted its price in measures in the Trade Union interest.

Several of the older Liberal statesmen died or retired or left the House of Commons during the regime to which they had looked forward, and a younger generation rose into prominence. When Mr. Asquith became Prime Minister, Mr. Morley was offered the Chancellorship of the Exchequer, but he retained the Indian Secretaryship to which he had been appointed by " C.B." and to the surprise of Radicals went to the Upper House.

Some one asked him how he liked being a lord. "The way of transgressors is hard," he replied with an enigmatic smile and shrug, but apparently he enjoyed his dignified surroundings. The Peers are more ready than the Commons to appreciate personal distinction won in other than Parliamentary fields, and much as they disagreed with him on domestic politics they held Viscount Morley in honour. They were amused rather than offended when he said : "You might as well talk to the House of Lords about land as talk to a butcher about Lent." He initiated far-reaching constitutional reforms in India by the enlargement of the Legislative Councils and the appointment of natives to high Executive office, and although his position in the Liberal party during the latter part of his career may not have been so conspicuous as it was in Gladstone's time, its esteem and admiration for him were fully maintained. "Honest John" he had been called, and honest he ever was in politics,—honest to his own conscience and honest to the world.

Although Mr. Lloyd George became Chancellor, Mr. Asquith's closest, most confidential colleagues were Mr. Haldane and Sir Edward Grey. The former, after distinguishing himself at the War Office by the creation of the Territorials and by other activities, succeeded Earl Loreburn, one of the last of the Gladstonians, on the woolsack, in 1912. He had been raised to the peerage in the previous year, but Sir Edward Grey was with his chief in the House of Commons till 1916. Grey's Foreign Secretaryship had contributed to the strength of the Administration by reason of the national confidence which he inspired. Old-fashioned diplomats may have thought him ill-

qualified for the position by his unsuspecting
nature.  He is one

> "Whose nature is so far from doing harms
> That he suspects none."

As one closely associated with him said, if you told
him that somebody was trying to deceive him, he
would be pained by your having such a suspicion
rather than inclined to share it.   Yet all recognized
not only his high-mindedness, but his determination, while labouring year after year in the cause of
international friendship, to maintain our own high
prestige.  His speeches, almost conversational in
form, have had no rich, warm colour.  "All is
silver grey."   And he has no expressive gestures
such as great orators use.  Cicero described Cæsar
"scratching his head with one finger," and Grey
while speaking scratches his neck with a finger tip.
But so deep has been the respect for his character that while he sat in the House of Commons
no other man's words were so likely to turn
votes.

Jealous observers of Mr. Asquith's pushful
colleagues, Mr. Lloyd George and Mr. Churchill,
thought that under their easy-going, tolerant chief
they got too much freedom.  Sympathetic observers,
on the other hand, attributed to their influence
much of the resource and driving power of the
Government.  Their comradeship was watched with
curiosity, and both being ambitious and restless,
candid friends wondered how long it would endure
and which would go the further.  Sometimes the
critics said that Mr. Churchill had more of the
philosophy of politics and would show the greater
staying power.  Mr. Lloyd George's friends, how-

ever, steadily grew in number and encouraged him in the race.

The personal animosity which Mr. Churchill aroused in the Unionist party when he turned against it and left it was maintained by his conduct in office. He was the member of " C.B.'s " Government most disliked by the Opposition. When as an Under-Secretary he denounced Mr. Balfour, the Unionists looked as if they wished to throw him from the House. And as a Cabinet Minister under Mr. Asquith, rising from the Board of Trade to the Home Office and the Admiralty, he kept alive this hostility on the part of his early associates by the pungency of his controversial methods. At the same time, prudent, if not jealous, Liberals were irritated by his imperious temper. With a consciousness of rare capacity he showed little consideration for mediocrity. He hurt the feelings of sensitive colleagues. They glared at him when, with head thrust forward and absorbed in his thoughts, he brushed them aside as he hurried past the Speaker's chair. There was, however, no more question of his ability than of his ambition. Industrious in administration and fertile in policy, he became one of the most finished and impressive speakers. The felicity and force of his language placed him high in Parliamentary oratory. His speeches from the Treasury bench, fastidiously prepared, had the sweep of Gibbon or Macaulay.

VETO OF THE PEERS.—There were many stirring and some disorderly scenes in the House of Commons during the struggle on the Peers' veto. One of the most animated occurred at the end of 1909, when the Liberals and their allies took up the challenge the Lords had thrown down by refusing to pass the Budget. The decision of the Government for an immediate dissolution set the parties in battle array. Mr. Asquith and Mr. Balfour, the opposing champions, were greeted with martial enthusiasm as they took their places, their respective followers rising to do them honour. There had been doubts as to whether the Prime Minister, a lover of compromise, who had no taste for violent issues, possessed the qualities for a fight to a finish. His action dispelled those doubts at this crisis. I have never known any leader by a speech excite a party to a higher pitch of political fervour. Even Gladstone never produced a greater effect.

Mr. Balfour stood by the Peers in a fearless attitude. He had been suffering from a chill, and while Mr. Asquith was speaking, he coughed and tapped his chest, took a tablet, and sniffed a restorative, but if his reply lacked vigour, it entertained the Opposition with its light-hearted irony. According to the Prime Minister, the Peers had referred the Budget to the people not because they loved the people, but because they hated the Budget. Thereupon the Unionist leader attributed to Liberals the election motto : " The Lords have insulted you by asking your opinion ; give such a vote that your opinion will never be asked again."

The general election of January, 1910, having resulted, although by a reduced majority, in favour of the Government, the Peers gave way on the Finance Bill, while the next stage in the constitutional struggle was opened. With ardent hopes on the part of Liberals and Nationalists, who expected to achieve all their aims when the hereditary House was brought to its knees, and who held up the hands of the Ministers when these appeared to waver, resolutions to curtail the veto of the Lords were, in spite of the resolute, undespairing resistance of the Unionists, adopted by the Commons. There was a long truce after the death of King Edward, as it was considered undesirable to vex a new, inexperienced Sovereign with the question of the contingent exercise of the royal prerogative to carry out the will of the people. A Conference of leading representatives of the Government and the Opposition made a protracted effort to settle the question, but after twenty-one sittings it ended without arriving at an agreement. Another appeal to the country followed in December, and this leaving the relative positions unchanged, Mr. Asquith proceeded to carry out his plans by means of the Parliament Bill.

MR. ASQUITH SILENCED.—The debates on the Bill in the summer of 1911 were very acrimonious and heated, and passion reached the boiling point when the Prime Minister intimated that the King was prepared to exercise his prerogative to secure its passage. This meant that if it were rejected by the Upper House, it would be re-introduced, and new Peers would be created in number sufficient to carry it. When the Prime Minister rose to make a statement in justification of the advice he had given to the Sovereign, the resentment of the Unionists was violently displayed. Except for the *mêlée* of 1893, it was the most disorderly scene witnessed till then by any living person. Persistent cries of " Divide " and taunting exclamations prevented Mr. Asquith from delivering his speech. For twenty minutes he stood at the table before he could get a sentence completed. He uttered a few words at every lull in the storm, but the lull was followed by a fresh outburst, and after struggling for nearly three-quarters of an hour he abandoned his attempt. Never before, in modern times at all events, had a leader of the House been thus silenced and insulted. Liberals did not retaliate during a speech from Mr. Balfour, but when, after a dignified rebuke to the Unionists from Sir Edward Grey, Mr. F. E. Smith, the future Lord Chancellor, tried to continue the controversy, they subjected him to Mr. Asquith's fate, and the Speaker was obliged to adjourn the House on account of the disorder.

Would the Lords who had clung tenaciously to their powers pass a bill to enable Acts of Parliament to be placed on the statute book without their assent ? Would they yield to the threat of a large creation of Peers, or would they take the risk of resistance to the death ? That was the question of an exciting year. Although the Commons had their impassioned debates on the Bill and their noisy scenes, as well as prolonged controversies on the National Insurance scheme, it was in the other place that the most dramatic and fateful events occurred.

THE MARQUIS OF LANSDOWNE.—At this crisis a heavy responsibility rested on the Marquis of Lansdowne. During the years of opposition to the Governments of Sir Henry Campbell-Bannerman and Mr. Asquith, he was the most influential figure in the House of Lords. With the exception of the short interval in which the Duke of Devonshire occupied the position, he had, since the Marquis of Salisbury's retirement, led the Unionist peers. Whoever might be the official leader at a time when

Liberalism was more hated and less powerful in the hereditary Chamber than ever before, its real leader was the Marquis of Lansdowne, who had an overwhelming force at his command.

There was something uncanny in his power. He was one of the masters of the State. The Government might propose, but he could dispose. Dapper in figure, with the manners of a French aristocrat, cold and precise, he treated Liberal Ministers with the polite condescension which Elizabeth Bennet disliked in Mr. Darcy. He had had a long and varied career. A Whig by descent and sentiment, and early in life a colleague of Gladstone, he had been Governor-General of Canada and Viceroy of India, and after a much-criticized term as Secretary for War in the Unionist Administration, he had found his true vocation in the office of Foreign Secretary. Subsequently, from the front Opposition bench, he directed the action of the Peers, his frigid phrases in scorn or defiance of the Government arousing as warlike cheers as might have followed Shakespeare's battle harangues.

On the Unionist side also were veterans who had begun their official careers under Disraeli— Lord St. Aldwyn, reserved but respected, and Lord Halsbury, an obstinate Tory with great force of character. Among Peers whose eyes were still to the future were Lord Curzon, the brilliant ex-Viceroy of India, with gifts of imagination and oratory, and Lord Selborne, an earnest-minded man of the familiar governing type, who had married a Cecil and shared the Cecil zeal for Church and who was regarded as a rival to Lord Curzon for the succession to the Unionist leadership of their House, while observers thought that the Earl of Derby, shrewd, smiling and safe, might go further than either. Facing them, as a rule, in the chief place on the Government bench, was the Marquis of Crewe, courteous and cultured, slow and fastidious in speech, rubbing and rolling his hands as he waited for the right, felicitous word. Lord Morley added distinction to that bench, and in Lord Crewe's illness it fell to the author of the " jingle " —as he called it—about ending or mending the House of Lords, to act as its leader and pilot through it a bill which neither ended nor mended it, but fettered it, while Lord Rosebery, who had tried his hand at mending, looked on sadly from the front cross seat.

Ever memorable was the scene in the Gilded Chamber when the fate of the Parliament Bill was decided. Viewing discretion as the better part of valour, the Marquis of Lansdowne, with the approval of Mr. Balfour, advised his friends not to insist on vital amendments. For once there was doubt whether his advice, so distasteful to the whole of the Unionists, would be taken by an adequate number. Lord Rosebery, although prepared to yield and then quit the scene of surrender, expressed the indignation of the vast majority of the House at the pressure which, as they assumed, had been put upon the King, recently seated on the throne, to assent to the creation of a large body of new peers. Like him, a considerable number of proud men subordinated their prepossessions to a sense of the danger of resistance. On the other hand, a section, led by Lord Halsbury, to whom encouragement was sent by Mr. Joseph Chamberlain from his retirement, were prepared to die in the last ditch in defence of their powers. Many who took no part in the ordinary business of the House, and who were rarely seen in it—the backwood peers they

were called—came up from the country to resist
and damn the consequences.

THE LAST ACT.—The division which, in Lord
Morley's words, ended the last act of this particular
play, took place at eleven o'clock on the night of
August 10, 1911. " Dramas are not made by
words, but are made by situations," remarked one
who had a good eye for a political drama, and
certainly the various scenes in the play now closing
had been thrilling enough. Till the curtain was
about to fall, the spectator did not know what the
end was to be. Lord Lansdowne, having decided
to take no part in the division, the majority of the
Unionist peers followed him out when the question
was put. There remained on the one side the die-
hards and on the other side the Liberals and such
Unionists as were prepared in prudence to vote
for a bill they detested. As the two lines emerged
from the division lobbies, one by the throne and
the other by the bar, abstaining peers watched the
scene through the glass of the doors at the upper
end of the Chamber. Peeresses looked down from
the balconies and members of the House of Commons
crowded their galleries. Ministers, after voting,
waited the result with anxious faces. It was seen
that the division was close, but when the last of
the die-hards had passed the tellers, the Government
were soon relieved to know that the number was
exceeded at the other exit. There were hurrahs
never before heard in our time in that stately
House when the Lord Chancellor announced the
figures, showing that by 131 to 114 the peers had
decided not to insist on their amendments.

UNIONIST LEADERSHIP.—When Mr. Balfour
resigned the Unionist leadership at the end of 1911,

his party were looking forward to office. He had faced the hostile Parliament of 1906 with patience and courage, and now his force was equal to the Liberals, although the Government had a large majority with the alliance of the Irish and Labour, but although he had always been equal to an emergency, his health was not able to bear a long, steady strain. Moreover, he had never secured the full confidence of the Tariff Reform " whole-hoggers," and a section of his followers wanted a more militant leadership than he displayed in connection with the Parliament Act. Probably he was less alarmed than they were by that revolutionary measure. But whatever may have been the considerations which influenced him, and whatever may have been the political views of his party, Mr. Asquith expressed the views of every section of the House when he spoke of the irreparable loss his resignation would cause in its daily life.

The succession to the leadership seemed to lie between Mr. Walter Long and Mr. Austen Chamberlain. Both were honourably ready to place their services at the disposal of the party. Mr. Long, an admirable specimen of the enlightened country squires who devote themselves to public affairs, had many qualifications for a post to which his long career gave him a claim. An experienced Parliamentarian and administrator, a champion of the landed interest and a resolute defender of the Union, a Conservative with an instinct for compromise, he would have made a safe, shrewd, sensible leader. Verbose but spirited in speech, he was skilful in the conduct of business, and in the warmest controversy fair and courteous to opponents. In the best sense " an English gentleman," he had been for many years one of the most popular figures in the House.

Mr. Austen Chamberlain, younger than Mr. Long, with a more finished style of speech, and the inheritor of his father's doctrines on Tariff Reform, was preferred by a section of the party. The son of a political leader suffers a disadvantage in the public view. His advancement is attributed to his father's influence. Mr. Austen Chamberlain owed his early opportunities to the fact that he was Mr. Joseph Chamberlain's son, and no doubt consideration for his father accelerated his promotion. But every office to which he was appointed he filled with credit. Conscientious and painstaking in his devotion to the life for which he had been trained from early years, he matured slowly but matured steadily.

When father and son were together in the House the one was the mirror of the other. Both were carefully " groomed." Till the lounge suit came into fashion, the young man, like the elder, wore a frock-coat, with the same sort of tie and collar as his father wore, and, like him, he used a single eye-glass, the only departure from paternal example being the absence of the orchid, which was so familiar to the last generation. Although Mr. Austen Chamberlain never attained his father's quickness or incisiveness in debate, his speeches grew in pith and effectiveness. With a capable grasp of business and a correct Parliamentary manner, he, too, would have been a leader of whom his party would not be ashamed. Ten years, however, passed before the post fell to him.

Mr. Bonar Law.—While the supporters—almost equally divided—of Mr. Long and Mr. Chamberlain

were canvassing their claims, the eyes of certain
members fell on Mr. Bonar Law, and it being found
that the party would unite on his election, the two
friendly rivals, recognizing that harm might be
done to the common cause by a ballot, which was
thought to be inevitable, withdrew their candidature.  Thus the Presbyterian minister's son, the
man trained in business, who was known only to a
limited circle before his election to Parliament in
1900, who had never been in a Cabinet, and was not
in the inner set at the direction of Unionist policy,
became the leader of the party of the Aristocracy,
the Church and the Land.  He had quickly made
his mark as a debater ; after being two years in the
House he had been drawn from below the gangway
to the Treasury Bench as Secretary to the Board
of Trade, and by strength of conviction and speech
he had, in and out of office, rapidly advanced in
repute, especially among Tariff Reformers.  Perhaps
some of those who acquiesced in his election looked
upon him as a stop-gap.  They may have acted
on the assumption that when their party obtained
office Lord Lansdowne would be Prime Minister
and that his choice of colleagues would determine
who should hold the chief place in the Commons.
So comparatively unfamiliar was the new leader's
name that after his appointment his private
secretary had to inform inquirers that Bonar was
sounded like Bonner.

As a speaker Mr. Bonar Law has distinguished
himself by dispensing with notes.  This is not an
unprecedented practice on the part of a great
Parliamentarian.  As Lord Rosebery has recorded,
Fox never used notes and Pitt rarely.  Palmerston's
famous " Roman citizen " speech in the Don
Pacifico debate, a speech which lasted " from the

dusk of one day to the dawn of the next," was
delivered without the help of a note. Neither
Disraeli nor the Marquis of Salisbury required
manuscript for their most polished speeches. Mr.
Fawcett, the blind Postmaster-General, showed
how a mass of figures can be stored and arranged
in the memory. Nevertheless, the feat on Mr.
Bonar Law's part has added to the impression of
his cleverness. One of his colleagues has described
how he " formulates in his mind the sequence of
his argument in the very words in which it is to be
expressed, and then by a series of mental rehearsals
makes himself as much master of the whole subject
as if he read it from a manuscript on the table."
The practice is not free from danger, and Mr.
Law has occasionally made mistakes in figures as
well as in literary quotations. His quotations,
although limited in range, are usually apt and
interesting. Carlyle, especially in *The French
Revolution*, has supplied him with many.

Mr. Bonar Law's leadership began with the
operation of the Parliament Act. To prevent the
passing of Home Rule, or any other opposed measure
under that obnoxious statute, was the object on
which he concentrated his efforts. He assured
Ulster of full Unionist support in her resistance,
Liberals charged him with encouragement of armed
rebellion,* and in respect of the Curragh incident
with encouragement of military revolt against
constitutional authority. Supported by what
became the largest party in the State he did not
waver or hesitate. He carried opposition to the
most extreme point, and his attacks on Ministers,
and especially on Mr. Asquith, exceeded in

* " If you like to call it rebellion," said Mr. Law, " no rebellion
which has ever taken place in the world was better justified."

vehemence and acrimony those hurled at Gladstone or Joseph Chamberlain.

Violent scenes were frequent in those days when Mr. Bonar Law stood at the table rapping the box, scolding the Government, pouring scorn on Mr. Churchill, telling Mr. Lloyd George that the one object of his life was the winning of elections, warning Mr. Asquith of the danger of being lynched on a lamp-post, declaring that the Ministers were bartering the interests of the State for party objects.  He brought charges of political corruption against them.  He called them tricksters and a set of gamblers, he attributed to them the methods of the Artful Dodger.  The more vehement his attacks the louder were the cheers of his followers.  Certain Conservative aristocrats, it was whispered, did not admire the Parliamentary style of their middle-class leader from the Clyde, " the uncontrolled of speech," like Thersites, but in the House of Commons the party as a rule followed him enthusiastically.  It has been said that members " grow, like hounds, fond of the man who shows them sport, and by whose halloo they are used to be encouraged."  The Unionists wanted sport and Mr. Bonar Law provided them with it.

THE PARLIAMENTARY MACHINE.—It seemed in November, 1912, that the Parliamentary machine might break down.  The Government, having been defeated on a financial resolution relating to the Home Rule Bill, proposed on the following day to rescind the decision which had been arrived at, as they contended, by a snap division.  This course led to deliberate disorder.  Mr. Bonar Law refused to recognize the occupants of the Treasury bench as the Government of the country.  They were, he said, simply a body of personages who by deception had usurped absolute power. When the Attorney General, Sir Rufus Isaacs, tried to reply, the uproar was so great that the sitting had to be suspended for an hour. On its resumption the disorder was renewed, and consequently the Speaker, declaring it was quite obvious the Opposition had determined not to allow further business, adjourned the House. After he left the chair many Unionists stood and jeered at the departing Ministers. An irate member of the Opposition took from the table a small volume and flung it at Mr. Churchill, striking him on the face. Mr. Churchill glared angrily and moved as if he would rush towards his assailant, but colleagues restrained him, and next day the offender made apology.

The strain on the machine was very great from 1912 to 1914. Truly our men in Parliament turned their sport to earnest

"With a visage of the sternest."

There was very little relaxation at any time in the sternness of the conflict. It was sustained with extreme bitterness and there were frequent hours of passion. While the Unionists were angry and resentful, seeking by every means to force an appeal to the country, the Liberals and their allies were dogged and determined, pressing forward to their goal. Radical and Labour members warned Mr. Bonar Law of the danger of his defiant doctrines, but he and his followers, believing the majority of the people of Great Britain were with them, never relaxed their resistance to the Government or their obstruction of the Home Rule Bill, the Welsh Disestablishment Bill and the Plural Voting Bill.

Mr. Lloyd George continued to be an object of attack. Criticism of his Insurance scheme was followed by severe censure of its administration and by denunciation of his land policy. Mr. Asquith was, however, most steadily assailed, as it was he who was chiefly responsible for the use made of the Parliament Act. On his own side he was staunchly supported, his conduct in the constitutional crisis and in the events which sprang out of it exciting enthusiasm in his party.

A scene in which the leader of the Opposition came into conflict with the Speaker occurred in May, 1914, at the third reading, in the third session, of the Home Rule Bill. There was a running fire of exclamations. The Ministers were bombarded with offensive epithets, and a Unionist, who was afterwards a member of Government, described the Premier as an old gentleman who could not make up his mind. Constant cries of " Adjourn " from scores of throats stopped the proceedings. At last the Speaker, turning to the leader of the Opposition, from whom assistance in the conduct of business is expected in normal times, gravely asked if the members behind him were acting with his assent and approval. Mr. Bonar Law rose at once to reply. " I would not presume to criticize what you consider your duty, Sir," he said, " but I know mine, and that is not to answer any such question." Reflection convinced the Speaker that he himself in the difficulty of the moment was " betrayed into an expression " which he ought not to have used, but the significant fact was that, when Mr. Bonar Law declined to assist him, many Unionists in delight sprang to their feet and shouted and waved hats and papers. On that occasion again, on account of the refusal of the Opposition to allow business to proceed, the sitting was suspended.

What would have happened if war had not for a time put an end to violent domestic dissension it is impossible to say.

# CHAPTER X

## THE WAYS OF A CABINET

THE excitement at the formation of a Cabinet has been vividly described by Sir George Trevelyan. He depicts " the stir; the gossip; the political clubs, swarming with groups of talkers, who exchange morsels of news and of criticism in eager whispers; the hansom cabs dashing about Belgravia and Mayfair, or waiting for hours together at the door of the incoming Premier; the ever increasing discomfort of eminent statesmen who sit in their studies, waiting for the possible arrival of a Treasury messenger; the cosy dinners at the houses of the new Ministers, growing larger and merrier daily as another and yet another Right Honourable gentleman is added to the number of the elect."* That is a picture drawn in the Victorian age, but although the area from which the " elect " are chosen is no longer limited to Mayfair and Belgravia the emotions are the same. The hopes and gratifications, the ambitions and disappointments of " eminent statesmen " ever provide matter for the gossip and speculation of the clubs and not less for the entertainment of the cynic. Certain men are sure of a summons and the most influential receive the positions they desire, but there are others who wait in their studies in vain.

* *Life and Letters of Lord Macaulay.*

Gladstone declared that the Cabinet as a great organ of government had in his time found its final shape, attributes, functions and permanent ordering. A daring spirit under the stress of war laid revolutionary hands on the system of tradition. In the organ of government with which Gladstone was content were included all the statesmen of the front rank closely associated with the Prime Minister and the heads of the principal departments, and each shared in and was responsible for the decisions of the whole. Mr. Lloyd George thrust convention aside when, instead of the body familiar in peace, he formed a War Cabinet consisting originally of only five members, all except one without portfolios. From this supreme set were excluded even the Secretaries of State, among whom was an ex-Premier, Mr. Balfour. " An inner Cabinet," as Lord Rosebery has noted, " is not unfamiliar to us ; and, as the members constituting Cabinets increase, it must become a recognized institution." What Mr. Lloyd George created was not an inner Cabinet. His War Cabinet was not responsible to, nor could its decisions be reviewed by, any larger organ of government.

To the " hoary quidnuncs of politics " this innovation gave a shock. Adopted as a war expedient, it would, if continued after the war, have been a step backward from the process that had gone on since Walpole established the Cabinet on a definite footing. A plan under which the heads of great departments and Ministers of first-rate importance ceased to meet regularly in Council and might have no share in the shaping of policy, tended, in the opinion of the hoary quidnuncs, to shake that joint responsibility which had enabled the Government to overcome the personal power of the Crown and was essential to the proper control of the Executive by the House of Commons. They were alarmed at the abandonment of an arrangement by which, as a historian observes, " the most important business of every office, and especially such business as is likely to be the subject of discussion in Parliament, is brought under the consideration of the whole Ministry." The adoption of the new plan and the debates on it brought into relief certain features of the inherited system and led ordinary persons to take a greater interest in that system and to appreciate its significance.

The Cabinet handed down by precedent and practice to the twentieth century has appealed to the imagination of the people by its power and prestige along with the mystery surrounding it. Admission to Downing Street has been the aim of all able and ambitious politicians. " In the closet," as Macaulay points out, " Ministers speak with the authority of men who stand high in the estimation of the representatives of the people. In Parliament they speak with the authority of men versed in great affairs and acquainted with all the secrets of State." And no less remarkable than the authority of the Cabinet has been its procedure. " A secret Council, on the Venetian model, and sworn to absolute silence "—that is a description of it given by Lord Rosebery. Its decisions are communicated first to the Sovereign and they are made publicly known when considered expedient by the head of the Government. A Minister on resigning who desires for his vindication to refer to its proceedings can only do so with the permission of the Sovereign. " I am not going to answer any question as to what was done in the Cabinet," said Mr. Asquith in March, 1914, when cross-examined

about a document which had been under consideration at Downing Street.

Where is Downing Street ? asks the keen
politician from the country. To him it is one of
the sights of London and it gives a thrill such as the
Abbey gives. " It is the smallest and at the same
time the greatest street in the world," said an
American ambassador at a Lord Mayor's banquet,
" because it lies at the hub of that gigantic wheel
which encircles the globe under the name of the
British Empire." Here, in the Prime Minister's
residence, the Cabinet has, as a rule, although not
always, met. Wellington held Cabinets at Apsley
House. The historic " Torpid Council " of June,
1854, at which the Government drifted into the
Crimean enterprise, took place at Lord John
Russell's residence, Pembroke Lodge, Richmond
Park. Sir Algernon West, who was Gladstone's
private secretary, has recalled the Ministers meeting
" everywhere." " In Bertram Currie's house in
Combe Wood is a brass tablet recording how a
Cabinet was held there during a visit of Mr. Gladstone's." The Cabinet at which Beaconsfield's
Government, in March, 1880, decided to dissolve,
met, on account of Salisbury's illness, at the Foreign
Secretary's house in Arlington Street. Mr. Lloyd
George on one occasion summoned Ministers to his
house at Cobham. Salisbury's Cabinets were held
at the Foreign Office and this arrangement was
continued by Mr. Balfour. It was there that
Ministers assembled in the autumn of 1903 when,
although their chief had Chamberlain's own resignation in his pocket, the Free Trade protagonists
also were allowed to resign. Usually, however, the
Cabinet has met in its room at No. 10, Downing Street, the plain, modest building with rail-

ings at the area and a knocker on the door.

No 10 has been described by a German writer as a mean-looking abode in a blind alley. Our own country visitors who expect to see a palatial building are astonished when it is pointed out to them. Viewed from the Horse Guards Parade its considerable size is better appreciated than in Downing Street. Yet from any point it is unpretentious enough to satisfy that pride of Englishmen which apes humility. They are gratified to think that so modest a house represents a world power so vast. Sir George Downing, an American colonist who came over to the mother country and held various posts under Cromwell and Charles the Second, received the grant of the ground from the merry monarch and built what were then considered mansions, with " back fronts " to St. James's Park. On its passing to the Crown in the next century a life tenancy of No. 10 was given to Bothmar, the Hanoverian Minister. When Bothmar died, George the Second offered the house to Walpole, and on his declining it as a personal gift, it was devoted in perpetuity to the use of the First Lord of the Treasury. In many cases, though not in all, since then it has been occupied by the head of the Government.

Here Pitt worked, read despatches and received his agents. Here Whigs and Tories alternated last century. Disraeli and Gladstone lived here. Salisbury preferred his own residence and did his work during the greater part of his Administration at the Foreign Office, going later to the Privy Seal Office. Campbell-Bannerman, as I have already noted, died at No. 10. Here Mr. Asquith's Cabinet held the fateful meetings which determined our entrance on the Great War and here Mr. Lloyd

George's War Cabinet met.  Portraits of departed Ministers look down in No. 10 on their successors, reminding them that while the State endures parties change and men pass, that reputations great to-day may be low to-morrow, that power and popularity are transitory, that in the long view of history he serves his party best who serves the country best.

" Went to Disraeli's after breakfast," wrote Lord Malmesbury in February, 1852, " and found him in a state of delight at the idea of coming into office. He said he ' felt just like a young girl going to her first ball,' constantly repeating, ' Now we have got a status.' " *  The letters and diaries of other statesmen record their self-complacency and pride on sitting for the first time at the table in the Council Chamber.  According to Theodore Hook " an hour's inhalation of the atmosphere of Downing Street affects some men with giddiness, others with blindness, and very frequently with the most oblivious forgetfulness."  As they take their places among His Majesty's confidential servants they feel a new sense of distinction and power.  Before they reach the Cabinet they may be often seen in the Lobby of the House of Commons.  Afterwards most of them disdain the company of ordinary mortals.  If they go to the Lobby they carry their greatness as a cloak, ostentatiously wrapping it around the secrets of State.

The Ministers, as Lord Chancellor Selborne has recorded and as is still the practice, usually sit in the same place, while Sir Algernon West has told us that Gladstone would sometimes draw on a sheet of paper a plan of the table with the seats to be occupied by himself and his colleagues indicated on it.  In the Coalition Cabinet of 1915–16 Mr.

* *Memoirs of an Ex-Minister.*

Asquith had the Marquis of Lansdowne on his right hand and Lord Kitchener on his left, and when the great soldier was drowned, Mr. Walter Long sat in his place. The counting of heads on a question of policy is probably rare. In the first two years after the war, as I have heard, there were at least half-a-dozen occasions on which a vote was taken, and it is said that not only was this done, but Mr. Lloyd George asked each colleague to give his reason. The ultimate decision, however, naturally rests with the Prime Minister. Those members of the Government who disagree with him resign, if the question is important enough. In the event of the majority of the Cabinet or a number of his principal colleagues refusing to acquiesce in his decision, he can bring the Government to an end or reconstruct it.

Till Mr. Lloyd George introduced a Secretariat no official record or minute of Cabinet proceedings was kept. Gladstone held that no member except the Prime Minister was entitled to make a note of what occurred. Biographies show that others kept diaries for their own vindication or the benefit of posterity. Lord Derby while Foreign Secretary in Disraeli's Government took notes at Cabinet meetings, holding that there was no objection to temporary memoranda for personal use, but he gave an undertaking to his chief that all would be destroyed.* The practice described by Gladstone was observed till the present reign. " It is the inflexible, unwritten rule," said Mr. Asquith, " that no member of the Cabinet should take any note or record of its decisions except the Prime Minister, and he does so for the purpose of sending his letter to the King." Presumably the motive of the rule

* *Life of Disraeli:* Buckle.

was that memoranda might fall into unauthorized and improper hands.

A lack of precision and clearness in the decisions if not in the deliberations of the Cabinet sometimes resulted from its procedure. Every one has heard the well-known story that at the end of the Council which agreed to propose a fixed duty on corn, Melbourne put his back to the door and said : " Now is it to lower the price of corn or isn't it ? It is not much matter which we say, but mind we must all say the same." Ministers have on various occasions carried away from their table conflicting recollections. This occurred, as Mr. Buckle has shown, in the case of a Cabinet meeting in 1878 regarding the Indian Expedition to the Mediterranean and the occupation of Cyprus. Again, in the case of the private negotiations with Parnell in 1882, Hartington wrote to Gladstone : " My impression was that the Council expressed a very strong opinion against their continuance," and the Prime Minister replied : " My recollection about the Cabinet is that there was informal conversation about it, but not any decision of any kind." * Misunderstanding among members of Mr. Balfour's Cabinet with regard to the resignations on the fiscal question led to controversy with the head of the Government. There appeared again to be looseness of procedure at No. 10 in respect of the Curragh affair in March, 1914. The Secretary for War was at the Palace while his colleagues were considering the draft of a letter to be handed to General Gough, and on returning to Downing Street after the other Ministers had gone to lunch, he added two paragraphs in consultation with Lord Morley who entered the Council room to note the

* *Life of the Duke of Devonshire* : Bernard Holland.

terms of the declaration which he was to make in the House of Lords. Subsequently the Cabinet repudiated the added paragraphs. Its management of this matter might have ruined it but for Mr. Asquith's Parliamentary adroitness.

Very modern people cavil at secrecy. They can understand why it should be insisted upon in grave international affairs, in fixing of taxes and military decisions, but in general domestic concerns they think Ministers make a fetish of secrecy for the sake of their self-importance or to gratify autocratic sentiment. Lovers of orderly government, on the other hand, approve of the traditional reserve. There are obvious reasons for the avoidance and dislike of publicity on Cabinet differences. These, it is believed, are likely to be accentuated if attended by Press " stunts " or popular clamour, because in such circumstances a minority at Downing Street may have increased difficulty in acquiescing in the view of the majority. Secrecy is insisted upon by the head of a Government also in cases of resignation or offers of resignation by colleagues. Resignation, described by Lord Rosebery as the *ultima ratio* of statesmen, is, as we know from memoirs, frequently threatened. Palmerston, it has been said, set his library chimney on fire in the process of burning Gladstone's letters of resignation, and it is suggested that in more recent times a similar effect might have been produced by similar letters from another restless Minister. These features of Cabinet life are as a rule hidden from public view. Their disclosure might disturb confidence in the Government. For its full authority a belief in its general harmony is necessary and opposition to its policy on any point might be strengthened by the knowledge that one of the Ministers ultimately responsible for that policy had so far resisted it at Downing Street as to tender his resignation.

The rule of silence has even on high affairs been now and again violated. For instance, there was complaint of a leakage of Cabinet secrets during the Russo-Turkish War. On the whole, however, as one Prime Minister after another has testified, the rule has been wonderfully observed. Long-enduring interest was excited by a supposed sensational breach of it. The revelation of Peel's intention to repeal the Corn Laws provided George Meredith with dramatic material for *Diana of the Crossways*. For many years rumour asserted that the secret was sold to the editor of *The Times* by Mrs. Norton, who had it from Sidney Herbert. This story owed a long life to Meredith's novel, but has been completely discredited. The fact is, that Peel's intention was communicated openly and deliberately to Delane by Lord Aberdeen with his chief's consent, in order, as Greville says, that the report might go over to America and influence the Oregon question. But even on that occasion all the facts were not disclosed. Delane, although told of Peel's decision in favour of Repeal, was not informed that the Ministry had resigned and that Lord John Russell was to be sent for.

" We know," the *Spectator* said some years ago, " of no instance of Cabinet gossip getting out owing to a wife's indiscretion." It may be suggested that secrets are kept by the wives of Ministers for the reason that they were kept by Harry Hotspur's wife—" thou wilt not utter what thou dost not know." This is a reflection on the discretion of the ladies. Published memoirs in various generations prove that members of Cabinets have written freely to their wives concerning State affairs, and it may be assumed that in conversation they have been equally confidential.

" I can't think who puts these things in," a Minister may sometimes say with better reason than Crummles. Occasionally irritation is caused to great men by the enterprise of the newspapers. Disraeli was extremely annoyed by the disclosure, on the morning before its introduction, of the details of the Reform Bill of 1859 ; and Gladstone, who was a stickler for all the Cabinet conventions, was very indignant at any leakage. Although there is less strictness in our own day and lobbyists of the House of Commons are occasionally privileged to give an intelligent forecast of Government intentions, reserve is still practised to a high degree on many matters. Not only is Parliament jealous of its right to the first information, but Ministers naturally dislike any revelation that would lessen interest in their own announcements. Such forecasts as they sanction only serve to whet anticipation. Secrecy is, as a rule, secured in the case of the Budget. Predictions of some of its contents may be made, but until it is opened by the Chancellor of the Exchequer the country is kept in doubt. This is a marked instance of the reserve of Downing Street, for the details must be known days if not weeks beforehand to a considerable number of persons. The Civil Servants, of course, are above suspicion, and however communicative members of a Cabinet may be on other subjects, they are usually impenetrable with regard to the finance proposals of the year.

Ministers have been charged with giving information to newspapers in order to secure support for their own plans or ambitions. The using of the Press in Cabinet controversy is considered improper by the fastidious, but it is too much to expect that statesmen with strong views will conceal them from sympathetic editors. Intimate relations between Ministers and the Press did not end with Delane nor begin with Lord Northcliffe. When Dilke became Under-Secretary for Foreign Affairs, John Morley, as editor of the *Pall Mall Gazette*, asked his friend to see him and give him information on the general position of foreign affairs and he consented to do so. " It would be worth silver and gold and jewels," Morley said, " if I could have ten minutes with you about three times a week." The similar privilege that Chamberlain gave him with reference to domestic policy " he used so well "—say Dilke's biographers *—" that no complaint ever arose in regard to it." There was a complaint in the case of the articles demanding Forster's withdrawal from the Irish Office, but Chamberlain, on being accused of inspiring these articles, replied that Morley was one of the most independent men in the kingdom. So is every great editor ! And Government is conducted on the assumption that every Minister is an honourable man. A breach of confidence hurtful to the State, an unscrupulous disclosure by a Minister prejudicial to a colleague has been of very rare occurrence. " It was," said Lord Morley, speaking as one who had acted in both capacities, " only those shallow ill-natures, who mistook ill-nature for knowledge of the world, who regarded with any suspicion or doubt the perfect fairness and the freedom from abuse of those relations which, so far as he knew, existed between Ministers and editors of powerful journals."

The relations of the Cabinet with the Sovereign are hedged round by convention. Sir Gilbert

* *The Life of Sir Charles W. Dilke.*

Elliot, writing in 1798 to Lady Elliot with reference to the marriage of William Windham, said : " It seems that there is an etiquette which requires that Cabinet Ministers should acquaint the King with their intention to marry and the King appears to have been his only confidant." Whether this etiquette has been observed in later times or not, we know that Queen Victoria exacted personal propriety of life from those employed as her confidential servants. The knowledge that she would object to a certain politician was sufficient to prevent his name being submitted for office. By this attitude indeed Her Majesty strengthened the prestige of the Cabinet and there is no reason to doubt that a high standard and strict observance of convention have been maintained by her successors.

In the Queen's reign the Cabinet seemed to be as sacred as an ark of the covenant. Her statesmen were content with it and the public regarded it with awe. No person living at the end of the Victorian era could have imagined that in less than twenty years a system so firmly set would by the stress of war be suspended.

CABINET IN WAR.—No such terrible question was ever discussed at Downing Street as that which demanded an instant answer from Mr. Asquith and his colleagues at the beginning of August, 1914. The next generation may obtain an account of their deliberations which will enable it to realize their individual thoughts and temper. People may learn then what differences there were and how opinion moved towards the great decision on the fateful Saturday and Sunday. Kinglake has asserted that most of the members of Lord Aberdeen's Cabinet were " overcome with sleep " on the summer

evening when the Duke of Newcastle read the
despatch recommending to Lord Raglan the expedition against Sebastopol, which received from
the Ministers " the kind of approval often awarded
to an unobjectionable sermon." A picture of
another decision between peace and war has been
presented by Lord Morley in the *Life of Gladstone*.
It relates to the question of our intervention on
behalf of Denmark against Prussia in 1864. At the
Council on that occasion Palmerston, the Prime
Minister, "held his head down while the talk
proceeded and then at last looking up said in a
neutral voice, ' I think the Cabinet is against war.' "
It will be interesting when the diaries and letters of
1914 give up their secrets to learn about the
demeanour of our statesmen when, largely through
the influence of Mr. Asquith and Sir Edward Grey,
they came without avoidable delay to the gravest
resolution in the history of the country.

A " collection of the heads of departments at
sparse intervals to discuss hurriedly topics, for
which they are often unprepared." There may
have been sarcasm in this description of the
Cabinet given by Lord Rosebery in 1899. If it were
exact, then indeed the system was inappropriate
to war. " A First Minister," Lord Rosebery further
wrote, " has only the influence with the Cabinet
which is given him by his personal arguments, his
personal qualities and his personal weight. But
this is not all. All his colleagues he must convince,
some he may have to humour, some even to cajole :
a harassing, laborious and ungracious task."* For
such a task Mr. Asquith was eminently fitted by tact,
judgment, patience and a spirit of compromise. But
it was not a task for which war gave opportunity.

* *Sir Robert Peel*, reproduced from *Anglo-Saxon Review*.

17

For about four months the higher direction of military operations, as the Dardanelles Commission reported, was vested in the Cabinet, assisted by the Committee of Imperial Defence. This was a Committee of Ministers with some experts added and " the responsibility for important decisions remained theoretically in all, and practically in most, cases with the united Cabinet." A War Council at the end of November, 1914, took the place of the Committee, and although not materially different in composition from it, practically decided the most important matters, but still, theoretically at least, the full body of Ministers retained the ultimate power. The formation of the Coalition by Mr. Asquith in May, 1915, was followed by the appointment of a War Committee of the Cabinet. It was stated on authority at a later period that the decisions of this Committee were never altered by the supreme twenty-three Ministers. At the time, however, the intervention of the twenty-three was suspected.

Cabinets had on account of the extension of Government cares and duties grown to an unwieldy size. Pitt carried on the great war against France with a Cabinet of seven or nine, although its exiguity in size, as Mr. Asquith pointed out, did not prevent it from committing great blunders or from suffering many strokes of ill-fortune. Peel's Cabinet of 1841 contained fifteen members and for half a century this number was considered adequate. There were only twelve in Disraeli's Cabinet in 1874 and fourteen in Gladstone's six years later. Salisbury's Coalition Cabinet of 1895 consisted of nineteen and on its reconstruction in 1900 it had twenty. There were nineteen in the Cabinet formed by Campbell-Bannerman. " The twenty-three " of Mr. Asquith's

Coalition, which included representatives of three parties, excited the daily sarcasms of scribes and politicians.

Critics held that his War Committee, consisting of seven or eight members, was too large and, moreover, they objected to its composition. While the Prime Minister was accused of a " Wait and See " temperament, his Cabinet, like that of Lord Aberdeen in the time of the Crimean War, was believed to be lacking in the dæmonic element. In war, said Mr. Lloyd George, you want quick decisions above everything ; and to obtain quick decisions when he himself was called to the helm he set up his small War Cabinet.

" It is good," wrote Bacon, " not to try experiments in States except the necessity be urgent or the utility evident." Whether the experiment of December, 1916, was thus justified was a question on which opinion never reached agreement. The concentration in the War Cabinet of absolute power over all affairs was watched with sympathy by those who had desired a change of Government and with critical curiosity by the Liberals who resented Mr. Asquith's overthrow. Its friends claimed for it that it proved an efficient instrument for the purpose for which it had been devised. On the other hand, independent statesmen of the old school, like the Marquis of Lansdowne, noting the absence from it of heads of departments, lamented the loss of " the good, sound doctrine of the collective responsibility of the Government of the day."

Differences of view and conflicts between departments have been frequent at all times at Downing Street, but, as a rule, a Minister holding opinions at variance with those of his colleagues submits to be overruled, and in such a case, as

Peel observed, he supports the measures which as
an Administration they promulgate.  This cohesion,
encouraged by, and in turn contributing to the
discipline of, the party system gave to the normal
Cabinet irresistible force.  Although collective responsibility was maintained in theory under the
novel regime set up by Mr. Lloyd George, there was
less opportunity than under the regular practice for
the co-ordination of the departments and the
Ministers outside the Cabinet had not quite the
same sense of responsibility for decisions taken at
Downing Street.  While all felt a common loyalty
to the Administration, each limited his concern to
his own office and in it was a law unto himself,
and this tendency was increased by the introduction of Controllers and Directors who were not
members of Parliament.  Some of these men
knew little and cared less about the traditional
Cabinet.

How, the " hoary quidnuncs " asked, were the
heads of the departments to arrange a common
policy without a Cabinet Council ?  It was face-
tiously suggested that the Ministers might meet
periodically at dinner.  This process would not
have lacked precedent.  Walpole, as Lord Morley
records, called meetings of the Cabinet as seldom
as possible.  " His habit was to invite two or three
of his colleagues specially acquainted with the
business in hand to dine with him and then he
settled it.  The regular Cabinet dinner was an
informal device of a later age, marked by the
peculiarity and possible convenience that no minute
of the topics of discussion was necessarily sent to
the Sovereign, as in the case of formal meetings
of the Cabinet.  The Cabinet dinner . . . was in
full vogue during the Aberdeen Government, but

fell into abeyance under Lord Palmerston, who always cared mainly for national defences and foreign relations, and did not choose to sacrifice a social evening to talk about miscellaneous business." For dinner Mr. Lloyd George substituted breakfast as an occasion for intimate consultation with colleagues, experts and friends. Now and again, moreover, there were formal meetings of certain Ministers outside with those inside the War Cabinet. They were summoned, as one of them explained, from time to time to deal with matters on which they were entitled to be heard.

A Domestic Cabinet, a Committee of the Government on Home Affairs, subject to the authority of the supreme body, was one of the innovations of the new system. In the absence of a Council in which Ministers could decide on a policy to which all were committed, they took different courses at some points and disputed in public instead of in private. When the Domestic Cabinet was set up, all home questions requiring the co-operation of two or more departments were referred to it, and it had the power of decision, although the larger matters of policy might be referred at the discretion of the Chairman to the War Cabinet. Little was heard of it in Parliament.

The system of which the War Cabinet formed the pivot was worked with good-will by the men associated with Mr. Lloyd George. Their official existence depended on it and, more important than that consideration, they knew that its failure or discredit would involve new constitutional and political difficulties at a time when attention should not be diverted for a day from the war. It was continued till the end of the struggle and for nearly a year afterwards.

IN PEACE.—For peace the traditional practice was demanded. The full Cabinet was restored in October, 1919, in response to appeals by Coalitionists who saw the defects of the war-time process and feared that the control of the House of Commons would be jeopardized. In form, at any rate, the old system was revived. Even in size the revived Cabinet was the same as in normal times. Whether it was restored in spirit was doubted by many observers. The changes made during the war were bound, as the Government admitted, to have lasting effects. It was doubtful if all the twenty members of the full Cabinet recovered the same opportunities of discussion and decision at Downing Street as the Victorian Ministers possessed. There was a greater tendency to settle matters by groups. Some of the Ministers who had no veneration for "hoary" practices might have been quite content if these were never re-established. They would, as they thought, be much better employed in their own departments than in listening in the Cabinet to discussions on questions about which they knew nothing and in which they had no interest. Anyhow, it seemed as if fuller power than in earlier days rested on a select group of oligarchs and especially on the Prime Minister and the leader of the House of Commons.

One important innovation introduced by Mr. Lloyd George was maintained by the employment of a Cabinet secretariat. Although any member of the Cabinet may secure the mention in the agenda of any question on which he requires a decision, it has been contended that the direct association of the secretariat with the Prime Minister has enhanced his personal power. That is a point to be tested by fuller experience. Meantime one is impressed by the daring character of the innovation. The Secretary, as the Prime Minister has explained, is entrusted with the keeping of national secrets in the same way as members of the Cabinet. All familiar with the old system will understand how complete a departure this is from its spirit. In the old days, as Lord Curzon has observed, the Cabinet was a sort of Star Chamber which sat with closed doors which no one was allowed to penetrate. Within the last few years it has been opened to outside experts. And now there sits regularly in the confidential Chamber one who is not a Minister of the Crown.

A Secretary was specially necessary during the war as a medium between the Cabinet and the departments when these were not represented in it, and his continued employment has been considered desirable for the methodical conduct of business. But that a person not a member of it should be entrusted with its secrets has appeared specially remarkable to those who recall the limitation placed by Queen Victoria on the communication of confidential State documents even to the Prince of Wales. You could imagine Peel and Palmerston, Beaconsfield, Gladstone and Salisbury looking down with amazement and horror on this innovation, just as they might look down with these feelings on the tape with the news of the hour recently introduced at No. 10. Everything new even at Downing Street is not necessarily bad.

# CHAPTER XI

## HOW PARLIAMENT STOOD THE TEST

IF it is a very hard thing, as George Eliot has observed, to say the exact truth even when you have no motive to be false, the difficulty is specially great in recording the strange political events of the time when the country was engaged in its life-and-death struggle and emotions were unusually tense and complicated. We are too near those events to view them with the cool, calm eye of the historian. History will say this, History will say that, confident men declare. But they do not really know. There are some who say—and perhaps believe—that Mr. Asquith, if he had remained in office, would have lost the war. There are others who say—and perhaps believe—that he was sacrificed to faction and intrigue. When opinions so different are held by observers equal in patriotism, the difficulty of saying the exact truth about the temper of Parliament during, and immediately after, the war is apparent.

I have described in the opening chapter the sacred union formed instantly by all parties to defend the State and the scene of lofty patriotism with which the session which opened with domestic dissension closed in September, 1914. At the outbreak of war there was general confidence in the principal members of the Government. In days " more trying perhaps," as Mr. Asquith said,

" than those any body of statesmen for a hundred years have had to pass through " they conducted affairs to the satisfaction of a country jealous of its honour. Mr. Asquith's rare qualities of intellect were recognized. Sir Edward Grey was regarded as the ideal Foreign Secretary. Mr. Lloyd George won the praise of opponents by his emergency financial measures. Mr. Churchill's gifts were supposed to be appropriate to the Admiralty. The heads of other departments were considered to be capable in administration. With the assistance of Lord Kitchener at the War Office the Ministers who had been in power when the emergency occurred were trusted to carry the country through it.

This feeling of confidence did not last long. When the House of Commons met for a fortnight in November the voice of criticism was raised. There were complaints of Government policy in respect of aliens and spies, of the Press Bureau, of the recruiting arrangements, of the allowances to soldiers' wives. Criticism, however, was not as a rule partisan. The Front Opposition Bench was prepared to give the Government a free hand as long as they prosecuted the war with vigour and Unionist statesmen patriotically assisted the Ministers. Mr. Austen Chamberlain, for instance, served on finance committees, and after the war Budget had been submitted, he co-operated with its author to make the proposals as workmanlike as possible, although he found himself so divided from the Chancellor of the Exchequer on the amount of the beer duty that he could not join in responsibility for it.

On the resumption of the session in February, 1915, criticism was loud and sharp. It came chiefly from back-bench Unionists, though also from a Liberal quarter. While the Prime Minister acknowledged the co-operation " patriotic in spirit and inestimable in value " of leading members of the Opposition, Mr. Bonar Law significantly made it clear that they did not share responsibility for the conduct of the war. There were controversies, not always without acrimony, on prices, the supplies of wheat, profiteering, industrial organization, the spy danger and the luxuries alleged to be provided for German officer prisoners. Complaints were made of a lack of vigorous impulse in the Cabinet and doubts began to be whispered with regard to the efficiency of Mr. Asquith's leadership.

SUPPLY OF MUNITIONS.—Spring, with its disappointments at the front, brought ominous signs of Parliamentary discontent. Old party controversies, it is true, were silent. They slumbered, if they were not dead. But many Unionists and a few Radicals, encouraged by a section of the Press, fired almost daily censures at the Government. In debate in April on the supply of explosive shells, Mr. Bonar Law himself was very critical. On this subject much uneasiness had been caused by newspaper articles and the talk of officers home from the front, and it was increased instead of being dispelled by the flat denial * which Mr. Asquith gave at Newcastle to a statement that the operations not only of our own Army, but of our Allies, were being hampered by our failure to provide the necessary munitions.

His denial produced in sceptical minds a feeling that he was not alive to the necessities of the situation, although the object of his visit to the Tyne

* This denial was based, as Mr. Asquith revealed in 1919, on a letter written by Lord Kitchener after a talk with Sir John French.

was to urge the vital need of a large and rapid increase in the output. Next day Mr. Lloyd George told Parliament of the " prodigious things that had been done " already and reproached the fault-finders with not being more generous in recognition of what had been accomplished. On the authority of Lord Kitchener he asserted that the production of high explosives in this country had been placed on a footing which relieved us of all anxiety. In view, however, of subsequent disclosures, Mr. Asquith's Newcastle denial was cast up against him in reproach and it was used to his prejudice.

Events took a sensational turn in the middle of May. On the 12th a Radical by means of a question suggested the admission to the Government of leading members of the various parties. The Prime Minister replied that this step was not contemplated. " I am not aware," he said, " that it would meet with general assent." A few days later *The Times* published a despatch from its military correspondent, Colonel Repington, who was at the front and had exceptional sources of information, containing the statement that the want of an unlimited supply of high explosive shells was a fatal bar to our success. This statement which there was reason to assume represented the feeling of our G.H.Q. in France produced a very great sensation.

It was not then generally known that Sir John French had taken means to have his complaint of a shortage of shells conveyed to leading members of the Opposition, but it became obvious to us all that they were reconsidering their attitude towards the Government. Their friends spoke in the Lobby of Mr. Bonar Law's intention to raise a debate and probably to move for a Committee of Inquiry. Such a motion would have been equivalent to a vote of no-confidence. At the same time, Mr. Lloyd George, who, like other members of the Cabinet Munitions Committee, had been insufficiently informed by Lord Kitchener, was believed to be on the point of resignation, and the difficulties of Downing Street were aggravated by the disagreement between Mr. Churchill and Lord Fisher, who suddenly gave up the post of First Sea Lord.

THE FIRST COALITION.—Exactly a week after he had said such a step was not contemplated, Mr. Asquith announced the reconstruction of the Government on a broader personal and political basis. He had, as he wrote to Mr. Bonar Law, definitely come to the conclusion that the conduct of the war to a successful and decisive issue could not be effectively carried on except by a Cabinet which represented all parties. To avoid dangerous dissension and to obtain " actual, visible co-operation " the first Coalition of Liberal, Unionist and Labour members was formed. The Nationalists declined to join.

The change of Government did not produce much alteration in the aspect of the House except on the front benches. As a rule Liberal and Labour members remained on the Government side and Unionists on the Opposition side. The mingling of leaders was the outward, impressive, significant evidence of Coalition. At first the presence of Mr. Bonar Law, Mr. Balfour, Mr. Walter Long and Mr. Austen Chamberlain, beside Mr. Asquith and Mr. Lloyd George, intrigued the House, but soon all became familiar with the spectacle. On the front bench on the left of the Chair were Privy Councillors of both sides. Mr. Henry Chaplin worthily performed the ceremonial duties of leader of the Opposition. He could speak for no party, but it was convenient and in accordance with tradition that some one should on behalf of the independent or unofficial members ask questions with regard to business, defend their rights, and second formal motions. For these functions Mr. Chaplin had the qualifications of a veteran trained in the Victorian school. So permeated was he with the practice of the time of the Queen that even in the reign of George the Fifth he spoke of *Her* Majesty's Government.

With Mr. Asquith and Mr. Bonar Law acting together Parliamentary concord seemed to be better assured than under a party Government, although a section of Liberals, who were always testifying to their principles like so many Mause Headriggs, regretted the new arrangement, and the Nationalists were suspicious of a Coalition in which Sir Edward Carson held office. Mr. Asquith still exercised high authority in the House. He was the unchallenged leader of his own party, he had the goodwill of the Nationalists, he was trusted more than any other Liberal or any Unionist by the Labour members. Value was attached to his influence and skill in gradually obtaining support from reluctant quarters to measures of compulsion. On the other hand, events soon proved that the Coalition was not firmly cemented. Mr. Bonar Law testified, after it had been in existence for fifteen months, that " our Liberal colleagues have dealt fairly with us," but after all it was a Government of groups which had different points of view and no thought of permanent association. There were sectional consultations, and the Unionist members of the Government, as their leader declared, were not under the ordinary allegiance to its head.

Critics, after a lull, raised their voices again. Questions became more numerous and speeches harsher. Mr. Asquith was exposed to attacks which Lord Curzon denounced as " cruel, slanderous and untrue," while Sir Edward Grey, in spite of his services and prestige, was censured on account of the failure of Allied diplomacy in the Balkans. Most of the Ministers who had been in office since 1906 were supposed to be tired and weary, and some of them were reproached for thinking too much of peace-time doctrines. " We are at war " was the reminder often tauntingly flung at the Treasury Bench. Not only was Mr. Bonar Law occasionally embarrassed by dissatisfied followers, but an increasing number of Liberals showed lack of confidence in the conduct of the war. This was not the section which resented the formation of the Coalition. It welcomed the Coalition, but was disappointed by the results and shared Unionist doubts of the energy of the Government, and particularly of its head. The " Ginger " Committees, formed by both the great parties, played an important part in the organization of opinion.

CRISES AND CABALS.—Throughout 1916 the House was troubled and restless. On questions of military compulsion and national service many members were now impatient at what they considered hesitation and timidity. It was evident by Spring that these critics were prepared for a change of Administration. They were alarmed at the position of affairs, and secret sessions produced no perceptible change of temper. Dissatisfaction with Lord Kitchener's management at the War Office, the

Dublin rebellion, the failure of negotiations with the Ulster and Nationalist leaders, division of opinion on votes for soldiers and a variety of other matters lowered the Ministerial prestige and loosened Coalition bonds which were never quite tight. There were, as Mr. (afterwards Lord Justice) Duke lamented, daily cabals. There were frequent reports of Cabinet crises and of Mr. Lloyd George's resignation.

Across the scene flitted the figure of Sir Edward Carson. No politician excited more conflicting feelings of devotion and repulsion than this cool, resolute man with the thin, pale face, and deep, protruding chin, who had come to Westminster with the reputation of a stern Crown Prosecutor in Ireland, who was first an Irish law officer and later an English law officer in Unionist Administrations, and who, as the fearless leader in the Ulster struggle against Home Rule, became one of the foremost figures in the House. The gifts of a great statesman were denied to him by opponents who saw in him only the epitome of the dour sentiments of Orangeism, but whatever he might lack in equipment, he did not lack force of character; he had personality and a high power of inspiring confidence. His authority in the Unionist party grew second only to that of Mr. Bonar Law, with whom he had been closely associated. He had therefore to be reckoned with when, in October, 1915, leaving his place as Attorney General in the Coalition on account of the failure to save Serbia and the loss of Allied capability in the Balkans, he became the chief spokesman of the discontents.

Another ex-Minister joined him on the front Opposition bench. Mr. Churchill, whose disagreement with Lord Fisher on the Dardanelles affair, had contributed to the troubles of the Liberal Government, was succeeded by Mr. Balfour at the Admiralty when the Coalition was formed, and received the office of Chancellor of the Duchy of Lancaster. No place being found for him in the War Council which Mr. Asquith instituted, he abandoned in November, 1915, the " well-paid inactivity " of a civilian Minister without departmental duties, and as an officer placed himself at the disposal of the military authorities, " observing," as he wrote in his letter of resignation, " that my regiment is in France." The fascination of Parliament, however, was strong upon him. On leave from the front he reappeared in the House early next year, taking part in naval debate in March, and on the disbandment of his battalion a few weeks later, he returned permanently to his familiar life. With Sir Edward Carson and Mr. Churchill on the front Opposition bench, from which Mr. Chaplin was elevated to the House of Lords, the Government were faced by competent critics.

A controversy, disturbing to Mr. Bonar Law, arose between himself and Sir Edward Carson on the sale of enemy properties in Nigeria. Sir Edward, severely attacking the Government, moved that there should be no sale except to British subjects. Mr. Law, then Colonial Secretary, firmly resisted the proposal, contending that it was no part of Mr. Joseph Chamberlain's fiscal policy to erect a Chinese wall around the Empire. What was embarrassing to the Unionist leader was the fact, as the debate and division showed, that Carson could divert from him a section of his party. He had declared that he could hold office only with the support of his own followers. To them he held himself responsible. It is possible that what occurred on this occasion influenced his future action.

Uneasiness in respect of the conduct of the war increased towards the end of 1916. We did not then know what was revealed by Ludendorff's book. We were depressed by the outlook. It is true that we had fought the battle of Jutland and sealed up the German High Seas Fleet, and that we had saved Verdun by our operations upon the Somme, but while the enemy was held in the West, his supremacy in the East had grown, and Roumania, whose intervention had revived our hopes, was beaten. The Zeppelin menace had been met, but an aeroplane had dropped bombs in the daylight on London. The submarine peril was increasing. There was alarm about our shipping and food. Critics demanded the more thorough organization of man power and the more effective control of prices. There were complaints of the luxurious meals still allowed in restaurants. In November Mr. Runciman, President of the Board of Trade, announced that a Food Controller was to be established, war bread was to be produced, and drastic measures were to be taken for dealing with milk and potatoes, and he hinted that food tickets might be necessary. The appointments of Jellicoe as First Sea Lord and of Beatty in supreme command of the Grand Fleet were well received. There was not, however, general confidence in the Cabinet. It was accused of a lack of war concentration and driving power. Its chief was suspected of a preference for middle courses, of compromises between sections of the Government when quick and unhesitating decisions were demanded.

The Press at this most critical period claimed

a conspicuous share in the direction of government. As in the time of George Meredith's Mr. Tonans, the journalist was bidding against the statesman; he was exercising a powerful lever on public, and not less on Parliamentary, opinion. And specially persistent in criticism were the newspapers controlled by Lord Northcliffe. Kinglake, in describing the part played by *The Times* in connection with the Crimean war, declared that its managers employed able writers to argue in support of the opinion which, as they believed, the country was already adopting. "On the Sabbath England had rest," he wrote, "but in the early morning of all other days the irrevocable words were poured forth and scattered abroad to the corners of the earth."

Whether—in the phrase of Diana of the Crossways—the morrow was manufactured by Printing House Square or it was the mirror of yesterday, *The Times* in 1916 undoubtedly influenced the course of events. Although it was silent on the Sabbath and poured forth its words only on the mornings of other days, it had allies which kept up the stream without ceasing. What the Northcliffe Press, and newspapers with similar views, said morning and evening, Sunday and week-day, was repeated by many members in Parliament. Gibes were flung daily at the Cabinet "23," Mr. Asquith was taunted every question hour with "Wait and See," the idea that any man or set of men was indispensable formed the text of countless sarcasms. Thus opinion was moulded or expressed.

If Mr. Asquith had been able to attend debate and keep in constant touch with the House of Commons, he might, to some extent, have met criticism and perceived the loss of confidence he was suffering. To do so was impossible. Although he continued to act as leader, he could give to his Parliamentary duties merely a fraction of his time and attention. Except on important occasions, he was present only during questions, and his answers frequently left a bad impression. He was accused of snubbing. That was not a deliberate fault on his part, but he seldom took the trouble to be conciliatory and his replies were skilful rather than informing. Impatient inquirers were not content to be told that there was no avoidable delay in dealing with what they considered urgent, nor were those who were anxious on a particular point content to hear that every relevant consideration was being taken into account.

A significant feature of the situation was that many of the members who complained of the Government, and especially of the Liberal Ministers, excepted from censure Mr. Lloyd George, who had succeeded Lord Kitchener as Secretary for War, and pointed to him as an alternative leader. He had indicated his own dissatisfaction with the conduct of affairs by a speech in December, 1915, which was never forgotten, confessing that in this or that important decision we had been " rather late." His stirring appeals, his determination, his energy as Minister of Munitions had won for him a personal measure of national confidence.

Events marched strangely as well as swiftly in December, 1916. The country and Parliament were excited on learning that proposals had been made by Mr. Lloyd George for the appointment of a small War Council of Ministers whose decisions would be immediately acted upon, that the composition of this body had been suggested to Mr. Asquith, and that his own position upon it was left ambiguous. The unfriendly Press rejoiced in the report that he might not necessarily be a member of it. On the second of December there was a rumour that Mr. Lloyd George—who, as he said three years later, felt that the Allied cause might be doomed unless we quickened our action and imparted new energy into the struggle—was packing up to leave Downing Street. On the third the Unionist Ministers, by a resolution which found its way into the Press, called for a change of Government. On the fourth Mr. Asquith informed Parliament that it was to be reconstructed, the assumption then being that he was to carry out a scheme on the lines suggested by his powerful colleague.

Next day great surprise was caused by the intimation that he had resigned. While he could not secure the continued co-operation of Mr. Lloyd George and Mr. Bonar Law without a change of system, he resented the humiliating interpretation placed upon the proposed arrangement by a newspaper supposed to be in the confidence of its promoters or supporters, and certain members of the Cabinet encouraged him to resist dictation in the belief that he would be called back. According to Mr. Lloyd George's statement to the Constitutional Club after the war, " they never intended to leave the Coalition ; they were only manœuvring to get rid of a troublesome colleague."

THE SECOND COALITION.—On the 6th of December Mr. Bonar Law having declined to form an Administration, Mr. Lloyd George, with his co-operation, attempted the task. It was obvious that an understanding had been arrived at between the Liberal statesman and leading Unionists. Detractors

called it an intrigue. The House of Commons
was a mere spectator of events which it did not
directly originate. On the 7th it adjourned while
Mr. Lloyd George was ascertaining whether he
could carry out His Majesty's commission. That
day, to the surprise and chagrin of those former
friends who had become ill-wishers, he secured
the alliance of the Labour party ; the Liberal War
Committee decided to support him, and assured
of Unionist assistance, he was able in the evening
to inform the King of his success. On the 12th
Parliament reassembled under the direction of
the new Government, with the small War Cabinet
(consisting originally of the Prime Minister, Lord
Curzon, Lord Milner, Mr. Arthur Henderson, and
Mr. Bonar Law, and subsequently increased to
seven members) as its novel, distinctive feature.
With the exception of Lord Lansdowne, the principal
Unionists joined the Administration, Sir Edward
Carson, who was credited with a large share in the
political revolution, going to the Admiralty, and
Mr. Balfour, who was believed to be an acquiescing
rather than an active figure in it, succeeding
Viscount Grey at the Foreign Office.

" How long will it last ? " the quidnuncs asked
in the Lobby. Bewildered by the rapid and
mysterious transformation, by the concentration
of absolute power in a small group of men, and by
the introduction of departmental chiefs through new
avenues instead of the path of politics, the House
of Commons was for a time uncertain in temper.
Some sections, Liberal and Nationalist, protested
against a change for which Parliament had not
formally asked, and sympathy was expressed for
the statesman who had for twenty-eight months
borne the heaviest burden ever laid on the shoulders

of a British Minister, who in dark days maintained the national unity, and whose ambition to hold his post till the end of the war was frustrated. In his retirement, although a considerable number of his followers took office under his successor, he retained the leadership of his party.

Soon we saw, however, that the House was prepared to give the Administration a fair trial. It was relieved to find a closer cohesion of the various parties on the Treasury bench, a fuller feeling of common interest, than in the first Coalition. While the country readily submitted to curtailments of its liberties and luxuries, to fewer and slower trains and an increase of railway fares, to standard bread, to a reduction of brewing, to a restriction of public meals, to a voluntary system of rationing, and to a narrowing of the mesh of exemption from military duty, the House recognized in such measures proof of the resource and vigour of the Government. National service and food production raised difficulties, and members who had been led by Mr. Lloyd George's language to hope for stronger securities for temperance than were adopted by his Cabinet, expressed disappointment, but on all points criticism, as a rule, was friendly and helpful.

While Liberals as a party had been the most reliable supporters of the first Coalition, Unionists, who obtained a larger proportion of important posts under Mr. Lloyd George and had acquired greater confidence in him than in his predecessor, were the warm friends of the second Coalition. Tradition was startled by the arrangement by which the Prime Minister, himself a member of the House of Commons, devolved its leadership upon a colleague. The entrusting, however, of that

function to Mr. Bonar Law secured the practical
solidarity of the Unionists, while it relieved Mr.
Lloyd George from duties which had encumbered
Mr. Asquith. On the other hand, the division
among Liberals became gradually more distinct.
An increasing number gave their allegiance to Mr.
Lloyd George, while the adherents of the fallen
Minister regarded his successor as a lost Liberal
leader, saying, as a previous generation had said
of Mr. Chamberlain : " We shall march prospering
—not through his presence." The Labour party
was so rent that it ceased for the time to be of any
Parliamentary account. Twice the number of its
members who had office under Mr. Asquith now
sat on the Treasury bench, other supporters of the
war maintained an attitude of friendly independence,
a third section was bitter in its pacifism.

The aspect of the House underwent a notable
change. There was a movement of Unionists from
the left of the Chair to the right. Those who
remained in their former places faced the Government with sympathetic eyes, while many crossed
the floor. Liberals were scattered in every quarter.
Mr. Asquith and his lieutenants who had declined,
or had not been offered office, took seats on the
front Opposition bench, where only one or two
Unionists lingered, and behind the ex-Premier
assembled the more steadfast of his followers. A
large number of Liberals kept their places on the
Ministerial side, two or three critical, some waiting
to see, others rallying to the support of the Government. A few associated with the anti-war Labour
group below the Opposition gangway.

The Irish Nationalists, who distrusted the first
Coalition, were more unfriendly to the second.
Early in 1917 they moved that the suspended Home

Rule Act should be brought into operation without further delay. Mr. Lloyd George's reply was to the effect that the Government (who subsequently set up a Convention of representative Irishmen to frame a constitution for their country) were willing to give Home Rule to any part of Ireland which desired it, but there must be no coercion of any part which wished to stay out. His speech was angrily interrupted by the Nationalists, who taunted him with being a turn-coat, and Mr. Redmond warned the Ministers that by their action they were playing into the hands of the revolutionists.

Although resentful Liberals and alienated Nationalists regarded the Government with ill-will, there was maintained, in face of the common danger, except in the insignificant pacifist quarter, a real sense of unity and comradeship. The new spirit produced by the war was displayed in the formal courtesies of Parliament. In normal times a member of one party was to members of other parties the honourable or right honourable gentle-man. Now each was honourable or right honour-able friend. This was a nice convention indicating that our own divisions had disappeared before the common enemy. Looking at itself the House could not forget the war. Many members were in uniform, and most of the strangers, if not in khaki, were in hospital blue, some with bandaged heads or hands, some with crutches.

REVOLUTION AND REFORM.—Advantage was taken of the subsidence of party feeling to extend the Parliamentary franchise, limit plural voting, and redistribute the constituencies. Questions, which under ordinary conditions would have occupied years of controversy, were settled by concession and compromise. A Conference on Electoral Reform, arranged during Mr. Asquith's Coalition and presided over by the Speaker, adopted a series of resolutions, and a motion calling for legislation on the lines thus laid down was submitted by the Liberal leader in the Spring of 1917. It excited the animosity of the stiffer Conservatives, who tried by loud demonstrations to intimidate the Ministers, but Mr. Lloyd George and Mr. Walter Long, the champions of opposite schools of political thought, exercised so much influence over the doubting and timid that, although as many as sixty-two Unionists went into the lobby against the motion, the majority in its favour was sufficiently overwhelming to enable the Government to carry the Representation of the People Bill through Parliament. Party prejudices were kept wonderfully under control, Liberals abating their demands and Conservatives yielding on various points. There was a division, it is true, on party lines, on the alternative vote. This was desired by Liberals, but Unionists, with the aid of the Peers, defeated it.

The movement for reform at home was quickened by the revolution in Russia. Late on a March night, when only a few score members were in attendance, Mr. Bonar Law, in his calmest manner, announced that great event and the abdication of the Tsar. Listeners were stunned with surprise at the tremendous upheaval, but were relieved to hear—what proved so erroneous a prediction—that it meant increased efficiency and energy by Russia in the war. Radicals and Nationalists hailed with enthusiasm the blow struck in "the cause of democracy." It was described by Mr. Lloyd George in a thrilling speech as "the first great triumph

for the principles for which we entered the war."
" Free peoples," as he said, " are the best defenders
of their own honour and safety." Reformers felt,
as their ancestors felt at the beginning of the
French Revolution, that

> "Bliss was it in that dawn to be alive."

Not reading the full lesson of what occurred in
France, they found in the Russian revolution a
" pleasant exercise of hope and joy." It convinced
even the Tories of the expediency of timely concession to democracy. Their startled senses were
alive to an ominous word in the air :

> " Methought the billows spoke and told me of it ;
> The winds did sing it to me."

WOMAN'S VICTORY.—Women at last secured
the Parliamentary franchise under the Representation of the People Bill. It was for them a notable
victory over former adversaries of the suffragette
cause. Mr. Asquith, who had been a stout opponent
of votes to women, changed his attitude, believing
that they had worked out their salvation by war
service and agreeing that their voices ought to be
heard in national reconstruction. Many other
members shared his conversion. They yielded
with grace what could no longer be resisted. The
Government left the question to the free decision
of the House of Commons, and the House, after a
final struggle, settled it in the only way in which it
could be settled.

The new political relationship of the sexes was
indicated by a structural change at St. Stephen's.
Between 1675 and 1778 women were occasionally
seen below the bar, but thereafter, in consequence
of the " violent and determined resistance " of

" fair intruders " to an order for the clearing of the House, they were excluded for a long period. In the later days of the old building, which was destroyed in 1834, two score ladies were admitted to an apartment called the ventilator above the ceiling, through the apertures of which, according to Townsend's *Memoirs*, they " saw and heard very well, but most inconveniently." In the House erected after the fire accommodation was provided for them in the gallery behind the Speaker's chair, with a metal lattice front.

Against this grille protests were often made. In one Parliament after another members urged that it should be removed on the ground that it was an insult to those who sat behind it and interfered with their seeing and hearing. Always it had been successfully defended. Old-fashioned men desired to maintain the seclusion of women for their own sake and objected to the House being " turned into a theatre." The movement for freedom was retarded by the action of suffragettes, who thrust banners through the grating and committed other disorders. It was torn down by the war. The summer session of 1917 ended with a small revolution and a great—the decision to remove the grille and the announcement of gradual self-government for India. The stone supports of the gallery remained a partial obstruction to the view, and women were still, to some extent, obscured, but the work of liberation had begun.

Other concessions followed. The strangers' gallery was opened to women so that they could sit by the side of men. Greatest of all the changes, of course, was the giving to the newly enfranchised sex the right of election to Parliament. A large number of members disliked the idea of women occupying the benches, addressing the Speaker, and voting in the lobbies, but on the eve of the first election in which they could exercise the franchise, man surrendered his exclusive privilege by a majority of 274 to 25. Meantime he became accustomed to the spectacle, so strange at first, of the two sexes sitting in the same public gallery. Formerly, when husband and wife came to hear a debate, they went to opposite ends of the House. When one became weary he or she had to signal discreetly to the other. Now they could keep each other company. Such an arrangement would have made old members tremble for the constitution. Soon the spectacle ceased to arrest the eye.

# CHAPTER XII

## WAR AND POLITICIANS

THE story of how Mr. Lloyd George, by energy and eloquence, strengthened and consolidated his position and eventually gained a rare and complete ascendancy in the House of Commons, forms a stirring chapter in its annals. His leadership of the nation in the conduct of the war, undertaken with the cordial co-operation of Mr. Bonar Law, soon secured the general confidence of Unionists— a confidence which ultimately became enthusiastic. But what about his own old political friends ? Could he always rely on any considerable number of the Liberals whose honoured chief he had overthrown ? Or would Mr. Asquith, in the event of a division, draw them as a party into the Opposition lobby, and with the aid of the Nationalists and of Labour members upset his Administration ? The answer to these questions seemed for a time in doubt.

Although during the greater part of 1917 no effort was put forth in any influential quarter to upset or embarrass the Government, it had its hours of Parliamentary stress, if not of peril. The concentration of power in the War Cabinet, the multiplicity of autocratic Directors and Controllers, some of whom did not know the ways of tradition, and the rareness of the visits of the Prime Minister alarmed men who were sensitive about the authority of the House of Commons. " We have certainly," said Mr. Churchill, " not gone to war with Prussia in order to capture her Constitution. It would be the irony of fate if we liberated Germany and enslaved ourselves." That was before he himself joined the novel Administration. Mr. Asquith, who after the change of Government pleaded for the continuance of national unity, set an example by deprecating " the idlest and most unpatriotic of all diversions "—that of recriminative comparison. But recrimination was hard to avoid, and personal rivalries were fostered by men sorely stricken by the events of December, 1916. The ex-Premier's more impatient followers, who thought he was too ready to support and too reluctant to find fault, hoped he would seize an occasion to strike, and after an interval their hope—with unexpected results— was fulfilled.

Meantime copious criticism came from various parts of the House. Two assiduous and able Radicals, Mr. Pringle and Mr. Hogge, who had been both vigilant and independent in discussion during the previous Administration, continued, while remaining on the Ministerial side, to take their own course with unflinching pertinacity. Pacifists below the Opposition gangway displayed their hate of the Government and all its doings. Sections of Unionists also found much to criticize, although not in a hostile spirit. There were controversies and daily questions on national service, on shirkers and conscientious objectors, on agricultural labour, on rationing, on the dearness and distribution of food, on submarine warfare, on racing and brewing, and on the air raids. There were secret sessions and hints of a general election. Conservatives muttered angrily when Mr. Churchill and Mr. Montagu were admitted to the Government. They disliked the strengthening of the Liberal element on the Treasury bench, which was so far predominantly Unionist, by the appointment to office of a states- man specially distrusted on account of his share in the enterprises of Antwerp and the Dardanelles, and of another who had been closely associated with Mr. Asquith.

Controversy involving pre-war principles arose on the Corn Production Bill, with its guaranteed prices for wheat and oats. In July, 1917, for the first time Mr. Asquith's lieutenants, with a large number of followers, voted for an amendment to a Ministerial measure. One hundred Liberal and Labour members went into the division lobby in support of a proposal to limit the guarantee to excess cultivation. Mr. Asquith's lieutenants voted also for an amendment, moved by a Labour member, who subsequently joined the Government, to raise the minimum wage of agricultural labourers, fixed in the bill at 25$s$., to 30$s$. The Government on this occasion issued an urgent whip, and officers were brought from the front for the division, which was treated as a test of confidence.

MR. ASQUITH'S CHALLENGE.—It was not till near the end of 1917 that Mr. Asquith himself challenged his successor. During the year the war had its fluctuations, its victories and defeats, its encourage- ments and disappointments. The French offensive, under General Nivelle, had failed, and but for the coming in of America with her financial and shipping resources, and the prospect of her armies, our Allies might have been gravely despondent. By the close of autumn the glamour of the new Coalition had somewhat faded. Victory seemed no nearer than when Mr. Lloyd George took control. Hope of further aid from Russia, entertained at the outbreak of the revolution, was shattered by the capture of power by the Bolsheviks, who entered into negotiations with Germany; Roumania was obliged to conclude a military armistice; the Italians had suffered a very severe defeat on the Isonzo and had fallen back on the Piave. At home people were annoyed by the air raids. The scarcity of food, the queues at the shops, the frequent intimation : "No butter, no margarine, no tea," the shading of lights of houses, and even the lessened illumination of the streets caused depression.

In this state of feeling a commotion threatening to the Government was produced in Parliamentary circles by new military arrangements. Mr. Lloyd George, having gone to Italy to assure her of assistance after her alarming set back, it was decided at a conference at Rapallo to create a supreme Allied Council, with a permanent Military Committee. The idea of a Council thus equipped, which might override our General Staff, disturbed national susceptibilities, and a disagreeable impression was made by a sensational speech delivered by the Prime Minister on his way home at Paris. In order to prove the necessity for allied co-ordination he described the situation with, as he said, " perhaps brutal frankness," and he drew an unflattering contrast between our achievements in the West and the victory of our enemies in Italy.

A Lobby crisis followed the Paris sensation. Dislike of the Military Committee was felt even by some of Mr. Lloyd George's Parliamentary friends. There was fear of friction between the Allies, there were rumours of disagreements at home between soldiers and politicians, and especially of an attempt by the Prime Minister to impose his own strategy on Sir William Robertson, the Chief of the Imperial General Staff. A stern demand by Mr. Asquith for information set tongues wagging. " How long," the quidnuncs again asked, " do you give the Government ? " " Twenty-four hours," said a clever Radical. Mr. Lloyd George's reading of the Rapallo agreement on his return from Paris lessened the apprehensions of friends, but still the Parliamentary attitude was uncertain. There were powerful Press influences against the Prime Minister. There were military and naval men against him. Who knew what the affair might not bring forth ?

On November 19, in a crowded House, with M. Venizelos and two American Admirals among the distinguished strangers, the first critical debate testing Mr. Lloyd George's position was held. Mr. Asquith, with his manuscript on the box, delivered his rounded, stately sentences. He spoke under the strain of the death of Sir Stanley Maude, of which he had heard on entering the House, and the death of Captain Neil Primrose, for whose father (Lord Rosebery) he sorrowed deeply. His language was measured, free from acrimony, suggestive rather than provocative. He laid down propositions on military control which received general assent ; he questioned Mr. Lloyd George's indictment of the strategy of the Allies ; he rebuked him for gauging the value of a campaign by " kilometric scale " ; he showed that our soldiers had " done great things under great commanders." But if not in tone, his speech was in effect a challenge.

MR. LLOYD GEORGE'S VICTORY.—Mr. Lloyd

George's reply was one of the decisive strokes of his career. He left unanswered, according to his skilful habit, some inconvenient questions and criticisms ; there were openings in his argument into which a lance might have been thrust. Several members, Unionist and Liberal, pointed out that the impression he now gave of the new Council was different from that derived from his Paris pronouncement. But whatever it was, he won overwhelming support for it. While repudiating the idea of a Generalissimo, he urged the necessity for greater unity of control and action, and explaining that he deliberately made his Paris speech disagreeable, he defended it as a successful piece of political strategy. This was not all. It could be said of Mr. Lloyd George, as Mr. Hutton said of Lord Salisbury, that he had an unpleasant dexterity in turning a defensive into an offensive warfare. Now he turned fiercely on the critics who had accused him of meddling with the work of the soldiers. These critics themselves he accused of an effort to sow dissension between soldiers and politicians and between France and Great Britain. His counter-attack was delivered with extraordinary energy and animation. Like Gladstone, he seemed as if he were to spring over the box ; his body was constantly in motion and the glowing face, the sweeping arms, the pointing finger, the clenched fist gave impetus to his words.

It was said in the Lobby that an occupant of the front Opposition bench, on being asked by a colleague what he thought of the Prime Minister's speech, whispered : " The first part eye-wash ; the second part balderdash." A very different verdict was given by the great majority of the House. The enthusiastic cheers which were raised

again and again, and the delight on the faces of Mr.
Lloyd George's friends, proved that there was no
need to think of a successor.

By his victory on this occasion his position was
consolidated. Hitherto he had been regarded by
unsympathetic observers as a Prime Minister on
sufferance. Without a party of his own, he was
supposed to be dependent on a Unionist force lent
by colleagues who could withdraw it at any time,
and on the forbearance of Mr. Asquith. Now
every one saw that he possessed the confidence of
the House, and that authority over it had passed
completely from his predecessor to himself. Hence-
forth the doubters and waverers moved to his side.

Those were days of historic events. A Mission
from the United States met the War Cabinet and
officials at No. 10, Downing Street, " in the very
room and round the very table "—as *The Times*
pointed out—" where one British Minister decided
to defy the American colonies and another consented to recognize their independence." The
co-operation of the United States, illustrated by
this picturesque incident, was the most hopeful
feature of a dark period. Except in Palestine,
where General Allenby was brilliantly successful,
the military theatres at the end of 1917 provided
little encouragement. The achievement of General
Byng's Army in breaking the Hindenburg line by
a surprise attack with tanks led to a ringing of
bells, which was followed by extreme reaction
when, after advancing close to Cambrai, we lost
much of the ground we had taken.

The Marquis of Lansdowne, who was in the first
Coalition but not in the second, amazed and startled
the country by the publication of a letter, declaring

that the prolongation of the war would spell ruin for the civilized world, and suggesting a reconsideration of Allied aims and a pact of the nations. As it was generally interpreted to point to the possibility of a negotiated peace it provoked indignant protests. There was scarcely any sympathy in Parliament, except in the pacifist quarter, with its temper. The prevailing feeling was that, as the Prime Minister said, "there was no half-way house between victory and defeat." Air alarms, annoying as they were, restricted meals, the submarine menace and even the secession of Russia and the proportionate increase of the enemy's strength in the West, failed to subdue the national spirit.

Although criticism was abundant in 1918 Mr. Lloyd George amply maintained the confidence he had won. At the beginning of the year he made to Labour representatives a plain, precise statement of our war aims and peace conditions, which received national approval. Even those who considered a fresh declaration unnecessary endorsed the terms that he presented, while Labour and Liberal circles expressed warm appreciation of his candour and explicitness, as well as of the democratic spirit of his policy. The need of unity was never more vital than at this period, when the question of man power was again delicate and urgent, and Mr. Lloyd George's leadership was accepted by a considerable number of members who were formerly distrustful.

An enlargement of the functions of the Allied War Council at Versailles, revealed in the report of its third session, led in February to an inquiry by Mr. Asquith. The Prime Minister at first pleaded the national interest for declining information, but a week later, in reply to a repeated challenge, he took it up and scored another Parliamentary triumph. Even the resignation of the office of Chief of the Imperial General Staff by Sir William Robertson, who objected to the Versailles control, did not frighten those who had placed their full confidence in the Government. Nor were they always tolerant of complaints of home measures. Attacks on the Controllers and the sometimes discordant Departments, which came from various quarters, were met by Ministerial enthusiasts with cries of " Get on with the war."

MR. REDMOND.—The House of Commons lost in March one of its most distinguished figures by the death of Mr. John Redmond. He was a great Parliament man, an orator of the old school. He knew when to strike and he knew how to wait. He was ever dignified, even when harassed by an independent section of Nationalists, led by Mr. William O'Brien and Mr. Tim Healy. A true friend of the British Empire, as well as an Irish patriot, he had won lasting gratitude by his support of the war. His son was in the Army and his brother, Major Willie Redmond, a fiery Nationalist, who, in the uniform of the King, delivered an earnest plea for conciliation to an intensely moved audience, had died of wounds in battle. But, in the delay of Home Rule, Sinn Fein had broken out and rapidly spread, the Convention set up by the Government to frame a Constitution for Ireland had failed to reach a sufficiently substantial agreement, Mr. Redmond's constitutional policy was repudiated by a large section of his Nationalist fellow-countrymen and he died broken-hearted. The one bright spot in Sir Edward Grey's survey

at the outbreak of war had become the darkest
spot when the Irish party led by Mr. Redmond's
successor, Mr. John Dillon, although still approving
the Allied cause, proved as hostile to the British
Government as it was under Mr. Parnell.

THE GERMAN OFFENSIVE.—On the night of
March 21 Mr. Lloyd George, looking very grave,
entered the House and had a conversation with
the Deputy Speaker, who was in the chair. The
ill news soon travelled through the corridors that
we had been forced to give way on the Somme.
This was the beginning of the great offensive by
the Germans. Anxiety lined the faces of members
during the weeks in which the enemy, putting
forth all his strength, replenished from the East,
made alarming progress. There was some taunting
of the Government and jeering at the Versailles
Council by military experts who had opposed the
weakening of the West for the sake of side shows,
and who now exclaimed " I told you so ! " but in
Parliament the sniping at the Ministers was
suspended while they took measures to meet the
new danger. Mr. Lloyd George had within half-
an-hour of the receipt of the news of the attack,
composed and dispatched an appeal—critics called
it a panic appeal—to the United States to send
reinforcements in the shortest possible time, and
in the emergency Marshal Foch was charged by
the British, French and American Governments
to co-ordinate the action of the Allied Armies.
Within a fortnight nearly a quarter of a million
troops from our own country were thrown across
the Channel. A drastic man-power measure was
introduced raising the military age, cancelling
exemptions of young men in industries, and extend-

ing conscription to Ireland. Although the Cabinet
promised to try to pass with the least possible
delay a bill for the establishment of self-government in Ireland, the Nationalists hotly resisted
the application of compulsion to their country,
but the service proposals were rapidly carried.

THE MAURICE DIVISION.—Mr. Asquith challenged
a division on May 9, 1918, for the first time since
he left office. This division served as a boundary
line between supporters and opponents of the
Coalition and had a permanent effect on political
fortunes. It related to one of the frequent controversies between distinguished officers and the
Government. Major-General Sir F. Maurice, till
a few weeks previously Director of Military Operations on the Imperial General Staff, in a published
letter, charged Ministers with a series of mis-
statements on our fighting strength on the eve of
the German offensive. A proposal by the Government to invite two judges to investigate his grave
allegations was received with general disfavour and
Mr. Asquith moved for the appointment of a
Parliamentary Committee of Inquiry. Thereupon
the Prime Minister, instead of setting up any
tribunal, appealed to the House for a vote of
confidence. He received it by a majority of 293
to 106. Even the Liberals as a party did not
support Mr. Asquith. While 99 voted with him,
72 went into the Government lobby.

The Maurice debate and division finally
established Mr. Lloyd George's paramount position.
It was now palpably evident that the vast majority
of the House, including a large force of Liberals,
was determined to stand by him. Very bitter
feeling was produced by the controversy  Intense

animosity against the Prime Minister was displayed by some former friends and colleagues. On the other hand, a galling distrust of Mr. Asquith was expressed in the ranks of the majority. There were fierce shouts of "Never! Never!" when reference was made to the possibility of his again becoming responsible for the affairs of the country. He listened unmoved to Mr. Lloyd George's triumphant speech, but on hearing these shouts his face twitched. To be so distrusted after all he had done may have exhibited to him a callous ingratitude. Only a few months previously Mr. Austen Chamberlain had testified that nothing in all his long public services became him more than the patriotism he had shown since his retirement from office.

While cynical observers remarked that Mr. Asquith for the first time in his career led on this occasion a forlorn hope, others, including a few of his own followers, said in censure or regret that he had allowed himself to be outmanœuvred, and it was assumed by opponents that under the influence of impatient colleagues he acted against his own judgment. One, however, in a position to know told me that from first to last he took firmly his own course in respect of the demand for a Parliamentary inquiry and that he was determined to challenge a division even if he should have to go into the lobby alone. From the Liberal point of view the misfortune of the vote was that it deepened and made more distinct the breach in the party.

Fortunately there was still no danger of a discord weakening the supreme purpose of the nation. Only the small group of pacifists opposed in that time of national ordeal the policy and pursuit of the war. Apart from them there was still a unanimous disposition to

> " Combine together 'gainst the enemy ;
> For these domestic and particular broils
> Are not the question here."

It was wonderful how the House went on with its daily business, passing the Education Bill and other domestic measures, discussing all sorts of subjects and asking scores of questions during the spring and early summer months, while the Germans approached Amiens and tried to separate the French and British armies, when the Channel ports seemed to be in danger, when one thrust after another was made at Paris, the target of long-distance guns, and when the great battle was fought between the Aisne and the Marne. No one who lived in London at that terrible time forgets the grave demeanour of the people, the anxiety with which they opened the newspapers, the compassion and pride they felt for the soldiers. Just as they relieved the strain by attending to the ordinary duties of life, so the House of Commons patiently did its work. Members took full interest in debate, gossiped in the Lobby, attended to correspondence, saw visitors, dined (according to ration), smoked and played chess.

THE LONG PARLIAMENT.—For the fifth time Parliament lengthened the span of its existence. Elected for seven years in December, 1910, it determined by the Parliament Act to substitute five for seven, but by a series of measures during the war it prolonged the term to eight. Few members believed in July, 1918, that the extension then decided upon would be the last. A general

election during hostilities would have been re-
pugnant to patriotic sentiment and another year,
if not two more years, of war was declared by critics
to be probable.  But although not eager to die, the
old House was weary, stale and *blasé*.  New men
were wanted with new ideas.  " I love everything
that's old," says Mr. Hardcastle, " old friends, old
times, old manners, old books, old wine."  Nobody
loves an old House of Commons—not even an old
member of it.  Only the supreme exigency saved
the Parliament of 1910 from dissolution within the
normal period.

Many of the old familiar faces, it is true, were
gone.  A large number of the members had died,
or resigned or received peerages or judicial appointments ; some had laid down their lives on the
battlefield.  There had been many by-elections.
But scarcely any of these during the war had tested
public opinion and few of the men returned had
brought a fresh impulse into the arena.  Chosen
by the caucus of the party to which the former
member belonged, they were looked at with a mild
curiosity when they stood at the bar waiting to
take their seats.  " Who is this ? " one observer
asked another.  Cheered with an effort by the
courteous veterans, the new men passed behind the
Speaker's chair and as a rule remained obscure.

END OF THE WAR.—The outlook of the world
was changed in that month when Parliament made
the last extension of its life by Foch's counter-stroke.
Thenceforth the tide of battle which had threatened
to overwhelm the Allies rolled back and on the day
that Parliament adjourned for the autumn recess
in August Haig began the offensive which never
ceased till he delivered the knock-out blow.  There

were Labour troubles at home while the soldiers of the Allies were fighting so hard and successfully. There was a strike of munition workers at Coventry and Birmingham in the last week of July. London was without omnibuses for several days in August on account of a strike of women and for two days the police left the capital in the protection of special constables. There was a strike of shipwrights on the Clyde at " the spring-tide of victory " in September. But we were all thrilled and inspired during that memorable autumn by the rapid succession of Allied attacks, the breaches of the Hindenburg line, the driving back of the Germans, the capture of vital positions, the American offensive, the collapse of the enemy in the Balkans, the Turkish *débâcle* in Palestine. The steady advance of our gallant troops filled us with pride. Each day people expected to hear of a new victory and each day gave the story of the recovery of a place engraved on the hearts of those whose husbands or sons, brothers or friends fell there in former battles.

Parliament, which adjourned in a hopeful but chastened mood in August, reassembled on October 15 in conditions surpassing the most sanguine expectations of the optimists. The surrender of Bulgaria at the end of September was, as Mr. Bonar Law said at the Guildhall, the beginning of the end. Germany's peace overtures to President Wilson, the increasing menace to her armies, the recovery of Cambrai, Ostend and Lille, the resignation of Ludendorff, who was to have dictated terms in Paris, the winning back of territory not only by the French and the Belgians, but also by the Italians, and the final defeat of Turkey filled October with excitement. It fell to the Home Secretary, Mr. Cave, in the absence of the Prime Minister and

Mr. Bonar Law at Versailles, to inform the House of Commons on the last day of October of the armistice with Turkey and members were specially gratified by the fact that the British Fleet was at last to pass to the Black Sea. A few days later they learned that Austria, beaten and broken, had in turn thrown up her hands. The terms of the armistice with that shattered Empire were communicated to the House on November 5 by the Prime Minister and there was a loud outburst of cheering at the intimation that the Allies had reached complete agreement on the conditions of an armistice with Germany and that her Government could ascertain them by making an application to Marshal Foch in the usual military form.

In the Lobby members speculated as to whether peace would come before Christmas or be deferred till next summer; they wondered what were the conditions to be imposed on our principal enemy and whether she would submit. And in the midst of these speculations they talked of the prospects of a general election. How would parties be affected by the experience of war and the coming of peace ? Would the old divisions be set up again ? If not, what would be the new grouping ? These were questions which had been asked since the time of the first Coalition. " No one can say," was for a long time the stereotyped answer. Many members had expressed the hope that union in the national interest would be maintained, but this hope became faint after the Maurice division and after the Labour party began to organize its own campaign in the country.

On November 11, in the House of Commons, Mr. Lloyd George read the terms of the armistice which Germany had signed that morning. Most of those present must have recalled the scene in August, 1914, when the House with defiant, determined cheers sanctioned our entrance into war. How little then did they foresee its length or its effects ! Thrones had fallen, Empires had been broken, the Tsar had perished, the Kaiser had taken refuge in Holland, a Socialist Government had been set up in Germany. At home there had been political changes which if prophesied in that fateful August would have seemed fantastic. Mr. Asquith, then the unchallenged leader of the Liberal party, the head of a powerful Government, trusted by Parliament and the country, was now on the front Opposition bench, with his authority over the House vanished and his party divided in allegiance. The Foreign Minister whose conduct of the negotiations on the eve of the war had on account of their firmness and dignity excited the nation's pride, was now an unofficial, silent peer. Supreme on the Treasury bench sat Mr. Asquith's former Radical lieutenant, beside him were colleagues who in peace had assailed him more than any other man, and behind him were Unionists as well as Liberals who hailed him as the saviour of the country.

It was for Mr. Lloyd George a moment such as few men in the world's history have experienced when he entered the House with the terms imposed on the beaten enemy. Members rose in his honour, Mr. Asquith and his colleagues joining in this tribute to the King's First Minister. He betrayed no exultation. He was solemn in his gratitude. At eleven o'clock that morning, as he recorded, came to an end the cruellest and most terrible war that had ever scourged mankind. And thus, he hoped, came to an end all wars. This as he said was not a time for words. " Our hearts are too full of a gratitude to which no tongue can give adequate expression." Mr. Asquith also was too much impressed to indulge in many phrases. Solemnly he joined in the aspiration that we had entered a new chapter of international history in which war would be recognized as an obsolete anachronism never to be repeated. While London was shouting in its relief and joy, Lords and Commons proceeded to St. Margaret's to give, as the Prime Minister suggested, humble and reverent thanks for the great deliverance of the world from its great peril. In the procession Mr. Lloyd George and Mr. Asquith walked side by side.

END OF UNION.—With dramatic swiftness the national unity of war ended with the coming of peace. Preparations for a general election were hurriedly made, while historic events continued throughout the world. On November 12 Emperor Karl of Austria abdicated, on the 17th the Allied armies began their movement to the Rhine, on the 19th the Tricolour flew over Metz, on the 21st the German High Seas Fleet surrendered off the Firth of Forth to Admiral Beatty, on the 22nd King Albert, after four years of exile, returned to Brussels, on the 24th French troops made formal entry into Strasburg and British reached the German frontier. The last Parliament of the United Kingdom chosen by man alone was dissolved on the 25th. Independent parties disputed the expediency of its dissolution before the peace terms were settled or even discussed and while the Army was still abroad. But it was a weary, war-worn Parliament. Few persons would for its own sake have wished " upon the rack of this tough world " to stretch it out longer.

To the country Mr. Lloyd George and Mr. Bonar Law and their Liberal and Unionist colleagues appealed as a Coalition. From the war-time combination the Labour party withdrew, although several of its members, disregarding its decision, remained in office. Unionists, while sanctioning the continuance of the Coalition, maintained, as Mr. Balfour noted, their "internal cohesion, and continuous identity." Liberals, on the other hand, entered the election with forces divided. A large number associated themselves with the appeal for authority to Mr. Lloyd George not only to go to the Peace Conference, but to begin the work of reconstruction. Others who held that no new mandate was required for the peace negotiations, vehemently protested against the Prime Minister taking advantage of the national enthusiasm for an electoral purpose. Supporters of the Government received from their allied leaders a letter endorsing their candidature— a " coupon " it was derisively called. Mr. Asquith stood as a Liberal " without prefix or suffix." He refused to countenance the setting up of any Liberal candidate against another Liberal adopted by the local Association, but those without the " coupon " were opposed by the Coalition. Only a few of the Liberals " without prefix or suffix " survived the contest. Mr. Asquith and his lieutenants fell.

# CHAPTER XIII

## AFTER THE WAR

A STRANGE House of Commons assembled on February 4, 1919. It was unfamiliar in composition and character, and most novel of all its features was the constitution of the Front Opposition Bench. For generations Whig and Tory, Liberal and Conservative, Unionist and Radical had in turn occupied the seat on the left of the Chair ready when their superior virtues were recognized to cross to the other side of the table. After the formation of the Asquith Coalition it had been shared by the two great parties, although in the final months of the war nearly all its occupants were Liberal. Now for the first time in history places were taken on it by the Privy Councillors and Whips of the Labour party. This was a political portent, signifying the advent of a new aspirant to office and power —a claimant to the reins of the State.

Never were there so many shades and sections of Parliament. There was the vast, overwhelming force of Coalition Unionists and Liberals, and within that force were the Ulster Unionists, led by Sir Edward Carson, while the ten National Democrats also, as a rule, acted with it; there were a few independent Unionists, including those who called themselves the National Party; and besides the Sinn Feiners, who did not attend, there were in Opposition the Labour members, about sixty in

number, somewhere between twenty-five and thirty
Independent Liberals, who derived from a section of
Scottish Presbyterianism the name of Wee Frees,
and the remnant of Irish Nationalists.

Coalitionists overflowed three-quarters of the
chamber, occupying not only the Ministerial side,
but also the benches below the Opposition gangway,
where formerly the Irish party had been
predominant. The Nationalists who for forty years
gave vivacity to Parliament were now reduced to
a group of seven, led by Mr. T. P. O'Connor, the
Father of the House. Those who had fallen before
the revolutionaries were missed by old British
colleagues, for whatever might have been thought
of their politics, they were, as a rule, personally
popular. The disappearance of the ex-Prime
Minister was the matter of greatest marvel. New
and bitter members felt " no need " of Mr. Asquith,
but his absence was deplored by generous opponents
trained in the Parliamentary school. The reserve
and dignity which he displayed in misfortune
extorted the respect even of men who felt no regret
for it. Like Wolsey he had " sounded all the
depths and shoals of honour " and like the fallen
Cardinal, he sought no sympathy. " Nay, and you
weep ; I am fallen indeed."

An epoch was marked in Parliamentary history
when Mr. Adamson, an ex-miner from Fifeshire,
rose as a leader from the front Opposition bench.
As the largest non-Coalition party in attendance in
the House, being exceeded in number only by the
absent Sinn Feiners, the Labour members claimed
the functions and rights of His Majesty's Opposition.
Their claim was sturdily, rather clumsily asserted
by Mr. Adamson. He had a skilful rival in Sir
Donald Maclean, the sessional chairman of the

Independent Liberals, who represented one of the great parties of tradition. Sir Donald and his Whips and those few colleagues who had been in office sat side by side with the Labour occupants of the front bench, sometimes in opinion disagreeing. They shared the duties of Opposition, the rival leaders asking the questions about business in alternate weeks and competing in debate for the eye of the Speaker.

Largely composed of rich men, well advanced in years and new to its life, the House early revealed considerable power of expert criticism in business affairs, but was naturally amenable to the influence of the Government. With its strange assortment of parties and the ambitious rôle of Labour, it presented fresh problems, but Mr. Lowther, who remained in the Chair for over two years to give it the benefit of his experience, found his task no more difficult than formerly. It was not, as a rule, a well-attended House. An unusually small proportion of the new men, unskilled and unpractised, were desirous of Parliamentary distinction or interested in the everyday work. Attendance was affected also by the development of the system of Grand Committees. Members who spent the early part of the day in the rooms upstairs had little desire to sit on the benches and listen to speeches in the evening.

Many matters caused anxiety to the Peace Parliament in its first session. There were demobilization troubles, Irish defiances of British rule, rent difficulties, profiteering complaints, the miners' demands, the cry of nationalization, the general industrial unrest, the threat of direct action by Labour for political objects and the national railway strike, behind which the Prime Minister found an " anarchist conspiracy," and in consequence of which, with stringent rationing, the prohibition of pastries, reduced lighting in the entertainment area, Hyde Park a milk depôt, and enrolment of special constables and transport drivers, London resumed some of the aspects and conditions of war time. There were problems of health and of housing which formed the subject of legislation. Our intervention in North Russia and the continuance of compulsory military service till peace was assured encountered opposition in Liberal and Labour quarters ; other measures tried the loyalty of this or that section of the Coalition, and the whole House was uneasy about high expenditure. Meantime an eye was steadily kept on the Peace Conference. Government supporters felt it necessary to stiffen the British representatives on the question of indemnities, over 200 members sending a telegram expressive of their anxiety to the Prime Minister while he was in Paris.

Linked only by recognition of the Prime Minister's services in the war, the huge majority suffered for a time from its very bigness and from its limited sense of political discipline. The party system in which, according to the formerly accepted doctrine of Morley's *Walpole*, lay " the secret of rule by Parliament," and without which, as Disraeli held, " you can have no Parliamentary government," had obvious defects, but it had the advantage of cohesion and concentration. It animated members in the pursuit or defence of a policy ; it gave them a cry and a flag. A Coalition of men of widely different principles and sentiments, who at the same time lacked the vivid consciousness of the need of unity which existed during the war, was inclined to be erratic and to indulge in sectional movements.

MASTER OF THE HOUSE.—The Prime Minister's hold on the House when put to the test proved to be complete. However restless it might be, he could rally it and excite its enthusiasm. During the first half of 1919 he spent most of his days in Paris at the Conference. He came over on flying visits. On one of these—in April—he replied to criticisms, inspired by a once friendly but now disparaging Press, with reference to the carrying out of his election pledges. The Prince of Wales, seated for the first time in the gallery behind the clock, heard the very vivacious speech in which he turned defiantly on assailants and attacked " a great newspaper proprietor " whose movements he likened to those of a grasshopper. Although censors found much of what he said irrelevant or flippant, it was for its purpose a shining success.

Certain speeches are conspicuous in the lives of statesmen as stages in their career or policy. Among such are Palmerston's *Civis Romanus sum* speech, Gladstone's unmuzzled speech after his defeat at Oxford and Chamberlain's first Tariff Reform speech at Birmingham. Mr. Lloyd George had secured his supremacy in the Parliament of the war by his victory in the Maurice debate. By his speech in April, 1919, he established and exhibited his hold over the Peace Parliament. It had a profound effect on the course of political opinion and the history of parties. Challenged by Coalition round-robins which had fluttered to Paris, the Prime Minister ridiculed and castigated those who inspired the telegrams ; and the members who had been muttering, if not threatening, protested they were really his best friends.

As an example of the orator's art there had been nothing quite so remarkable since Gladstone's achievement in submitting a Vote of Credit, when members who intended to move amendments forgot to move them. Political success, it is often said, depends too much on the gift of the tongue. But Parliament is a speaking place and so long as we have Parliamentary government, policy must be vindicated in words. Mr. Lloyd George's vindication of his Peace Conference policy weaved the spell which is exercised only by the true orator. From rhetoric and invective it ranged to satire and humour. It was finely phrased and although it had been written out, the orator did not lean over his manuscript. Every sentence he uttered with appropriate expression and his gestures were free and dramatic. Again the pointed finger, the clenched fist, the outstretched arms, the shrug, the thump on the box, the gleam of the eye, the twitch of the mouth set off the accusing, the appealing or the mocking word.

The passage on Lord Northcliffe was the most sensational feature of the speech. Some of the Coalition members heard it with sorrow. Valuing highly the part which *The Times* had played in the war their faces showed that they were puzzled and pained by the vehemence of the attack on an old friend. On the other hand, it gave satisfaction to men of the type of Mr. Austen Chamberlain, who while temporarily out of office had deplored the close association of Mr. Lloyd George and his Government with the Press. Amused listeners considered it significant of a new direction in policy. " I would rather have a good Peace than a good Press," said Mr. Lloyd George with an arch and smiling gesture. Coalitionists saw in his attitude fresh proof of his courage, and Independent Liberals were pleased when he fell out with the great news-

paper controller who had contributed to their own
leader's downfall, a " setter up and plucker down "
of statesmen who might be expected in wrath to
say of the present Prime Minister : " Had he none
else to make a stale but me ? "

SUPREME TRIUMPH.—Mr. Lloyd George's supreme
triumph was attained in mid-summer at the signing
of the Treaty of Peace at Versailles.  There had
been doubts, as there were before the Armistice,
whether Germany would sign.  The Allied armies
were concentrated on the Rhine and all was ready
for action.  Germany whined and blustered and
wriggled, but on June 28 the Treaty was signed.
Next day the Prime Minister, on his return from
Paris, was met at the railway station by the King,
and on the 30th he had an extraordinary reception
in the House of Commons.   Almost all the members
rose in his honour and as he sat on the Treasury
bench, looking worn and weary, Coalitionists stood
at the benches, at the bar and by the Chair cheering
warmly, waving the Orders of the Day and gazing at
the national leader with pride and gratitude.

Once more there was a patriotic demonstration
such as occurred at the opening of the war.  With
all its frankness and freedom the House has an
inherited distaste for anything theatrical or for any
display of feeling except in its own traditional way,
but in its emotion on this occasion it joined readily
—on the initiative, as in September, 1914, of Mr.
Will Crooks—in " God Save the King."   Five
years previously the Anthem was sung with solemn
anxiety ; now it was sung with devout thankfulness.
There was as deep feeling in the singing after the
perils of the war were over as there had been when
we began dimly to see them.

AUTHORITY OF PARLIAMENT. — Although the Coalition showed no sign of weakening after the signing of Peace, many members protested against the continuance of some of the Ministerial war-time practices. One grievance was that the head of the Government appeared in Parliament only on the rare occasions when he had an important statement to make. All recognized that his days and hours were mortgaged by other calls, international and domestic. At the same time, the leadership of Mr. Bonar Law was generally acceptable. Mr. Law humoured the House and offered in its business arrangements to do what it might desire, with the result that usually he got his own way ; and in debate, although his style lacked the succinctness and polish of his predecessor's, he knew when to be conciliatory and persuasive and when to be forcible and resolute. His unaffected, unassuming manners, his candour and amiability won the esteem of all parties. Rarely had a leader of the House been on such easy terms with followers as Mr. Law, who enjoyed a pipe and a chat in the smoking-room, and perhaps no leader had been regarded with kindlier feelings by opponents. The acrimony which he formerly excited had melted away. This was proved even by the interesting fact that he was entertained at one of their weekly lunches by the Independent Liberals.

But no member of the Government, however agreeable and eminent, could take the place of its head. No Prime Minister since Gladstone had towered so greatly above colleagues in personal authority and prestige. It was to support Mr. Lloyd George that the House was elected and to him it looked for inspiration and guidance. If it was to be kept fully effective for the work of reconstruction and if it was to set aside sectional considerations, his presence and voice were necessary. It desired to see him on the Treasury bench more regularly. Accordingly, he arranged to attend on certain days to answer questions and his intervention in debate became more frequent.

Complaint was made long before the war that the powers of the House of Commons were being transferred to Downing Street. Parliament, it was asserted in one decade after another, had become a mere machine for registering the decisions of the Cabinet. This was a rather superficial view. There are, it is true, issues on which the House of Commons has either to confirm what the Ministers decide or to face the alternative of a new Government, but all familiar with its life and work know that in the vast majority of cases the Cabinet, as Mr. Churchill has confessed, defers to its wishes and opinions by a process of intelligent anticipation. That is to say, Downing Street is influenced in the decisions it takes by a knowledge of what Parliament will accept. Then, after the policy has been submitted, it is modified—and sometimes completely changed—not so much by vote or even by debate as by committee-room meetings, representations through the Whips and all the other agencies which are constantly at work.

Undoubtedly during the war and especially during the dictatorship of the small Cabinet, Parliament played an unusually submissive rôle and was content on most matters to register decisions, but it recovered, at any rate, some of its control when the full Cabinet of twenty members was restored, when Ministers felt again a common responsibility and when the heads of Departments ceased to be a law unto themselves. While the closure and other

modern devices for limiting debate have lessened
the powers of minorities, those watching the House
of Commons year by year know how jealous it is of
its authority.  A Minister may disregard it for a
time, but in the end he submits or falls.  " Say
what we will," wrote Lord Morley when Indian
Secretary to his friend the Viceroy, " the House of
Commons is your master and mine, and we have got
to keep terms with it."

GREAT CHANGES.—In a single week the House
passed, by a majority of more than five to one, a
resolution in favour of the creation of subordinate
legislatures in the United Kingdom and without a
division read the second time a bill to start India
on the road towards the substitution of " government by vote " for " government by despatch."
The imagination of Burke would be required to
point the significance of the scene on a sunny
afternoon when tall Mr. Montagu, bending over the
box beside the mace, and dropping and replacing
his single eyeglass, expounded to a few score members the measure in which 315 million people were
interested, while a group of Indian princes, some in
khaki and some in robe and turban, looked over
the rail of the gallery.

Significant from the domestic point of view was
the speech delivered in support of the devolution
motion by Mr. Walter Long.  The country squire
supposed to be personified in Mr. Long has retained
the tradition of centuries.  What he was in the days
of Addison and Steele he remained to some extent
in the pages of Jane Austen, and to our own day
in those of Mr. Galsworthy.  At Worsted Skeynes
Mr. Galsworthy exhibits a harmonious edifice of
ideas and prejudice and aspiration.  " I believe

that we have made the country, and shall keep the country what it is. And I believe in my social equals and the country house, and in things as they are, for ever and ever." That was the creed of Mr. Pendyce, and shaken although it may be by taxes and Labour parties, the old ideas are not without representation even now in Parliament. But Mr. Walter Long, the Conservative, discerned the signs of the times. Statesman as well as squire, he led in the way of devolution.

Two picturesque personal incidents marked very interesting stages of political development in 1919. One was the appointment of Lord Sinha, the first native of our great Dependency to hold office in the British Government, as Under-Secretary of State for India. His elevation to the peerage was in itself a memorable event and to see him among the white men on the Ministerial bench in the Upper House was a lesson in the history of our Imperial system. It was his privilege to sit in the Royal Commission in front of the Throne when the assent of the Crown was given to the Government of India Act.

A WOMAN IN THE HOUSE.—The other wonderful incident was the introduction of a woman to the House of Commons. Sinn Feiners had taken the lead in returning a member of the newly-enfranchised sex at the general election, but she did not come to Westminster. The first to occupy a seat was Lady Astor, who on the succession of her husband to the peerage, was chosen in his place for Plymouth. Old-fashioned members and journalists found themselves in a new world, a world at which some of them marvelled uncomfortably, when she came within the great doors and when two women reporters made notes in the Press Gallery, hitherto as strictly reserved to men as the House itself. All present will ever remember Lady Astor's appearance at the bar, wearing a black, tailor-made costume with white collar and a toque, her obeisances as she advanced between the Prime Minister and Mr. Balfour, and her writing of the first woman's name in the great book kept in the table. As she stood by the Chair with her hand in the Speaker's welcoming grasp, while peers (among whom was her husband), strangers, and the American Ambassador looked down on the scene, the whole House cheered or smiled. If the men who held that home was the place and domestic management the occupation for women felt any prejudice when the new member took her seat among themselves they concealed their feeling.

Change had come with an irresistible rush. The passing of the Sex Disqualification (Removal) Bill at the end of the year showed how the barriers, formerly so staunchly maintained, were being thrown down. Already all the Parliamentary disqualifications had been removed. Woman could sit in the open gallery, she could vote for a member, she could herself be elected. And she was taking advantage of her liberation in every respect. Now for the first time in the speech read from the throne at the prorogation of Parliament, the King, instead of addressing My Lords and " Gentlemen," addressed My Lords and " Members of the House of Commons."

NOTABLE FIGURES.—No new figure with the promise of a great career was revealed in the early stage of the Peace Parliament except Sir Robert Horne, a shrewd, genial and cheery Scottish Advocate and an excellent *raconteur*, who proved his administrative ability during the war and subsequently as a Cabinet minister recommended himself so much to the House by firmness and clear-headedness, that in the scarcity of brilliant men he was soon named as a likely Unionist leader for the future. The back-bench members who attracted most attention were Sir Edward Carson and Lord Robert Cecil. Sir Edward after little more than a year in Mr. Lloyd George's War Government, had retired in order to be unfettered in dealing with any situation which might arise out of the Irish Convention. While exercising strong influence over the stiffer section of Unionists and capable of embarrassing their leader, he watched the Administration with a friendly eye and placed special confidence in the Prime Minister.

Lord Robert Cecil had left the Government at the general election because he disapproved of its policy in respect of the Welsh Church. With head and figure recalling his father's, he inherited Lord Salisbury's unconventional manners and high character and some of his mental qualities. An able, industrious Parliamentarian, vigorous although not piquant or polished in speech, strong in opinion and earnest in conviction, he displayed an independence which gradually estranged him from the Coalition. His zeal for the League of Nations and his sentiments on many other subjects, domestic and international, appealed to the Opposition, but Ministers did not fear him, for scarcely any section on either side agreed with him at all points. While on certain subjects he went to the left, on others he shifted back to the right with extreme Conservatives and Churchmen.

To many of the Labour members the Parliamentary art was new and as a rule they were slow

in acquiring it. Several of the more experienced
men had been in office during the war and had
learned the rudiments of government; there were
a few, and notably Mr. Arthur Henderson, skilled
in political organization and tactics, there were
authoritative spokesmen for their Unions like Mr.
J. H. Thomas, there were one or two good debaters,
one or two with the gift of eloquence, and most of
them were naturally well versed in industrial affairs,
but their hours and thoughts were largely given to
sectional considerations and to movements outside
Parliament. Mr. Clynes was regarded as one of the
rare statesmen of the party, and even before he
succeeded Mr. Adamson as leader, he was frequently
the exponent of its views on general politics.
Reared in the factory and self-educated, his speeches
were couched in language worthy of a graduate
of Oxford trained from early years at St. Stephen's,
and although his thoughts, like Cowper's, were
" clad in a sober livery, for the most part as grave
as that of a bishop's servants " and his manner of
uttering them was as sedate, he secured attention
and respect.

Much of the humdrum work of an Opposition,
the daily criticism, the framing and moving of
amendments, the examination of estimates, was
left to the smaller body of Independent Liberals
who regarded the continuance in peace of a Coalition
of men of conflicting principles as not only unnecessary, but dishonest and unprofitable to the
State. Mr. Asquith's friends, in the absence of
their chief and of his principal lieutenants in exile,
were fortunate in obtaining Sir Donald Maclean
as their Parliamentary leader. Sir Donald, who
had never held office except as Deputy Chairman of
Ways and Means, astonished almost every one by

the manner in which he rose to a great emergency. The House at first smiled with amusement at the non-commissioned officer with lithe figure and refined, agreeable face, who took command of the remnant of a shattered party, but its amusement was soon turned into good-will and admiration. He was neither a great speaker nor a ready debater, but he was always in his place, always watchful of events, always ready to apply Liberal principles, and although he was invariably courteous and considerate, never taking part in personal recrimination, never doing or saying anything unworthy of a great gentleman, he criticized frankly, freely and forcibly, and he displayed a courage and constancy which recalled Campbell-Bannerman. Yet nobody was better pleased than Sir Donald when the ex-Premier himself returned to the House.

MR. ASQUITH'S RETURN.—" *Heureux qui, comme Ulysse, a fait un beau voyage !* " but the wanderer, after his successful adventure at Paisley, had no such welcome as his distinction would have justified as he passed along the front Opposition bench in search of a seat. Mr. Adamson clung doggedly to the chief place, and when a colleague made way for Mr. Asquith, he found himself between the Labour leader and a Labour Whip. Lord Morley said of Joseph Chamberlain, with reference to the office he received from Gladstone in 1886, that whatever his place in the hierarchy he knew that he could trust himself to make it as important as he pleased. And whatever Mr. Asquith's place on the bench to which he returned, he could make it almost what he pleased. When he intervened in debate he was, of course, easily the most important and interesting figure on the Opposition side. But

while his claim to the Speaker's eye continued
occasionally to be challenged by the Labour
spokesman, he derived no encouragement from the
House in controversies in which he was opposed
to the Government.

Scarcely any effect was produced by Mr. Asquith's
reappearance on the attitude and relationship of
parties.    When he attacked the Government policy
on such important issues as Ireland and Mesopo-
tamia, the Prime Minister replied in scornful speeches
which pleased the whole Coalition.    The Coalition
Liberals hardened their hearts against their former
leader.    Instead of going over to his side, they
showed more clearly than before that their fate was
linked to the Prime Minister's.    Some stir was
caused when the Lord Chancellor, Lord Birkenhead,
in a newspaper article, described the Coalition as
an invertebrate and undefined body, and called
for the early formation of a national party.    There
was a movement for the fusion of its two sections.
For this neither was altogether ready, but by the
course of events, sharing the dangers of political
warfare, their alliance was steadily strengthened.

1920.—The session of 1920 was very productive
in legislation—too productive, as many members
thought.    Its chief feature was the measure for
setting up two Parliaments in Ireland.    This marked
a notable new chapter in the history of parties.
The first Home Rule Bill was rejected by the House
of Commons, the second was thrown aside by the
Peers, the third was carried over their head to the
statute book, where it was displaced by the fourth.
In recent years the last obstacle to Home Rule had
lain in Ulster, and this was overcome by giving
the province a Parliament of her own.    Lord

Rosebery and Lord Morley were the only survivors of the Cabinet responsible for the proposal of 1886, but among the members of the House of Commons were several who had taken part in the controversy since its start, and now they found themselves in a new world.   There was a minority of unrepentant, unbending Unionists who used the old arguments, and the bill which the Irish Nationalists spurned was opposed by Independent Liberal and Labour members on the ground that it would not settle the question, Mr. Asquith still proposing to give a single Parliament to Ireland with county option, but the Coalition Liberals agreed with the Prime Minister that the Government scheme was the best calculated to lead to ultimate union between North and South.   Acquiesced in by Sir Edward Carson, it was carried by great majorities.

Numerous again were the trying problems and anxieties of the session.   Industrial troubles ran through it, culminating in the miners' strike.   The war between the Authorities and the armed rebels in Ireland, and the reprisals charged against servants of the Crown, led to innumerable questions and hot debates.   In the course of one of these, when the House was under the influence of the emotion excited by the murder of British officers in Dublin, a Unionist was so irritated by Mr. Devlin's vehement protest against the shooting of civilians, that he seized the impassioned Nationalist by the back of the neck and almost pulled him down, and in the scuffle another member received a blow in the face.   It was not only from the Opposition that complaint and criticism came. A large number of Unionists voted against the Government on the case of General Dyer, who had been deprived of military employment for his

action in the Amritsar riots, and many Coalitionists
were disturbed by the negotiation of trade relations
with " blood-stained " Bolsheviks, by our attitude
towards Poland, when, in her struggle with Russia,
we gave her peaceful counsels, by the question of
reparations and by temporary friction with France,
while the increased Excess Profits Duty swelled
the storm against high expenditure.

The Prime Minister's authority was not shaken
either by criticism on his own side or by censures
from the other. Opposition attacks rallied his
friends just as in pre-war times they had rallied
the partisans of a Government. His optimism,
amid all the cares of the country and the world,
continued to shine. " I believe," he said, " we
are working our way out of the whirlpool." This
optimism encouraged many to retain their faith in
his leadership.

1921.—Getting out of the whirlpool, however,
has been a slow process. The strangers' gallery
of the House of Commons, which was in consequence
of police information closed at the end of 1920,
gloomily testified by its empty seats in the following
session to the continuance of one of the troubles
and humiliations of the State. Privileged persons
were admitted to the special gallery, and the ladies
gallery was in summer opened to members' wives,
but for fear, presumably, of Sinn Fein outrage,
ordinary admissions were stopped and strangers
were excluded also from the Lobby. The House
had, in 1921, many other causes of anxiety. It was
disturbed by the situation arising from the failure
of Germany to execute the Peace Treaty with
regard, especially, to reparations, but in its attitude
on this subject it displayed a practical unanimity

such as existed during the war, and fortunately at last Germany yielded to an ultimatum and accepted the demands of the Allies.   The protracted stoppage of the mines in consequence of the dispute on the system and rate of wages which were to follow de-control, the danger to the pits by the withdrawal of pumpmen, the threat of a sympathetic strike by railway and other transport workers, the declaration of a state of emergency, the calling out of the Reserves and enlistment of a Defence Force, the curtailment of industries and public services for lack of coal, and the immense increase of unemployment and of the burden on the Exchequer were watched with very grave concern by the House.

It could do little but watch. Although it discussed the emergency at several stages, and the dramatic intervention of a meeting of members—who sent a conciliatory suggestion by the secretary of the Miners' Federation to Downing Street at midnight—led the other Unions to cancel their order for a strike, negotiation was naturally left to the Government and the parties. Meanwhile the echoes of old fiscal controversies were heard in debate on legislation for the prevention of dumping of low-priced imports.

PERSONNEL.—In the front rank of Unionists important changes occurred this year. Lord Robert Cecil, accompanied by his brother, Lord Hugh, took a more independent and convenient position as a persistent critic of the Government by crossing from the Ministerial side to the front Opposition bench, where, as a Privy Councillor, he was entitled to sit. Mr. Walter Long, having on account of ill-health resigned office, received

a peerage, and Sir Edward Carson, now that his
work for Ulster was done, also went to the other
place, as a Lord of Appeal.  While the crossing of
the floor by Lord Robert, the most conspicuous
of the Cecils, was an event of political significance,
the departure of the two older statesmen from
the House in which they had long played a prominent
part marked the end of a Parliamentary generation.
New men came more into view.

There was a still more notable change.  I have
scarcely ever seen the House so surprised and
shocked as it was in March, when the Prime
Minister, in a sobbing voice, read a letter from Mr.
Bonar Law, announcing that he was no longer able
to continue his political work.  For several years
it had been very heavy.  " I am quite worn out,"
Mr. Law wrote, " and my medical advisers have
warned me that my physical condition is such that,
unless I have an immediate and long rest, an
early and complete breakdown is inevitable."  The
Prime Minister was overcome by the feelings he
tried to express, and Mr. Asquith was also deeply
moved.  Members in all quarters felt a sense of
personal loss.  They realized at that moment that
they had liked Mr. Law better even than they
knew.  He gave up not only his office in the
Government, but also the Unionist leadership, and
went abroad for months, although he retained his
seat as a member of Parliament.

To the Prime Minister the loss of the well-tried
ally who had worked with him so harmoniously
was almost irreparable.  There had been established between them a friendship more intimate
and cordial than exists as a rule in the case of life-
long colleagues.  As Mr. Asquith said, the Coalition
was like a pair of scissors that had lost one of its

blades. The Unionist members promptly and unanimously elected Mr. Austen Chamberlain to the party leadership, to which he aspired nine years previously, and on the invitation of the Prime Minister he became also leader of the House. The new blade, as Mr. Lloyd George retorted to Mr. Asquith, was of the best English steel. Experience alone, however, would prove if it could act with the other part of the scissors so evenly and efficiently as the old blade.

On Mr. Lloyd George to an increasing extent attention is riveted. He alone excites the curiosity aroused by the political celebrities of the past. Country visitors gather at the gates of Palace Yard when he is expected to visit the House just as their fathers assembled to catch a glimpse of Gladstone. Mr. Balfour especially, when he was the rising hope of his party, and Joseph Chamberlain, at the sensational stages of his career, aroused similar curiosity, but Lord Salisbury and Mr. Asquith never made this popular appeal. They did not seem able, like Henry Hereford, to dive into the hearts of the common people. When Mr. Lloyd George appears on the Treasury bench there is a quickening of interest in the House, and for the representatives of the Press he is a welcome and enduring topic. In the last generation they always found " copy " in Gladstone. His face, his movements, even his collars provided countless paragraphs. So also does Mr. Lloyd George supply endless material. When he comes unexpectedly all wonder why he has come. They see as much in his smile or shrug as Mr. Puff saw in Lord Burleigh's nod.

Now my task in trying to hold a mirror up to

Parliament is done. The life of the House of
Commons is much more strenuous than it was in
former generations. Since the Liberals attained
power nearly sixteen years ago it has had crises
and excitements sufficient for a century. In all
the years, except two, since 1905, autumn sittings
have been necessary. And not only are the modern
sessions long and the counts-out few, but the strain
upon members has been increased by the gravity
and urgency of the questions demanding settlement.
Parliamentary life has lost its attraction as a social
pastime for the idlers and human clothes-horses
scorned by Carlyle. It is full of labour and
burdened by care.

Critics say that the House of Commons has
deteriorated. That is no new saying. It has been
heard in successive generations. As Lord Boodle
told Sir Leicester Dedlock : " A debate is not what
a debate used to be ; the House is not what the
House used to be ; even a Cabinet is not what it
formerly was." " The House of Commons," says
Mr. Ormsby in *Sybil*, " is not the House of Commons
of my time." Recently a member of the Cabinet
noted a decline in distinguished figures and in the
quality of debate. Truly there are few figures
in the present Parliament which catch the popular
eye, and few of its debates are conducted in the
grand style. It is a transition Parliament elected
under conditions which make it exceptional. It
lacks the dramatic element of two strong opposing
parties which in the past enlivened debate and
stimulated the interest of the people. But to say
that the House of Commons has permanently
deteriorated is to say what the new decade may
refute. It has not yielded its rights nor abated
its pretensions. Its authority has been unsuccess-

fully challenged by ambitious departments. How far the challenge of Direct Action will be carried remains to be seen.

I have brought down my unpretentious record— the record of a mere reporter I again admit—to the strange times through which we are passing. But who can say what History will write of these times and of the men who are playing the leading parts ? And who will venture to predict what sort of Parliament and Government the country may have a quarter of a century hence ?

" The past is a dream," wrote Disraeli, " and the future is a mystery."

THE END

# INDEX

56 ; characteristics, 56 ; early career, 57 ; high position and popularity, 57–8 ; distrust of his leadership, 58 ; relations with colleagues, 58–9 ; ploughs the furrow alone, 60 ; picturesque excursions, 138 ; rejects Home Rule banner, 61 ; speeches, 62 ; cross-bench attitude, 63 ; withdrawal from House of Lords, 63–4 ; on Cabinet system, 245, 257

*Printed in Great Britain by* Butler & Tanner, *Frome and London*